Roland Barthélemy
Arnaud Sperat-Czar

Cheeses of the World

A season by season
guide to buying,
storing and serving

Photography:
Daniel Czap
Jacques Guillard

HACHETTE
illustrated

Contents

Foreword

Looking back at my earliest memories, my love of cheese dates from the time when my father used to take me, holding on tightly to his hand, to Les Halles, the central food market – at that time situated right in the heart of Paris. I must have been about six or seven years old and I was absolutely fascinated by the unbelievable, gargantuan spectacle of literally tons of cheese and butter from every corner of France, being sorted, weighed, packed, carted and piled up one on the other, straight on the ground. (People were less preoccupied with hygiene than they are now.) The vast assortment of shapes made me feel quite dizzy: the massive wheels of Emmenthal overshadowing the little Crottins; Brie, from Meaux and elsewhere, giving lessons in elegance to the stocky Fourmes d'Auvergne; the distinguished pyramids of goat's milk cheeses turning up their noses at the boorish Pavés from northern France.

The profusion of colours – orange, black, red, brown, yellow, cream – and the intoxicating vegetal, buttery, sulphurous and earthy smells were all it took to awaken my senses. Curious, amazed and impressed, I let my father lead me through this shambles. My eyes must have sparkled with delight. The throbbing life of the place, typified by the *forts des Halles* – the strapping porters, brimming with energy – formed part of the spectacle. Their cheeky humour, the tone of their voices, their accents, were all clues to their regional origins, but I was too carried away by all this exoticism to recognize them.

To me, the son of a man from Cantal, proud of his roots, this initiation gave me a taste for diversity that was radical and conclusive. Les Halles was a fabulous crossroads where all the countries of Europe came together. I learned to see cheeses as so much more than a mere promise of gastronomic pleasure. Each one represented a condensed universe, a prism through which I could watch the evolution of men, atmospheres, seasons, memories… And this wealth, this profusion is what I would like to help you discover; just as I hope, in the course of this book, to infect you with my passion and to share all my favourites with you.

R Barthélemy

Roland Barthélemy, aged seven,
with his father Jean-François at
Les Halles in Paris.

The magic of white gold

To all those who are fearful that internationalism means standardization, banality, levelling-down, this book should bring some comfort and reasons not to give up hope: the steamroller of modernity will have a hard job standardizing this tremendous heritage, which combines traditions and innovation, loyalty and change. In the pages that follow we list some 1,200 cheeses. Many come from France – one of those countries where one only has to travel 30 kilometres (20 miles) to have the impression of having crossed a frontier; and from other parts of Europe, of course: several European countries claim the title of 'the other homeland of cheese'. Cheeses from all over the world are also included, even if, being of more recent origin, they are less well known.

Our 1,200 cheeses represent only a small part of a universe under perpetual development. New products are created everyday, replacing those that disappear. Countries such as Great Britain, which had neglected their cheese heritage, are suddenly undergoing a renaissance, digging out ancient magic spells and resuscitating forgotten recipes. Since the 1970s the citizens of Quebec, brought up in the Anglo-Saxon Cheddar culture, have become infatuated with more authentic products.

Their passion for cheeses made from unpasteurized milk began less than ten years ago. As a result, many interesting products have seen the light of day in the 'Beautiful Province' since the 1990s, such as Victor et Berthold, Ciel de Charlevoix or Saint-Basile – the very names are an invitation to travel.

The United States, too, since the beginning of the 1990s has boasted an association of farmhouse cheese producers at Madison, in Michigan, set up under the auspices of the *Guilde des Fromagers* (Cheesemakers' Guild) of which Roland Barthélemy is president. Countries with no history of cheese-making, such as Japan, are also acquiring the taste: a group from Normandy has recently taught the Japanese how to make Camembert from a traditional recipe.

Traditions patiently handed down, gestures repeated a hundred times: cheeses like Parmesan seem to originate from the dawn of time. In the half-light of the cellars, men watch over the slow burgeoning of the flavours (Rolando Rossi cheese dairy).

The places evoked, the products described, the men and women mentioned in this book have all been chosen by Roland Barthélemy, famous Parisian retailer and *affineur* (ripener) of fine cheeses, who has opened up his address book and the doors of his imagination to you. His cheese shop is one of the most popular in the world and also the most unpretentious. Seen from outside, its cream façade is like a rural engraving: a few terracotta tiles and two tiny shop windows, which are dressed afresh each week. Inside, the space is positively cramped; the employees have to contort themselves to allow the customers to see the shelves, which go right up to the ceiling. Beneath one of the display shelves, a steep ladder plummets to the cellar, where cheeses are patiently ripened before emerging into the light of day. This is not a shop: it's a hideout, a den – a delightfully orderly little universe of marble, glass, wood and earthenware, harbouring the cheese treasures of the world.

Number 51, Rue de Grenelle, is a source of constant wonder and astonishment. In his novel, *Palomar*, Italian writer Italo Calvino paints a magnificent picture of this Ali Baba's cave of cheeses, this Pandora's box of flavours. Discriminating palates appreciate the way the products are rigorously selected at their peak of perfection, while admiring businessmen calculate the increased value of the property. Born into a family of cheesemakers in Cantal, Roland Barthélemy was 20 when he moved in here, to be joined three years later by Nicole, his wife. They take turns overseeing the business from the back of the shop, between two columns of cheeses. Claire, their daughter, is also there at Christmas and New Year.

Like all his colleagues, Roland Barthélemy has lived through extreme changes in the cheese world. The movement towards modernization and concentration of production that began after the Second World War has gone on ever since, fuelled by the rarely challenged drive to increase volume while maintaining standards of hygiene (one answer to this was pasteurization).

In the pastures of Paye d'Auge, in Normandy, or in chalets in the Swiss Alps on the Gstaad heights, the success of the alchemy of cheese depends on meticulous care and intimate knowledge of the raw material.

10

Cheese, don't forget, was originally made on the farm; cheesemaking took place right there, immediately after milking, so as not to leave time for unwelcome bacteria to develop. The setting up of dairies to collect the milk from several sources, and from ever-widening areas, radically changed the situation: the milk had to be chilled and was sometimes not processed until 48 to 72 hours later, and so had to be protected from unwanted microbiological activity.

Take a look at the route taken by the milk in a modern installation: the milking is done by machines – cleaned and disinfected daily – that deliver the milk straight into stainless-steel tanks, allowing no contact with the surrounding atmosphere. It is then cooled to around 4°C (39°F); this reduces bacteriological activity but, since the tanker sometimes only collects every other day, some of the fermenting agents are lost, leaving the milk poorer in bacteria, both good and bad.

The various batches of milk, mixed together in the tankers, are then transported to the dairy, and sent to be pasteurized, to destroy those pathogenic bacteria that are not affected by low temperatures, since microorganisms that thrive at low temperatures generally produce a bitter flavour. Pasteurization – heating the milk to above 70°C (158°F) for a few seconds – gets rid of them, leaving the milk ultra-clean; in other words, dead!

New ferments, carefully selected to restore the typical flavours of cheese, have to be added. This has some advantages; industrially produced cheeses are destined for big outlets, where a constant flavour throughout the year is the criterion of quality and reference; with a product that is easy to identify and recognize, the customers know exactly where they stand. But however well chosen, a few ferments are not enough to give the cheese fullness and complexity. While it is possible, with just a few molecules, to give it an aroma that is reasonably close to that of the original farmhouse product, it will always lack character and depth. A cheese made from pasteurized milk has immeasurably less flavour than one made from raw milk. The one is standardized, the other varies with the seasons.

But we must avoid idealizing a past era where quality was, to say the least, uneven. There is no doubt that the scale of values has narrowed and the overall quality of products has improved considerably. One only has to read a passage in Emile Zola's book *Le Ventre de Paris*: in it he evokes cheeses with their retinue of 'stinks' and 'sulphur fumes', maggots, etc. Delightful surprises are perhaps

page opposite, Salers being made at the Salat farm at Cussac.
above, turning a Cabécou de Thiers in its mould at the Bergerettes' farm.

Affectionately known as 'La Mamma',
Madame Brunelli has handed on the
art of making Brocciu to her son, but
still likes to lend a hand.

fewer and farther between but gone, too, are products
liable to upset the modern stomach.

Roland Barthélemy has built his reputation on the
scrupulous choice of authentic cheeses with strong
distinguishing characteristics, almost exclusively made
from unpasteurized milk. You will find a great many of
them on the pages that follow. In putting this book
together, the selection he made was inevitably incomplete
and subjective to boot. It is the fruit of his travels and
his love of the subject…and of his memory lapses, too!
The cheeses he is particularly fond of are noted in
'favourites' boxes – gastronomic nuggets inserted here
and there in the pages. Each cheese carries the handprint
of the man – or very often woman – who devised, made

and ripened it. Farming tradition has it that the men till the
fields and tend the stock, while the women make and take
care of the cheeses. Since the days of Marie Harel, official
creator of Camembert, all the great cheese dynasties owe
much to women who transform milk into 'white gold'.
Among them are: La Mère Richard, who did so much for
Saint-Marcellin in Lyons, and whose daughter has taken
over from her; Jaqueline Chévenet, small producer of
farmhouse cheeses in the Mâcon area, whose son aims
to establish the largest goat-rearing concern in Europe;
Bernadette Arnaud, at Poligny – her son has just acquired
the Fort de Rousses, a sumptuous, peaceful haven for
thousands of *meules* (millstones or 'wheels') of Compté.
At Lapoutroie, in the Vosges, is yet another woman,
Virginie Haxaire, who has taken over her father's business
and runs it brilliantly. Inventive geniuses or inspired heirs –
all these women are guardians of a cheese-making
culture and they, more than anyone, have the know-how
to hand it on.

Some of the most enterprising cheesemakers are
foreigners who have fallen in love with a particular area
of France and set up production here. Less 'legitimate'
initially, they had everything to prove. A name comes to
mind at random: a German couple called Claudia and
Wolfgang Reuss, who produce an excellent Bruyère de

A cheese dairy in
Haute-Provence, on
the Valensole plateau.
Traditionally the men
work in the fields and
tend the stock, and the
women make the cheese.

The secret of large cheeses lies for the most part in the way they are handled in the latter stages of ripening. Here: brushing the Saint-Nectaire in the Jaubert cellar (Saint-Nectaire).

Joursac in a lost corner of Cantal, at an altitude of 1,100 metres (3,600 feet). In the Ariège, at Col de Fach, is a Canadian woman, Marie-Suzanne Garros, whose idea of making a goat's milk version of Vacherin produced astonishing results. That is one of the constants in the history of agriculture: renewal very often comes from outside. Is not Charles Chabot, 'adopted son' of Provence over at Forcalquier, the most fervent ambassador for Banon, the historic local cheese?

These are fascinating people. They live their passion intensely and feel personally affected if someone is disappointed with their last consignment – this can happen with farmhouse products, which are more capricious than industrial ones. To show you this fascinating world, we have chosen to approach it on a seasonal basis. This will allow you to understand why and how the market stalls change their appearance as the year wears on. It will help you to become more adept at choosing products that are at their best. It will show you the daily reality of stockbreeders, producers and *affineurs* – the experts who take care of the cheeses as they ripen. With the passing months you will enter the arcane world of the cheesemaker, discover the secrets of the men and women who make the cheeses, and

come to understand its limitations and the origins of its incredible diversity.

At the end of the book are minutely detailed annexes listing the cheeses in alphabetical order and according to 'family' groupings.

This book pays homage to a trade which Roland Barthélemy has practised with passion for 30 years, that of a cheese *affineur*: a specialized trade requiring meticulous care and close attention to detail. Homage, too, to the warm, colourful, generous world that daily surrounds him – that of the people who produce the milk and transform it. Homage to milk itself, an extraordinarily malleable material, capable of metamorphosing into a wealth of treasures with as many different shapes as it has flavours. Homage to an ethic, humility: for all the players in this book are nothing without the support of the others. Homage to a history, finally: that of all those who, since the dawn of time, have worked this magic.

Jean François Brunelli
(*above*), in the cellar where he makes his Corsican Tommes.

Spring

The exquisite smell of fresh grass

The arrival of spring brings an explosion of flavours to the market stalls. Animals that have been confined to cow sheds, sheepfolds or goat pens throughout the winter are let out to rediscover the fresh air and fresh grass. The result is an abundant supply of full-flavoured milk.

In common with all my fellow cheese *affineurs*, my year doesn't begin until April. Spring fills up the cheese cellars in a matter of a few weeks. An uninterrupted procession of products floods in from every corner of France and other parts of Europe. Nature throws off its winter sluggishness and is suddenly bursting with generosity. The weather is fine and the animals are out to pasture. No more hay or dry winter fodder; fresh grass is back on the menu and the milk flows freely into the churns.

GOAT'S MILK CHEESES, ABOVE ALL, ARE BACK. Reduced to a tiny share of the market in winter, now they have to be restrained from overwhelming the market stalls. Traditionally, nanny goats give milk for only 280 days in the year, from February to the end of October, possibly to mid-November when the gestation cycle begins. They give birth at the end of January and in early February but, though their udders are swollen with an onrush of milk, one must wait a while longer; at the start of lactation the milk contains colostrum – excellent for the growth of the kids but no good for making cheese. Ever-provident Nature arranges for good, nourishing fresh grass to be available the moment the young are ready to start grazing.

THE EARLIEST OF THE GOATS' MILK CHEESES come – logically – from the warmer, sunnier regions, in other words from the Mediterranean. The same applies to Pecorino, Bra and Robiola from Italy, Aragon and Ibores from Spain and the Portuguese Evora. In France, the Drôme, Gard, Ardèche and Haut Provence regions are the forerunners: Pélardons, Picodons and other Banons are the first to be ready. Those from central France need a little more time to reach perfection before gracing my shelves.

At Rotolo, near Ajaccio, the Brunelli family raise 120 ewes. Because of the very favourable climate, their Brocciu are very early arrivals on the market stalls. *Pages 18–19*: the herd of goats on the Bergerettes' farm at Thiers.

The mountain pastures, accessible
only in fine weather, are reputed to
provide the fullest-flavoured milk.
Opposite page: Morbier being made
at La Chapelle-du-Bois.

IN THE CASE OF EWES, the rhythm is slightly different; their lactation period is shorter and they normally give milk only from mid-December to mid-June. The lambs are born around November 15th and the shepherds begin milking around December 15th. In Corsica, my friend, cheese-maker Jean-François Brunelli, processes the milk from November through to July. His first Broccios are flown in at the start of the year. His ewes do not give huge quantities of milk, but it is particularly rich in protein (twice that of cow's milk). Over a year, a ewe will give 200 litres (350 pints) of milk, whereas a goat can provide as much as 1,000 litres (1,760 pints) and a cow up to 9,000 – even 10,000 – litres (15,800 to 17,600 pints), at a rate of 20 to 30 litres (35 to 50 pints) a day. The date the animals are put out to grass varies with the altitude. In mountainous areas, they can only be out for about 100 days in the year, since they must wait for the thaw to make the high mountain pastures accessible. The highest mountain pastures, often snow-covered until the end of spring, only become available in June and by the end of summer the grass is yellowed by the heat. These mountain pastures, in the Alps, the Pyrenees and the Voges, or even the Jura, contain an abundance of wild flowers which are reputed to produce milk with a fuller, richer flavour.

YEARS OF EXPERIENCE give me the authority to state categorically that nothing equals milk from animals fed on fresh grass. For me the year is a binary affair, divided into two great seasons: that of fresh grass and that of hay. The milk is at its best during the second half of spring. Before that, the intense biological activity generated by Nature's reawakening results in excessive fermentation, which can be prejudicial to the cheese (despite the grass being an appetizing pale green). When the animals first

Jean-François Brunelli's
pedigree Corsican ewes –
a species perfectly adapted to
the local climate and vegetation.

Don't ask the impossible!

Please don't ask me for goat's milk cheeses for your Christmas and New Year cheeseboard, or for an 'excellent' Camembert in February, even if I do find it difficult to refuse. Cheese, especially that from farms and small producers, is a seasonal product which has its ups and downs and even the occasional absence. You must forgive it and let it arrive in its own good time. Mont d'Or is only made from August 15th to March 15th, and Salers just from April 15th to November 15th. It's a shame that the period of most prolific production does not coincide with the period of greatest demand. You eat far more cheese in winter than when the weather is fine!

The best of springtime

Spring is by far the best season for most cheeses. Here are a few tips to help you get the most out of this good period.

• *Goat's milk cheeses* return with a flourish. Their short ripening period (ten days to one month) makes them quickly available. They come flowing in from central France (Saint-Maure-de-Touraine, Selle-sur-Cher, Crottin de Chavignol), from Poitou-Charentes (Chabichou), the Rhône-Alpes region (Brique du Forez, Chevrotin, Persillé de Aravis), from the south of the Massif Central (Rocamadour, Picodon, Pélardon), and from Provence (Banon, Tomme d'Annot, Brousse). An embarrassment of riches!

• *Soft cheeses*, with a bloomy rind (Camembert, Brie, Chaorce) or washed rind (Maroilles, Livarot, Epoisses), rarely take less than a month to ripen. They are at their best on the market stalls during the month of May.

• *Pressed, uncooked soft cheeses* (Saint-Nectaire, Reblochon) only reach their peak condition later, since they need longer to ripen. Sometimes they are not at their best until the middle of June.

Hard cheeses Comté, Gruyère, Emmenthal), produced the previous summer, start to become very interesting. And the Tommes from Auvergne or the Pyrenees are not far behind.

go out to grass, the milk lacks the solids – casein, a phosphoprotein, in particular – that give the cheese its appearance. It is at its best following a period of stabilization, after which the quality drops gradually over the course of the summer – though this varies greatly with the climate. The changes in the composition and richness of the milk are so great that the cheese-maker is obliged to use quite different methods of production from those applied in winter.

On the following pages, I give details of six cheeses which, when made in the traditional way, are (happily) noticeably influenced by the seasons. For some years now, these seasonal variations have tended to become less marked, since so many producers now alter the breeding pattern of their stock to produce the young at periods that ensure a regular volume of milk throughout the year. This practice is already almost universal in the case of dairy cows and becoming more and more frequent among goat and sheep breeders. Is it to be regretted? I'm not sure: the quality of the cheese is not affected but I am concerned about animals being kept indoors the whole year round.

Saint-Marcellin draining on grooved shelves at the Etoile de Vercor cheese dairy on the banks of the Isère.

Brocciu

France (Corsica)
**Milk and whey from ewes
and goats**

A seasonal cheese, Brocciu is at its best in spring. A modest product from an arid area, it is made from the whey left over from the making of the Tommes. With the addition of a little whole milk, this still contains enough proteins to make a cheese, no matter which animal species the milk came from.

In Corsica, as elsewhere, ewes only give milk during the first part of the year. From spring through to autumn it is the goats' turn. Even today, the producers still vary the proportions according to availability.

It requires a temperature of around 80°C (176°F) for the proteins to come together (floculate). The liquid must also be whisked vigorously; the name Brocciu comes from the French *brousser*, meaning to beat or to whip. After about an hour the flakes of curd come to the surface and are skimmed off and put into moulds. Traditionally these were little rush baskets, called *caciagia*, but nowadays plastic cheese-strainers are increasingly used. Brocciu is generally eaten very fresh, but some people prefer it *passu*, that is, quite dry.

Cabri Ariégeois

France (Southern Pyrenees)
Goat's milk

Its binding and wooden box make this cheese look just like a little Mont-d'Or, but beneath its corrugated rind is a deliciously runny cheese made from goat's milk – an amazing technical achievement by 68-year-old Philippe Garros, who is constantly on the lookout for something new. He runs a herd of 80 goats in a valley in the Comté de Foix, 4 kilometres (2½ miles) from his nearest neighbour. His products are a happy blend of spruce tannins and goat's milk. The cheese is ripened for four or five weeks, at the end of which time it weighs about one pound. Fed on natural food, the goats give no milk from mid-November to mid-January, so production ceases in winter. The cheeses begin to reappear in March, and rapidly come to their peak. They need careful handling (the rinds must be washed every day or two) and rigorous supervision at all stages in their fabrication – goat's milk not being the ideal medium for this type of production. Apart from that they have to be bound, turned and put into boxes. Philippe maintains that his wife, Marie-Suzanne, does these things much better than he. 'A real labour of love,' he tells us. And no doubt that is why Cabri Ariégeois has flourished.

Pont-l'Evêque

France (Lower Normandy)
Cow's milk

Seemingly cramped in its square box, which it has a tendency to over-flow, Pont-l'Evêque is a generous cheese, like the rich Normandy pastures that it transforms to perfection. It comes from the Paye d'Auge, a prodigious farming region that also gave us Livarot and Camembert. Pont l'Evêque is the name of a little town between Deauville and Lisieux. The area covered by the appellation contains 16 producers, of which half are producers of farmhouse cheeses. There are two types of Pont l'Evêque, depending on the method chosen to mature them. The first is brushed regularly during ripening: the fine, light-coloured mould that grows on its rind takes on a pinkish-grey hue, with reddish streaks. The cheese has a characteristic nutty flavour. This type is the one most frequently sold in supermarkets, because of its excellent keeping qualities. The second – which I prefer – is washed regularly in salt water during its time in the cellar. This encourages the development of 'red' ferment that gives an orange tint to the rind and a firmer texture to the cheese. A good Pont l'Evêque only comes to its full richness after five or six weeks but, as your taste buds will tell you, it is well worth the wait!

Saint-Marcellin
France (Rhône-Alpes)
Cow's milk

Dating back several centuries, it used to be made with goat's milk, but Saint-Marcellin is now exclusively cow's milk, as the nanny goats browsing cheaply on roadside grass verges have progressively disappeared from the countryside. This cheese, deliciously creamy when well ripened, has always attracted prestigious fans. The governor of the Dauphiné – the future Louis XI – assured its future in 1445 when, after a spirited hunt, he found himself alone and facing a bear. He was rescued by two woodcutters, who later introduced him to the local cheese, which delighted him. Demand took off when the railway arrived at Saint-Marcellin between 1860 and 1870, giving access to the big city markets.

The supply of goat's milk, by then no longer sufficient, was augmented with cow's milk; after a few decades it was abandoned completely.

At Lyons, Paul Bocuse and La Mère Richard did a great deal to popularize Saint-Marcellin, which was soon granted an AOC (*Appellation d'Origine Controlée* – label of origin) centred on the Dauphiné. Made with rich spring milk, this cheese is at its best and quite irresistible. It needs to be served in a small, deep dish. I choose those from the Etoile de Vercors cheese dairy, where some of the *hâloirs* (ripening rooms) give directly onto the Isère – the river that runs beside the dairy. The atmosphere is perfect for these cheeses, which like humidity.

Stilton
**United Kingdom
(central England)**
Cow's milk

Not as salty as the Aveyron Roquefort, less creamy than Gorgonzola from Lombardy, Stilton is the softest of the great trilogy of European blue-veined cheeses, particularly in spring and summer. Very balanced, strong without being piquant when ripened in accordance with the rules, it offers a quite extraordinary length of flavour on the palate. It is this fullness that justifies its title of 'King of English cheeses'. Its origins – much more recent than the 1,000 years or so of Roquefort and Gorgonzola – go back three or four centuries. Originally the blue mould happened spontaneously and, to the cheese-makers' dismay, could not be relied upon. Today the production of Stilton is confined to a dozen or so dairies in Leicestershire, Derbyshire and Nottinghamshire, all of which, sadly, have given up using raw milk. It reaches its best after being ripened for 10 to 15 weeks. At the end of that time it has darkened, become marbled, and certain aromas have begun to disappear. It is impossible to mention Stilton without citing its magical affinity for port wine; the practice of stirring the wine into the cheese itself is, however, less universally appreciated.

Pougne Cendré
France (Poitou-Charentes)
Goat's milk

Pougne Cendré has been in existence for at least 20 years. Though it looks like a smaller version of Selle-sur-Cher it is, in fact, modelled on a Cendré de Niort. A mature Pougne Cendré weighs about 150 grams (5 ounces). It is made only by one young farmer, Sébastien Gé, using a fairly traditional method. Each cheese requires 1.25 litres (2¼ pints) of milk, which is processed immediately after milking. It is moulded with a ladle 24 to 28 hours after coagulation. It is *cendré* (dusted with vegetable charcoal) between 24 and 36 hours after being moulded. Pougne – the name comes from an ancient region amalgamated with Hérisson – is eaten fresh (excellent in spring) or matured. Local people like it quite dry, after it has ripened for six to eight weeks. Sébastien Gé doesn't aim for a bluish bloom on the rind; instead he encourages the growth of a white down (*geotrichum*) that, combined with the powdered charcoal, gives a greyish colour to the rind, which tends to form slight ridges. Cheese-producers call this 'curling' and say it is a sign of quality.

Cheeses neatly line up in the half-light of the cellar

On the retailer's shelves cheeses jostle each other contentedly, their smells and colours mingling in a swirling ballet. But in the cool humidity of the cellar everything is much more orderly. Come with me…

Oh, the joyful month of May! The shelves in my cellar are overflowing with slowly ripening cheeses. One corner smells of green apples and mushrooms, another of yeast.

An extraordinary variety of smells, shapes and colours, linked to the different *terroirs* where they are produced, the different production methods and the characteristics of different kinds of milk. Goat's milk cheeses, you may have noticed, are often very small. Cow's milk cheeses, ranging from the great wheels of Beaufort to the tiny Langres, seem to come in all sizes. As for cheeses made from ewe's milk, they only rarely venture into the realms of soft-textured cheeses (Pérail is an exception), seeming more at home in the hard-pressed category, like the ewe's milk cheeses of the Pyrenees.

CHEESEMAKERS today are able to make all types of cheese with any kind of milk, from the softest to the hardest, the mildest to the strongest. There is no reason, given a little research and a few adaptations, why one should not make Gruyère from goat's milk. It is made in Crete, under the name *Graviera*, but the fact remains that it is fairly exceptional. Traditionally, herds of goats are rarely large enough to furnish the 500 litres (880 pints) of milk needed to make a wheel of, say, Comté. It would require nearly 200 goats – an unusually high number – to produce that amount in a single day.

ANOTHER IMPORTANT FACTOR: goat's milk is relatively low in protein, the substance that gives the cheese its structure. At the moulding stage, a very large goat's milk cheese would risk being unable to hold its shape, of spreading, or breaking when taken out of the mould. In France, a Tomme 20 centimetres (8 inches) in diameter is the

The countries around the Mediterranean (*pictured left*, the countryside around Nuoro, in Sardinia) are the most noted for sheep and goats.
Page opposite: Pecorino cheeses in Podda dairy in Sardinia.

From milk to cheese: the minimum you need to know

The result of a combination of practical experience and scientific fact, cheesemaking rests on an unchanging sequence of events: all cheese is milk that has been coagulated, drained to a greater or lesser degree and if necessary, ripened.

• *The milk* is often partially skimmed (traditionally the cream was used to make butter). In principle, full-cream milk gives suppleness to the curd. Raw milk has the maximum flavour-potential; milk that has undergone full or partial pasteurization will generally give a more standardized product.
The by-products of milk – whey and buttermilk – contain residual proteins and can also be made into cheese.

• *Coagulation* is the process that causes the milk proteins to link together. It happens spontaneously when the milk is left at ambient temperature: its own ferments and the bacteria present in the atmosphere cause it to 'turn' and curdle. To help the process the cheesemaker may add other milk ferments (this is essential when the milk is poor quality or has been pasteurized), or even natural rennet, taken from the stomachs of young calves, or microbiological coagulant enzymes. Curd made using predominantly lactic ferments makes, for the most part, cheeses that harden and dry as they mature (this applies to most goat's milk cheeses), while curd made mainly with rennet (also called 'soft curd') is better for softer textures, such as Brie or Munster.

• *The curd,* once it is put into moulds (to give it the desired shape), must be drained of its liquids, to a greater or lesser degree according to the result required: the less moisture it retains, the longer it will keep. The drainage can be slow and spontaneous or accelerated by chopping, crumbling or pressing the curd, or even heating it to around 50°C (120°F).

• *Ripening* is done by the action of different microorganisms, such as bacteria, moulds or yeasts, which work either on the surface or within the curd. The rind forms, with the aid of salt, the curd is transformed and the flavour asserts itself.

largest goat's milk cheese made. This is also the reason why Saint-Maure-de-Touraine has a straw running through it – not to aerate it but to reinforce it.

THE VARIOUS KINDS OF MILK therefore, have qualities that make them more or less easy to adapt to certain recipes. The practised eye can recognize this immediately the milk arrives at the dairy. It is a question of consistency. Milk from cows and goats is quite white in colour and appears much more fluid than ewe's milk, which is opaque, viscous and fragrant. Such a texture, purely from its appearance, reveals good cheese-making qualities. A litre (1¾ pints) of this milk will produce twice as much cheese as a litre of cow's milk. Ewes are the champions when it comes to cheese-production.

IN THE MATTER OF SMELL, on the other hand, all types of milk tend to be similar initially. It takes time for their singular characteristics to emerge. In the case of goat's milk it needs either to be kept cold for a lengthy period or to be made into cheese before the 'goat taste' has a chance to develop. This odour is linked largely to certain fatty acids. The Bleu de Causses (cow's milk) and Roquefort (ewe's milk), first cousins in terms of production are, however, very different because the fatty acids they contain are different. It is the fat content of the milk that both fixes and develops the aromas. Butter's unfortunate capacity for taking on all the other odours in the refrigerator is a clear indication of this. Fat soaks up smells like a sponge.

ON THE SHELVES, depending on the season, I arrange cheeses by milk type or according to size. In the cellar the order is strictly governed by the recipe used in their making; cheeses are matured in family groups, each in the conditions most suited to it.

IT WOULD BE OUT OF THE QUESTION, for example, to put washed-rind cheeses that need cool, damp conditions (Munster, Epoisses, Maroilles, etc.), beside most goat's milk cheeses, which do better in a dry atmosphere. A Caprini from Piedmont would not improve for being covered, in the space of a few days, by the reddish mould from an all-pervading Belgian Herve.

THAT IS WHY, IN THE CELLAR, it makes no sense to arrange the cheeses by milk type or according to their *terroir* of origin. The cow's milk Saint-Marcellins can share cellar-space with Pérails (ewe's milk) and Gramats (goat), while the Tommes from the Bauges (cow's milk) can go with Tommes from the Pyrenees (ewe) or the Chevrolins from Aravis (goat). It is a question of affinity and similar production methods.

IF ONE WERE TO COMPILE a 'Noah's Ark' of cheeses, like that conceived by the Italian association 'Slow Food' (an organization created as an antidote to 'Fast Food'

and a great enthusiast of diversity), it would need to be guided by good professionals or it would be a shambles. Each one would have to be placed where it could best retain its essential character, its colour and its flavour. I recall some Normandy Camemberts accidentally colonized by the blue mould from goat's milk cheeses from Touraine: really not presentable!

ON THE FOLLOWING PAGES are cheeses that are in sparkling form in spring: cheeses with natural rind (Crottins), brushed rind (Chevrotin), bloomy rind (Royal Briard), washed rind (Vieux-Boulogne), etc. While they can be safely placed together for a buffet, such an arrangement would be unthinkable in the cellar, as you will have realized.

Chevrotins des Bauges in Denis Provent's cellars at Chambéry. The cheeses are brushed in the last stages of ripening.

Crottin de Chavignol

France (Centre)
Goat's milk

Chavignol, a little village in the centre of France, can be seen from the top of Sancerre, beside the Loire. There are vineyards everywhere. The history of this cheese is closely linked with that of the wine: goats are the 'poor man's cow' for these small wine-growers. The Crottin de Chavignol is now very hackneyed; all the French regions make 'Crottins'. I put my trust in a young farmer, Magali Legras, located at the edge of the vineyards in Pays-Fort, an undulating and fairly damp, wooded area of pastureland. The estate, with its typical black stone Berry farmhouse, is ringed by a poplar grove. Its 90 goats are put out to grass during the summer period – a rare sight in the region these days. The Crottins produced there gradually develop – as Crottins should – a fine blue mould, without losing their freshness. Magali, tired of complaints that his cheeses are 'excessively rich', is thinking of giving up his AOC label (label of origin). If necessary, I will follow his example and call his cheeses 'Farmhouse Crottins'. It you visit the region, don't hesitate to ask to taste his *repassées* Crottins, which are ripened for as long as three months in earthenware pots; they are creamy in the centre, just like they were in the old days. Sensitive palates should abstain!

Chevrotin des Bauges

France (Rhône-Alpes)
Goat's milk

This one has all the virtues! Chevrotin des Bauges, made always with the full-flavoured milk from the mountains, exudes natural goodness with its thick, greyish rind and yellow or red growth of mould, according to season – even pink, in the summer. Four or five cheese-makers produce it at Les Bauges, highlands that form a natural, well-defined entity between Annecy, Chambéry and Albertville, partly in Savoie and partly in Haute Savoie. Les Bauges rises to an altitude of 2,200 metres (7,200 feet) and the villages are situated at between 600 and 1,100 metres (2,000 and 3,600 feet). This region, though known for its cow's milk Tommes, has been producing this goat's milk version for a long time now. A Chevrotin uses about 6 litres (10 pints) of milk and needs a good two months of ripening for the cheese to soften. I leave this in the hands of Denis Provent, *affineur* at Chambéry, who knows every nook and cranny of the mountains. He works principally with a producer who has divided his herd into three groups to stagger the lactation periods and avoid spending long months out of production … which frustrates the winter-sports enthusiasts who come to the area! Denis assures me that a bottle of Gamay from Savoie goes very well with Chevrotin. You must try it!

Dôme du Poitou

France (Poitou-Charentes)
Goat's milk

Dôme, though an unusual shape for a cheese, nevertheless offers excellent results: it is ripened in a perfectly standard way and its pyramid shape makes it much easier to cut. Hélène Servant has been making this small, very creamy cheese in that shape for seven years at Melle, in Deux-Sèvres, an important goat-breeding area. A customer who wanted cheeses made in that format brought her a model of the mould and, with a few years experience behind her, Hélène decided to concentrate exclusively on cheese production (she makes 15 different kinds); she no longer keeps her own goats but buys her milk from a neighbouring stockbreeder. Her methods are entirely traditional: use of raw milk, ladle moulding, no industrial ferments used, etc. Hélène is heart-broken when customers ask her for *fromage frais*; she recommends at least two months ripening for her Dôme de Poitou. This cheese, whose rind only very occasionally turns bluish, is also made in a *cendré* version, sprinkled with powdered charcoal. This is a cheese which, though mild to the palate, nevertheless has an authentic, farm-product identity and cuts a fine figure on the table.

Pecorino Sardo
Italy (Sardinia)
Ewe's milk

In Italy, the name *Pecorino* covers a prolific and very varied family of cheeses, most of which are used grated, sliced or cut into slivers to flavour and embellish not only pasta but many other dishes. While we use them fresh, the Italians like them as hard as stone. Their origins are lost in the mists of time (they were known to Pliny the Elder). The only thing they have in common is their name, which means 'cheese made from ewe's milk'. Almost every region produces its own version, the best-known being Pecorino Romano (made both in Latium and Sardinia), Pecorino Toscano (made in Tuscany) and this Pecorino Sardo (also called Fiore Sardo), which is one of the most frequently exported varieties.
It is made in the form of a cylinder with a nicely curved crust; it can weigh up to 4 kilos (9 pounds) and rarely less than 1.5 kilos (3½ pounds).
Benefiting from an *Appellation d'Origine Contrôlée* (label of origin), it is a seasonal cheese, made largely in the early part of the year. The mild, *dolce* version, ripened from 20 to 60 days, has a soft centre; the hard, brittle *Maturo* must have been matured for at least a year. Like a great many hard-pressed ewe's milk cheeses, Pecorino Sardo releases slightly lemony aromas when young and can become piquant as it ages.

Vieux-Boulogne
France (North)
Cow's milk

The north-western quarter of France is the home of soft and washed-rind cheeses, and Philippe Olivier, my fellow *affineur*, has become their harbinger. He was behind the production of Vieux-Boulogne. He and a young cheesemaker made many preliminary attempts and for the first time, in 1982, he introduced this cheese, which is similar in appearance to a Pont-l'Evèque. Since then, three small producers have begun making Vieux-Boulogne (the 'Vieux-' name-form is common in the north, where there is also a Vieux-Lille and a Vieux-Gris-de-Lille). The cows are pastured between Blanc-Nez and Gris-Nez, where the often strong winds blow the damp, salty air onto the grass and give rise to a very specific kind of fungal growth. The lightly pressed cheese is very close-textured and permits the formation of fermentation holes, while the rind is washed with Saint-Leonard beer – an original touch. The ripening period is two months on average.
I should stress that here we have a cheese with both character and presence – a happy development that demonstrates the vitality of the farming world. While traditional products, often dating from a long way back, are disappearing regularly, others are being brought forward and forming new traditions.

Royal Briard
France (Ile de France)
Cow's milk

All the cheese-*affineurs* in the Paris region offer their own version of Brillat-Savarin, triple-cream cheese invented at the start of the last century. This is not because they are attempting to usurp it for their own purposes, but because great skill is required to *affiner* this fairly delicate type of product. It can form bitter, soapy flavours beneath the rind if not properly handled. Practically speaking, everything hangs on the first days after the cheese is made. In particular, the *affineur* must pay close attention to the onset of mould and the way in which the cheese gives up its water-content in the *haloirs* (drying rooms). Gerard Gratiot, *affineur* in Hauts-de-Seine and specialist in soft and bloomy-rind cheeses from Ile de France, offers this Royal Briard, made in Seine-et-Marne and ripened in his cellars at Asnières. He works on it for four to six weeks. The cheese gradually loses weight in the *haloir*, sometimes going from 600 grams (20 ounces) down to 450 grams (16 ounces). Its rich, creamy texture makes it truly a 'special occasion' cheese. Indeed, most of it is sold at Christmas and New Year or Easter.

33

Away up to the high pastures!

At the end of spring in the mountains, the herds are taken to the high pastures, where they will remain for about a hundred days. Although, increasingly, the animals are taken up in cattle trucks, this seasonal migration to the high ground, is still a lively process. And a promise of quality!

This is an enduring ritual: at the end of spring, in all the mountainous regions of Europe, the animals are taken up to feed on the rich grass of the high mountain pastures. I always try to get to Allanches, in my own region of Cantal, to join in this colourful spectacle.

AS THEY LEAVE THE COW SHEDS, there is great excitement and much clattering of hooves on the ground. At first the animals gambol – literally – take the quickest route, trot along briskly, but as the sun rises higher in the sky the pace begins to slacken. When the going gets steeper the herd thins out and straggles along in single file. Tongues start to loll out and the animals stop to rest in the shade and take a moment as they round a bend to glance back towards the village, now lost among the greenery.

Transhumance festivities in Aubrac, in the Massif Central. Cows decked in their best trappings to go to their summer quarters.

stored for the winter. They stay in the high pastures for about three months, and while nowadays they are generally transferred by lorry, without any festivity, the work carried on at high altitude is still just as demanding and involves long working days. The stock has to be tended, the summer pastureland maintained and twice a day the milk must be made into cheese. (See pages 92 to 100).

IN THE ALPINE MOUNTAINS, the mechanics of the transfer are quite sophisticated; the animals are taken up the slopes in carefully calculated successive stages, to altitudes ranging from 1,500 to 2,500 metres (5,000 to 8,000 feet) (2,800 metres (9,000 feet) in some circumstances). The growth cycles of vegetation are more rapid on mountain slopes. The first cycle begins with the thaw and lasts about a month. The grass grows for 10 to 15 days once the snow has cleared and is ready for grazing one week later. If there is enough rain, the middle of summer sees a small re-growth that can be used three weeks later.

THE ANIMALS thus follow this progressive growth of the grass, which occurs later and later as the altitude increases, and by around the middle of August they have arrived at the highest point. On the way down they

THIS TRANSFER OF LIVESTOCK is frequently accompanied by festivities. The cows are decked out with large bells and ribbons and set out for the high pastures followed by an old-fashioned procession. This is a tradition dating back to the Middle Ages and is still very much alive in the French Alps and the Pyrenees, and also in Auvergne, the Vosges and the Jura. The reason for it is practical: the need to make the best use of available resources. Taking the animals to feed on high pastures means that the grass in the lowlands can be made into hay and

Pastures at Jarsy, in the Massif des Bauges. The practice of grazing the high pastures in summer is still very much alive in the whole of the Alpine region. *Opposite page: bottom left: ancient wooden mould in the Maison du Val d'Abondance museum.*

What faith can we put in labels of quality?

Red label, AOC, farmhouse cheese, unpasteurized milk, organically produced, manufacturer's guarantee of quality: all these indications of quality appear on labels. It is difficult to find your way around them and know how much you can rely on them. Cheese is, in fact, the result of a very long production chain that involves a number of trades and a lot of know-how, from the stockbreeder, through the cheese-*affineur* to the retailer. A Camembert made from the finest milk can be insipid if it is not properly ripened. Added to that, like any living, unpredictable natural product, the quality of cheese can vary greatly from one week to the next, especially if it is made from raw milk. And so, any label purporting to guarantee unreservedly the intrinsic quality of a traditional cheese, is guilty of misleading advertising. To my mind it is wiser to rely on the competence of the professional at the end of the chain – the retailer. He knows his wares, the conditions they were made under and for how long they have been ripened. He sorts them regularly, selects those which are at their best – or will be on a given day – will share his favourites with you and give valid reasons for his choices; and all without recourse to this or that label or title. These indications of quality are, however, both necessary and useful. They offer guidelines, not guarantees. They can point you in the right direction: the mention of pasteurized milk promises nothing special, but the logo of some of the more exacting AOCs (not all of them are) are reassuring. Remember, too, that first impressions are generally reliable: a cheese that doesn't immediately appeal to you is unlikely to offer any wonderful surprises.

Transhumance festivities at Allanches, in the Cantal region. A great ritual gathering.

stop to eat the re-grown grass at the place they grazed in July and, finally, that of the stage where they were in June.

SAVOIE, for example, has 80 farmhouse cheesemakers working in the high pastures, producing Beaufort, Tomme de Savoie, Tome des Bauges, Reblochon, Bleu de Termignon, Chevorotin des Aravis or Persillé de Sainte-Foy. With almost a thousand of these high pastures, ranging in size from 30 to 800 hectares (74 to 1,980 acres), it is one of the most important areas of seasonal migration (or transhumance) in France.

THE PRACTICE has undergone a certain revival since the 1970s, when the high mountain pastures were greatly under-used. Contrary to popular belief, the high pastures of Savoie are used predominantly by sheep and goats – 150,000 of them, against 38,000 cattle. Ninety thousand come from the South of

Pictured right and opposite page: farmhouse production of Abondance in the Chablais Massif, at André Girard's establishment. Temperature of the vat: almost 50°C (120°F).

France, principally from Bouches-du-Rhône, in herds easily numbering a thousand animals. Only 1,400 cattle make the same trip. Many of the stock-breeders in the south are – and this is no coincidence – expatriates from Savoie. Seasonal migration takes place principally in the Maures and Tarentaise valleys. The Beaufortin herds remain at pasture there from the end of spring to the middle of summer, then transfer to the Tarentaise, returning to the Beaufortin at the beginning of September.

IN THE VOSGES, where the hills are less rugged, there is no ascent by stages, no changing of valleys: in less than two hours the herds of cows have reached the *chaumes* – the pastures up at a height of 1,000 metres (3,300 feet) in the Voges. After going through the pine forests, then the beech groves, they come to a thick carpet of green dotted with splashes of colour: forget-me-nots, carnations, marguerites, dandelions, hounds-tongue, arnicas. There, as elsewhere, the chosen date owes nothing to chance: 'The transfer must take place on Tuesday, Thursday or Saturday,' a stockbreeder once told me. The other days are considered unlucky: it is said that witches have a hand in the business!

IN SWITZERLAND, at Martigny, the return to the valley in the autumn is the occasion for a quaint spectacle – the ritual battle of the 'queens'. During the summer, there is always one cow that establishes itself as head of every herd and these are set against each other in the town's Gallo-Roman arena. After some preliminary heats and much kicking and goring, a hierarchy develops and the final battle decides which cow is the 'queen of queens'.

TRANSHUMANCE, this great seasonal movement, is based on secular traditions, but the system has been badly weakened by the industrialization of agriculture and the exodus from rural areas which marked the last century. The importance currently being given to improvement in the countryside is bringing it to the fore again. And we cheesemakers will not be the ones to complain about that!

Pressing the cheeses speeds up the draining process and gives them a perfect shape. A characteristic of Abondance: a concave rind.

Idiazabal

Spain

(Basque provinces and Navarre)

Ewe's milk

Idiazabal came from the high Pyrenees, where the ewes of the Lacha and Caranzana breeds ranged freely over the mountains in the summer. In September, when the weather turned and the first cold spells arrived, the shepherds came back down to the valleys with their cargo of cheeses, slightly smoked after their prolonged stay in mountain cabins heated by log fires. There is still a smoked version of *Idiazabal*, made by farmers and small cheesemakers; producers on an industrial scale aren't aware of this variety. This characteristic product, which often carries Basque emblems printed on its rind, is made in a fairly stocky, cylindrical form. The cheese is starred with a scattering of small holes; its texture is quite dry but softens after ripening for six months. In many ways it resembles the ewe's milk Tommes from the French slopes but, on both sides of the frontier, local loyalties have permitted each to retain its truly individual character.

Grataron d'Arèches

France (Rhône-Alpes)

Goat's milk

Warning, a cheese in the process of disappearing! Denis Provent, cheese-*affineur* at Chambéry, never stops reminding me: the last three producers of Grataron d'Arèches are already getting on in years and their holdings are too small to be of interest to a possible rescuer. It would be a damaging loss, for this very attractive product is quite unique. To the best of Denis's knowledge it is the only soft, washed-rind goat's milk cheese in the whole of the Alps. It is produced at an altitude of about 1,500 metres (5,000 feet), at the heart of Beaufortin, on a valley floor, and it has never been imitated outside that area. At the start of the twentieth century it was made in every house. The peasants washed it – probably to remove the 'cat's hair' (the grey mould characteristic of Tommes de Savoie), which becomes intrusive in very damp weather. It was made mostly in winter. In the summer, when there was an abundance of milk, the production of Tommes took over. In the cellar, the cheese is regularly washed with a sponge soaked in salt water. The rind slowly takes on an orange to ochre colour, and the texture is soft. It is reminiscent of Reblochon, but with the flavour of Tomme and a little extra touch of salt that makes it very good indeed.

Abondance

France (Rhône-Alps)

Cow's milk

It needs 60 to 70 litres (100 to 120 pints) of milk to make a wheel of Abondance, easily recognized by its inward-curving sides, which are reminiscent of a Beaufort. Abondance comes from Chablais, in the Northern Alps, below Lake Léman.

It is made in much the same way as Gruyère, with the essential difference that the curd is slightly heated, giving a softer texture. This means that Abondance doesn't take as long to ripen as Beaufort – six weeks is enough for it to be at its best. It has a characteristic supple, even melting, texture. The farmhouse cheeses have a square patch of blue casein on the rind; those made in the dairy have an oval one. My friend Daniel Boujon, retailer at Thonon-les-Bains and great cheese connoisseur of Savoie cheeses, likes the very typical little bitter touch found in Abondance and reserves his praise for cheeses made by small producers in the high pastures. He often says, 'Dairy produced cheeses are like a beautifully-written page with no crossings-out – totally without character. The farmhouse product develops an aroma that even the best of the dairy products never achieves. Admittedly it occasionally has flaws, perhaps lacks the perfect little round holes required by the *Appellation d'Origine Contrôlée*, but these defects often give it richness and are the sign of a great cheese.' I couldn't agree more.

Saint-Nectaire

France (Auvergne)
Cow's milk

Saint-Nectaire has the good smell of earth and humus. Beneath its rind – sometimes covered with yellowish or reddish mould, the supple, soft cheese combines delicacy with a full flavour. It is sophisticated and distinguished. It once graced the table of Louis XIV, the Sun King, taken there around 1655 by Henri de la Ferté-Senneterre, Marshall of France, who gave it its name. Made in the Massif du Mont-Dore, in central Auvergne, its *terroir* is made up of volcanic earth covered by rich pastures. While the bulk of production nowadays is industrial, some 500 farmhouse cheesemakers ensure its vitality. Until 1990, my friend Philippe Jaubert, *affineur*, whose business was created by his grandfather in 1908, used the ancient, traditional method of ripening on rye straw laid on beaten earth. In natural cellars that are 150 years old, he ripens the cheeses from six or seven producers, some of whom still take their herds to the high pastures in summer. Saint-Nectaire is made either with a greyish, brushed rind, like those made by the peasants in the mountains, or a washed rind with an orange tinge, like those made on the plain. Each one has its adherents.

Persillé de Tignes

France (Rhônes-Alpes)
Goat's milk

This cheese gives me the opportunity, prompted by Denis Provent, to correct a common misconception: a *pâte-persillée* cheese is not a blue-veined cheese, but the product of curd which has been *recuit*, as one used to say in old French – meaning re-cooked. And the curd of this Persillé de Tignes is uniformly white! The recipe for re-cooked curd is a mountain speciality found also in Auvergne: the cheesemaker leaves the curd for a whole day then re-heats it together with a freshly coagulated batch the following day. It is then broken up again and re-moulded. This technique, derived entirely from practical experience, produces cheeses that keep for much longer. Produced in the Tignes valley and recognizable by its fairly definite flavour, this Persillé was saved from probable extinction by the success of the nearby winter-sports centre. The tourists keep coming back for more and the three or four farmhouse producers have trouble keeping up with demand, while the *affineur* can barely manage to keep the cheeses in his cellars for a month. In the old days they were ripened for six months, at the end of which time blue had developed in the cheese.

Tome des Bauges

France (Rhône-Alpes)
Cow's milk

Even though urbanization is gradually invading the outer slopes, Les Bauges is still traditionally inhabited by mountain people. This is the home of the very best Tommes de Savoie – a cheese that mass-production is making increasingly commonplace. The award of an AOC – 'Tome des Bauges' – based on serious criteria, is a step in the right direction: only raw milk to be used, supplementary ferments banned, priority given to local breeds (Tarine or Abondance cows), use of curd pumps banned as too harsh, minimum ripening period of five weeks in the appellation zone, etc. The Tomes des Bauges that I offer my customers are matured for more than two months, prepared for me by Denis Provent who goes to collect them, sometimes from up the mountains, from Alfred, Dominique, Stéphane, René, François and the others, some of the 20 or so producers who ensure the continued vitality of this cheese. Like all the other Tommes, Tome des Bauges has a greyish rind, with a pronounced mushroom flavour, enclosing a fairly soft cheese. In summer, the rind is sometimes tinged with pink, and in winter with traces of sulphur-yellow. It can also be unpredictable, like all farmhouse cheeses.

Do you know how many cheeses there are?

Nobody has ever been able to make a complete inventory of cheese; it is a constantly changing world. One thing is certain, however: France continues to offer an unequalled variety – though perhaps not one that could never be rivalled.

I am often asked how many cheeses there are, in France and elsewhere. I don't have an answer. A precise number would seem impossible to arrive at, since their definition raises so many problems. If every little farmhouse cheese, named after its maker or the place where it is made, is deemed worthy of inclusion in the census, they must number several thousand in France alone. Did you know that, just in France, there are about 25,000 farmhouse cheesemakers, of which more than 17,000 rear their own goats? Just counting the recipes used (sometimes very similar from one farm to another), considerably lessens the number. The art of cheese-making is embodied by its richness, its infinite number of forms and variations, as demonstrated by the six cheeses I have chosen to tell you about at the end of this chapter.

DEPENDING ON THE AVAILABILITY OF ANIMAL FEED, geographical variations and attitude, countries differ greatly in the degree of inventiveness they show. One could claim – though it would be a gross distortion – that the Dutch only make one kind of cheese: Gouda. Or that the Swiss limit their production to variations of the Gruyère family, while the Spaniards stick almost exclusively to goat's milk Tommes. On the other hand, countries like France, Italy and – to a lesser degree – the United Kingdom, are happy to employ a number of different techniques.

IN MY SHOP I always have around 250 different kinds. One of the biggest wholesalers in the Rungis food market estimates that his own stock exceeds 2,500 products. Many of them are new lines, produced during the last two decades when milk quotas encouraged dairy-farmers to get better value from their milk. This happened in France and, even more spectacularly, in Great Britain, where a veritable cheese renaissance took place. At the same time other products have disappeared, either because there was nobody to take over the business, or compliance with the new hygiene regulations proved too costly.

Newly unmoulded Picodons draining; the holes left by the cheese strainers are still visible on the surface.

Ladle-moulding – just a tradition, or a necessity?

It is a process that has not changed over more than two centuries. In thousands of farms and small cheese dairies where goat's and ewe's milk cheeses and small, soft cow's milk cheeses are made, the ladle is an indispensable implement to the cheesemaker – who is very often a woman. This little action requires precision, consistency and delicacy, so as not to break the curd. In the making of Camembert, for example, the cheesemaker begins by filling the ladle from the bowl of coagulated milk covered with a thin layer of whey, using a rapid, fluid action of the wrist. Hundreds of moulds, about 20 centimetres (8 inches) deep, are lined up on the moulding table in front of her. She deposits one ladleful into the bottom of each mould with a clean, precise gesture. This must be repeated a total of five times, at intervals of one hour, to make a Camembert. Why so much care and precision? The whey must drain from the cheese very slowly, over almost ten hours. If the curd is broken the drainage occurs too rapidly and when this happens the resulting cheese is drier, with a tendency to crumble. For goat's milk cheeses, ladle-moulding gives them a perfectly smooth texture. The technique of moulding by portioning (the curd is poured straight onto the moulding table) is unfortunately becoming more widespread; it saves a great deal of time and manpower – and woman-power – but the cheeses do not have quite the same excellent appearance. Curd treated with less care becomes gritty and gives a granular, irregular, less integrated texture. Another worry is that in some industrial dairies, particularly those within the Camembert AOC, the moulding is done by machine, which considerably speeds up production. The remaining small producers are demanding that labels marked 'ladle-moulded' should be restricted to that done by hand. This is understandable.

IN THIS PERPETUALLY EVOLVING SCENE, not a day goes by without the loss or gain of a cheese. It's very difficult, therefore, to settle on a definite number. On the other hand, there is no doubt that France is the 'land of cheese', the only one to offer, month in and month out, a choice of vastly differing products. You are familiar, of course, with Camembert, Brie, Roquefort, but have you tasted l'Ecir de l'Aubrac, Tomme Capra or Cœur Téotski? Behind each of these names is a very specific *micro-terroir* that has successfully cultivated and preserved its identity down the centuries.

THIS RICHNESS GOES BACK TO MIDDLE AGES, as I learned from the writings of Jean-Robert Pitte, professor of history at the Sorbonne. He recounts how, in that era, France became very inward-looking and restricted its commercial contacts – a regressive attitude when compared with the Gallo-Roman period, which had seen a movement towards unification of the regions. In this new context, cheese-production was largely destined for the home market, which accounts for its extraordinary diversity – a reflection of the variety of geological areas. In each one, however small, milk, pastures, natural ferments and production techniques were different.

In the Cevennes mountains of the Ardèche, the broom and heather are a great treat for the nanny goats, whose cheeses flood the local markets in March.

Valençays Cendrés from the De Diou farm. Vegetable charcoal is used to coat these cheeses in ash.

From the mountain pastures of Savoie to the rich meadows of Northern France and inland Provence, tourists who come to France never cease to be astonished by the richness of the countryside and diversity of climate.

BENEATH THIS PROFUSION nevertheless, lie basic rules and constants. Jean-Robert Pitte is really saying that a close look at the map of France discloses two major types of region: one producing predominantly fresh or soft cheeses, usually small in size; the other, mainly much larger, hard cheeses. The first occupy the low-lying areas, the second, the mountains. The main explanation for this is entirely attributable

to transport problems. The cheeses made in high pastures cannot be marketed until they are brought down to the valley at the end of the season, and only hard cheeses will keep for several months in that way (see pages 84 to 91).

LITTLE BY LITTLE, the historian explains, a choice came into play: those cheeses that were perishable and delicate to transport were produced near towns; hard cheeses and pressed-curd (raw or cooked) or pâte-persillée cheeses came from the farming areas situated far from towns, mainly in mountainous regions. The transport revolution and new methods of preserving food-stuffs have drastically altered the situation. For example, Brittany, which produced butter but for a long time made no fermented cheeses, now makes a large part of the Emmenthal consumed in France.

Sprinkled with fennel seeds and herbs, Gardian is eaten on the day it is made. *Above right* Ewe's milk Tomme from Arles, made on the same soil.

Picodon
France (Rhône-Alpes)
Goat's milk

Made in the Ardèche and Drôme, but also in a small part of Gard and Vaucluse, Picodon is at its best from March onwards. Its AOC is somewhat wide-ranging and fairly mixed in terms of quality. Anyway, it is the only cheese to have circled the world in the space shuttle: the French astronaut Jean-Jaques Favier took 14 Picodon cheeses with him aboard the Columbia in April, 1996. It is true that, at 7 centimetres (2¾ inches) in diameter it doesn't take up much room (in the Languedoc dialect *picho* means 'small'). The one I prefer comes from the Peytot farm in the Ardèche Cévennes. Christian Moyersoen keeps some 120 goats, looked after by a shepherdess among the chestnut woods, heather and broom. The farm stands at an altitude of about 750 metres (2,500 feet) at the end of a forest track. Christian arrives at local markets, where most of his sales are made, with 15 different kinds of cheeses in separate boxes: blue Picodons, brown ones, black, white, rather dull-looking cheeses ripened by the *méthode Dieulefit* (ripening in a damp cellar), etc. There is a positive explosion of cheeses from February to April, but the bulk of consumption is in summer, when the tourists arrive, and during end-of-year festivities. Which is why he is obliged to keep his cheeses and, therefore, to be aware of how best to ripen them – which he does brilliantly.

Gardian
France (Provence-Côte d'Azur)
Goat's milk

Christian Fleury belongs to the 'neo-rural' generation; he acquired his first goats in 1968. Since 1976 he has been farming the fields of Comtat Venaisson, near Saint-Rémy-de-Provence, outside Arles. He keeps a herd of 50 or so goats, which are fed essentially on excellent hay from the neighbouring meadows of Crau. In particular he makes a small Tomme Fraîche called Le Gardian, which I strongly recommend. This very mild cheese is topped with a bay leaf and sprinkled with fennel seeds, pepper and often a few seeds of aniseed too; not forgetting a drizzle of olive oil. Very fresh on the palate, it is typical of a cheese that should be eaten at the start of a meal rather than at the end. If you want to eat it at the end anyway, I suggest you have it as a dessert, with a touch of something sweet, like honey. Gardian is sold the day it is made. It also comes in a ripened version that, after three weeks, has an unctuous, almost creamy texture. That is the one they prefer in the area around Arles. At one time, when the *mistral* blew, the cheese had a tendency to dry out. In the farmhouses it was moistened with white wine or eau-de-vie then put to macerate in an earthenware jar so that it didn't put a strain on the eater's jaws.

Selles-sur-Cher
France (Centre)
Goat's milk

Selle-sur-Cher is a cheese that I recommend be eaten fairly young, particularly in spring and summer, when its aromas are at their most developed. That is when, in my opinion, its subtlety and lightness are at their best. It is a quite unusual shape: a bevelled disk about 10 centimetres (4 inches) in diameter and 3 centimetres (1 inch) high. It is made like this to distinguish it from its many neighbours, such as Chavignol (crottin), Sainte-Maure-de-Touraine (log-shaped) and Pouligny-Saint-Pierre and Valençay – both pyramids. The AOC zone is centred around the village of Selles-sur-Cher in the Loir-et-Cher department. It includes Basse Sologne, Champagne Berrichonne and the central valley of the Cher. Recognizable by its nutty flavour, enhanced by a touch of salt, Selle-sur-Cher is essentially made by farms and small dairies. Its *cendré* rind and its lack of depth make it unsuitable for cooking, so don't put it in the oven. You could, however, put it in a green salad, cut into thin slivers, together with pine nuts and walnuts, for instance. It has a natural affinity for the Sauvignon wines of the Loire, and also for Chardonnay from Burgundy.

Besace, made with pure goat's milk
France (Rhône-Alpes)
Goat's milk

This cheese, with its indeterminate shape, was created by an imaginative farmer in the Tarentaise. It is a 'pre-drained goat's milk cheese' which brings to mind the recipe for mozzarella. After coagulating the milk, he hangs the curd in cloths suspended from the ceiling and leaves it to drain. This is the so-called 'pre-draining' process, an ancient method also used for Tarentais, as well as for Persillé from the Haute Tarentaise. After a while, he mixes the curd again in a bowl with some hot whey and a little salt, then he squeezes it energetically, just once, in a cloth. A few crafty people, attracted by his success, have tried to copy him, but they were wasting their time! The cloth is removed immediately after the pressing.

The shape of the cheese, which weighs about 250 grams (9 ounces), is reminiscent of a *besace* (shepherd's pouch), which, understandably enough, is the name they gave it. In the course of ripening (three to four weeks at the most), a fine, whitish rind forms, as light as that of the Saint-Marcellin. The finest feature of this Besace is its softness on the palate.

Charolais
France (Burgundy)
Goat's milk

In all the Charolais mountain areas goats are overshadowed by the prestigious local cattle, the Charolais. The announcement that an AOC was to be granted for the local goat's milk cheese, Charolais, gained the nanny goats a little bit more respect. And they can be proud of their classy cheese, made in the form of a tower, which is notable for its dense and compact texture. Bernard Sivignon – a successor to the *racotiers* of years gone by, who went from farm to farm collecting cheeses, chickens, eggs and rabbits – is one of the great architects of this development. He ripens (under the name of Clacbitou) the produce from 50 or so farmers, mostly women who have followed in their mothers' footsteps. It needs 2 to 2.5 litres (3½ to 4½ pints) of milk to make one cheese according to a method which demands patience and delicacy (slow coagulation, hand-ladling into moulds, draining over several days, and so on). That's the price that must be paid for a texture that is very smooth and homogeneous without being brittle. Well-ripened (up to four weeks), Charolais offers aromas of almonds and hazelnuts. The presence of a blue mould on the rind – as long as it is not too pronounced – gives it the taste of mushrooms and of the cellar.

Feta
Greece
Goat's or ewe's milk

Feta is a very ancient Greek cheese whose origins are lost in antiquity. But today it is the Danes who produce it in the greatest volume. French producers are not far behind, particularly near Roquefort, where they have taken to making it with any surplus goat's or ewe's milk. One can even find Feta made with pasteurized cow's milk. This is the consequence of not patenting the name of an ancient recipe soon enough. The European Union is currently seeking a remedy that will give back to Greece the exclusive right to its heritage. But to return to the source: like the whole of the Mediterranean basin, Greece, with its poor and arid soil, is dedicated to extensive stock-breeding, which suits goats and sheep very well. On account of the heat, the milk is set to coagulate immediately after milking, using rennet. Then it is separated from the whey by drainage and light pressure, in cloth bags or in moulds, before being plunged into salt water. Once it has become firm it is ready to eat. It's that simple. Refreshing, widely used in summer salads, Feta can even have a very aromatic and slightly acidic flavour. But to judge it properly one has to go to markets in Greece, where farmers' wives still sell it from round, woven baskets.

It's the season for fairs!

Cheese, like wine, is made for sharing and creating a convivial atmosphere. From the end of spring onwards, all manner of fairs, gatherings and shows are held to celebrate this bounty with feasting.

With the influx of tourists, the end of spring is the right time to hold great gastronomic fairs. Many of them celebrate local cheeses with much pomp, not forgetting the wines that accompany them so well. In Estremadura, the *Fiera Nationale de Caso di Trujillo* is like a fair in medieval times. In France one of the most famous fairs is that of Sainte-Maure-de-Touraine, a few kilometres from Tours, which is held on the first weekend in June every year, and brings forth a great show of farmhouse cheeses. In the same month, Ambert, in Auvergne, welcomes the 'Fourmofolies'. But perhaps, at that time of year, you would prefer to visit Rocamadour and the celebrations to honour the local Petit Palet du Chevre.

RIGHT UP TO THE END OF SUMMER not a single weekend passes without some kind of celebration of a local cheese. Chosen at random, there is the *Fête du Picodon* at Saou, in the middle of July, Auvergne's *Fête Bleu*

at Riom-es-Montagnes in August, or the *Fête des Terroirs Fromagers d'Europe* in September, at Lausanne. The procession is endless, right until October, with the *Fête de la Fourme* at Montbrison. Not forgetting, of course, the many 'transhumance' festivals, which can begin in May, and all the little local fairs where cheese, and other products, are honoured guests.

THE PICTURE WOULD BE INCOMPLETE if I didn't invite you to attend one of the gatherings of the *Guilde des Fromagers-Confrérie de Saint-Uguzon* (Cheesemakers' Guild – Brotherhood of Saint-Uguzon) organization, of which I have the honour to be President of the Provost's Council since 1992. More than 4,000 people are, or were, members of the Guild (it is reserved for professionals) and of the Brotherhood, which is for amateurs. Present

The very picturesque cheese fair at Alkmaar is now just for tourists rather than traders (Netherlands).

in 32 countries, this association is often asked to preside over, or organize cheese shows. It also regularly organizes gatherings of its own (more than 300 since it started in 1969). These meetings alternate between visits to sites where cheeses are made, festivities and relaxing moments, all in honour of cheese – sometimes in unusual places. Walking shoes are often recommended!

SOME RECENT EXAMPLES? Events have taken us to Bessin, beside the salt marshes of Isigny or the high mountain pastures of Gstaad, in Switzerland; into the sacred atmosphere of Orval Abbey in Belgium and the majestic venue of the monumental cellars beneath the ancient military fort of Rousses in the Jura (with a prodigious play of light around the thousands of wheels of Comté); to sea, off the Ile de Ré, or to the top of Mont d'Or. We have been to the *maquis* on the Ile de Beauté and to the lakes of Quebec; to the United States, to defend traditional cheeses made from raw milk and to Saint-Jean-de-Cuculles, in Cevennes, to celebrate the marriage of wines and Pélardon cheeses… The exceptional heritage of cheese truly offers a wide variety of pleasures.

ALL THESE GATHERINGS – a dozen or so every year – take place under the auspices of Saint Uguzon, a shepherd with a big heart brought out of obscurity by Father Androuët, one of the founder members of the Guild. This shepherd kept a flock of sheep in Lombardy, near the present town of Cavargna and was in the habit of distributing cheese and lambs to the poor, only to be finally killed by his somewhat intolerant master. Legend recounts that a spring burst forth at the scene of the crime, whose healing waters were beneficial in the treatment of eye diseases. There is a shrine dedicated to the shepherd saint on the Swiss-Italian border, to which the Guild has already organized two pilgrimages. The feast of Saint Uguzon is celebrated on July 12th.

Holstein cows in the area around Alkmaar. Intensive stock-breeding is a great tradition in the Netherlands.

50

At the Alkmaar cheese fair:
the Edam and Gouda cheeses
are laid on mats on the ground.

APART FROM THE TITLES CONFERRED BY THE CONFRÉRIES –
Companion, *Garde et Juré* (an official), *Prud'homme*
('man of experience and integrity'), Master-cheesemaker –
and some good-natured folklore (at official reunions its
members wear the historic dress of
Parisian merchants), the Guild is
built, first of all, on a generous
philosophy that brings together all
members of the cheese-making
world, from the shepherd right
through to the lover of good food.

TO HELP YOU UNDERSTAND WHAT MOTIVATES our
association, I would like to tell you about the journey
undertaken by one of our members, Ian Picard, a young
man from Quebec. Under our auspices, he went on a
year-long tour to get to know France which took him,
in the true spirit of the Guild, to the doors of professionals
from the whole cheese-making membership of the Guild
network: producers, *affineurs*, retailers, etc. His father,
Marc, an ice-hockey coach, discovered cheese when
he went to Switzerland to take charge of a team there.
He decided to make it his trade and open a shop in
Montreal. With us, his son toured Normandy, the Loire
valley, Quercy and Cevennes, and the Pyrenees.
Now, on the other side of the Atlantic, he is one of the
most dynamic representatives of the traditional cheese
trade and, from his base in Montreal, is not unhopeful of
converting North America to 'real cheeses'.

Worth a visit – the fair at Alkmaar

Between 10 am and midday every Thursday
morning, from April to the end of September, the
main square in the little town of Alkmaar, north of
Amsterdam, is covered with hundreds of yellow
globes of Edam and wheels of Gouda. This
cheese market is one of the most famous in the
Netherlands. While it has lost its original function
– that of a market where the cheesemakers of the
area sold their produce to wholesalers and retailers
– it has become a great tourist attraction. With its
Brotherhood of Cheese Porters it is a first-rate
traditional spectacle. Dressed all in white, with
coloured bands around their dark hats, they work in
pairs, carrying the cheeses on a litter slung from their
shoulders by ropes. Arms spread and knees lifted
high at each step, they cross the square in a rapid,
jerky, sometimes synchronized style to transport their
precious cargo to the waiting merchants' carts.
A splendid building with a crenellated frontage
overhangs the square; this houses the public scales
where the cheeses were weighed to determine the
amount of tax due to the municipality. The Alkmaar
public weighing facility dates back four centuries
and was the most important one in the whole of
the Netherlands. Very few towns were allowed to
have one, and that of Alkmaar was still in use at
the beginning of the last century.

Master cheesemaker of France!

Since 1998, cheesemakers have competed for
the prestigious award of Master Cheesemaker of
France, along the lines of that granted to so many
great chefs.
In September 2000, four of my colleagues were
awarded this precious ribbon: Marie Quatrehomme,
of Paris (the first woman to qualify in the food-related
category); Christian Janier, from Lyons; Hervé Mons
from Roanne, and Parisian, Laurent Dubois. The
most spectacular part of the competition consists
of producing a 'pyramid of flavours', an 'aesthetic
creation made up of several large cheeses
accompanied by a number of small ones, either
whole or in pieces'. I have been personally involved
for 15 years in trying to convince the authorities to
open the competition to the trade of cheese-making.
What a long way we have come since the years
immediately after the war, when retailers of cheese,
butter and eggs had a very poor image. One only
has to read Jean Dutour's work, *Au bon beurre*
'I can recall remarks made by my schoolmates,
who used to call me "the son of a dairyman".'
It is a source of personal pride that I have made
some contribution towards obtaining recognition
of my trade, in the form of a State diploma, and
towards making it a synonym of excellence.

Rocamadour

France (Midi-Pyrénées)
Goat's milk

This little round disk is covered with a fine, ivory-coloured, slightly velvety growth. It belongs to an illustrious family – the Cabécou, a goat's milk cheese from the South whose origins probably go back to the Arab invasions. In the Languedoc dialect *cabécou* means 'little goat'. Rocamadour gets its name from the magnificent village in the Lot, perched on the side of a cliff. This very popular tourist destination, one of the traditional halts on the road to Santiago di Compostela, rests on a chalk plateau where goats browse on vegetation that is very varied and rich in aromatic plants. Rocamadour needs a dozen or so days to ripen. After that its rind tends to give way; if you want to keep it nice and creamy, wrap it and put it in a cool, dry place. But it is far better to eat it as soon as possible, with a light, fragrant, dry white wine – a Sauvignon, perhaps. This is, par excellence, a springtime and summer cheese (the Rocamadour fair is held in June) but it is still delicious right up to autumn. A concentrated pleasure.

Farmhouse Gouda

Netherlands
Cow's milk

The whole world is familiar with Dutch cheeses made from pasteurized milk and destined for export. But this country, a champion of intensive production and stock-rearing, also produces farmhouse cheeses that are rather less 'all-purpose'. There are no less than 600 cheesemakers producing Farmhouse Gouda from raw milk – the *Boërenkaas*, for example, made near a nature reserve to the north of Amsterdam. Gouda, named after a small port near Rotterdam, is shaped like a millstone and coated with yellow paraffin wax. The ancient trading tradition of the Netherlands favours the production of cheeses that will stand up to transporting over long distances, in other words, firm cheeses. Soft and mild when young, Gouda becomes hard and brittle as it ages, with a slightly salty and piquant flavour. The best ones can be ripened for two years or more. The rind is almost always impeccably waxed, though in some instances herbs and spices are discernible. Cumin, paprika, nettle, black pepper, garlic, rosemary, mustard seed – Dutch cheesemakers are well aware of their fellow-citizens' taste for the exotic. Their best showcase is the fair at Alkmaar (see page 51), which is as picturesque as it is entertaining.

Fourme d'Ambert

France (Auvergne)
Cow's milk

Married for a time, Fourme d'Ambert and Fourme de Montbrison have decided to go their separate ways: both covered by the same AOC, they wish to resume their 'maiden names' to avoid being mistaken for each other, as happened with Munster and Géromé, or with Valençay and Levroux. While they both come from the slopes of the Mont du Forez, Montbrison faces east and Ambert west. The latter is recognized by its dry, grey rind, with occasional little red patches. The former, ripened on pine racks, is an attractive, orange-ish colour. The paste of Fourme d'Ambert is 'wilder', more veined with blue than that of Montbrison. This amicable divorce, which has already resulted in them holding separate fairs, is not just a 'Clochemerle' affair; it comes within the framework of the renaissance movement, and demonstrates how culturally attached local people are to their product. In 1996, after a twenty-year absence, a farmhouse Fourme d'Ambert – made with raw milk – has re-emerged. I make no secret of my support for these cheese-producers who have an acute sense of *terroir*.

Maquis Brunelli

France (Corsica)
Ewe's milk

Rosemary, savory, juniper berries, peppers, oregano – from Bastia to Bonifacio, Corte to Ajaccio, the herbs and spices of the maquis abound in the markets of this beautiful island. Corsican cheesemakers traditionally use them to flavour and improve the keeping qualities of their Tommes, as well as the Brocciu Passu. This technique allows them to set aside some of their produce during abundant months to be consumed later. The cheeses are put to dry and rolled in herbs and spices. Sometimes they are macerated in local marc, which gives them a fuller flavour. Jean-François Brunelli and I have perfected this little cheese, a fresh Tomme coated in a mixture of herbs exactly three days after it is made. It is a seasonal cheese – Jean-François' flock of 120 ewes only gives milk from November to July. They all belong to the Corsican breed, a rustic species ranging in colour from white to black, passing though grey and brown, and hardy enough to stay out winter and summer alike. The milk from this flock is of an excellent quality for cheese-making – this Maquis is the resounding proof of that. Each year in April it is very much on view at a show which is becoming increasingly important in Corsica – that of the farmhouse cheese-producers of Cauro, a village 10 kilometres (6 miles) from Porticcio.

Pavé de Gâtine

France (Poitou-Charente)
Goat's milk

Pavé de Gâtine was created by 30-year-old farmer, Sébastien Gé. His parents came to Deux-Sèvres in 1976, with no previous knowledge of cheese-making but with plenty of willingness to learn. Sébastien took over from them in 1995 and keeps a herd of about a hundred goats, the whole of whose milk yield he makes into cheese. The farm is 25 kilometres (16 miles) north of Niort, in an area that is very like Brittany, with standing stones weighing several tons resembling menhirs. Sébastien makes about 200 cheeses a day, including this square-shaped Pavé de Gâtine, which is made from raw milk and ladled into the mould. It takes 2 litres (3½ pints) of milk to make one Pavé. Because the cheese is not very thick, it must be ripened with great care. A slight white down of *Geotrichum* forms on the surface with a scattering of blue penicillium. Once the cheese is well-drained in the *hâloir* (drying room), Sébastien places it on a chestnut leaf for presentation. He collects the leaves from the trees himself in the autumn and dries them by the fire, then stores them in a fairly dry place. His reward is the reputation of this smooth, creamy Pavé, fêted year after year at the regional goat's milk cheese fair held at Niort at the beginning of May.

Sainte-Maure-de-Touraine

France (Central)
Cow's milk

Far from the flamboyance of the Mediterranean and the opulence of Normandy, Touraine delights in restrained measures and a refined ambience, as illustrated by the sun rising on the morning mists over the Loire. The 'garden of France' has produced a cheese that fits this image of refinement and finesse: Sainte-Maure-de-Touraine. Made from raw milk, it is identified by its balanced flavour and its very fine grain. About 30 centimetres (12 inches) long, it is usually pierced from end to end by a straw which in former days allowed farmers to stick broken cheeses back together again or reinforce them. Woe betide anyone who cuts the first piece from the narrow end; according to an old saying, this is 'cutting the goat's udder'. Almost a hundred farmers produce this delicate cheese, imitated throughout France under the name of 'Sainte-Maure'. The flavour is influenced by the seasons; in summer it gives off aromas of dried hay, changing to nutty flavours in the autumn. It is white when young and bluish after ripening for three weeks to a month, or it can be *cendré* according to an old technique that improves its keeping qualities. A sparkling Vouvray is always a happy accompaniment.

53

The difference is in the ripening

While a bad affineur *can ruin an excellent cheese, a good* affineur *can never hope to restore quality and vivacity to a lacklustre or mediocre one. This trade, which fosters talent in a manner worthy of Pygmalion, is as crucial as it is unrecognized.*

Cheese should be served at its best and no other way, that is to say, ripened and brought to perfect maturity: neither too much nor too little. In the case of fruit everybody understands this – no one chooses a pear that is still unripe or an apricot that's as hard as stone. And it's the same with wine, even if we are impatient and want to open the bottles before they are really ready. But when it comes to cheese, it has to be admitted that people still need

educating. What delights are narrowly missed, or glimpsed only faintly, when one eats a cheese that is unripe, still insipid and flat! Believe me – most cheeses improve with ripening, but it is a process that demands know-how.

THE JOB OF THE *AFFINEUR* requires an intimate knowledge of his cheeses, their life cycle and the conditions in which they are happiest. Like most of my colleagues, I learned the trade on the job, watching, listening, touching. The path that leads from just-coagulated milk to the cheese merchant's shelves can be a very long one – as much as three years for some cheeses.

WHEN THEY COME FROM THE CHEESEMAKER'S WORKPLACE the cheeses have already been moulded and been given their definitive shape, but they are as naked as a cheese in a cheese-strainer. They have an acid, lactic, sour taste. *Affinage* consists of giving them a rind, making their texture agreeable to the palate and revealing the aromas and flavours locked inside them. A job worthy of an obstetrician!

Patrick Beaumont, who created Lavort. This cannonball-shaped cheese should only be ripened for four months. Beyond that the rind becomes too thick, to the detriment of the cheese.

Making Lavort: the milk is
set in big troughs to coagulate
with the aid of rennet.

I WON'T CLUTTER YOUR HEAD with too many technical details, for each family of cheeses requires a specific approach and each cheese in every species is different. This work is, by its very nature, a 'bespoke' trade that uses all the senses: the eye, to give the alarm when the rind of the cheese sinks too far, or mould growths develop abnormally; the nose, to detect excessive fermentation; the hand, to divine the texture of the cheese simply by pressing it; finally the ear, to 'listen to' the texture of, for example, a ball of Mimolette when it is tapped. Only experience teaches one to identify the difference.

TO SUM UP: first of all the cheese dries as the water left behind after draining evaporates. At the same time, yeasts and moulds gradually develop on the surface, forming first a silky down and then a rind. This protects the cheese from excessive drying and helps the flavours to develop. Almost all cheeses need turning regularly so that the humidity is lost evenly, and some are washed with a sponge impregnated with salt water (Maroilles, Taleggio, Swiss Vacherin, Epoisses, etc.), or rubbed with a mixture of other products (secret to each cheesemaker), like the mixed herbs used in the making of Appenzell. Some even require brushing, as happens to many of the Tommes.

Can one ripen cheese at home?

It is fruitless to try to improve the condition of cheese in the refrigerator; the temperature is too low and the humidity insufficient for even ripening to continue.

The sole purpose of a refrigerator is keeping things fresh. If you are the fortunate owner of a good cellar there are certain cheeses you could perhaps consider ripening. The temperature needs to be about 10°C (50°F) and the humidity quite high and more or less constant. However, you must stick to cheeses that require no specialized care, such as those with a bloomy rind, that can be kept in an insect-proof food-safe. In that case there is hope that at the end of a week, a chalky Camembert would have softened or the flavour of a too-mild Brie de Meaux would be enhanced.

Goat's milk cheeses should not be put in the cellar; they prefer dry cold and risk fermenting in humid conditions. Nor should cheeses with washed rinds, such as Munster, be put in the cellar – unless wrapped in clingfilm the damp will quickly cause mould to develop. Large cheeses, such as whole Gruyère, are less at risk (unless a passing mouse, lured by the smell, manages to sink its teeth into them!)

Common sense dictates that you buy cheeses that are ready for eating from a good cheese merchant, and consume them fairly quickly; which is what most people who have been disappointed by risky experiments in the past end up doing. Remember that cheese is a delicate living substance that demands good bacteriological conditions and resist the temptation to play 'sorcerer's apprentice'!

At the supermarket

The large outlets find it difficult to offer cheese in peak condition, partly on account of lack of equipment and know-how, but also because of commercial considerations: their constant aim of high volume and low prices, as well as the need for quick turnover of stock, does not allow the cheeses to be handled in the way they deserve. It is therefore difficult to find top-quality cheeses (which are more often than not those made from raw milk) in this type of retail outlet. On the shelves, and even on counters selling them by weight, cheeses are generally kept at a constant 4°C (39°F), without the slightest possibility of further ripening or development. Therefore it is fresh, or quick-ripening cheeses that will disappoint you least. If you are looking for a cheese with which to end a good meal, I can't recommend too strongly that you buy it from a retailer who is also an *affineur*.

Page opposite, another stage in the making of Lavort: dairy hands cut the agglomerated globules of curd into rectangular pieces and put them into moulds (*pictured on the left*).

WHILE THE SURFACE OF THE CHEESE is turning into a crust, the texture, flavour and aromas are also developing. Acidity, which starts off like that found in fresh white cheese, gradually fades, owing to the partial disappearance of lactic acid. Fat globules are transformed and become the main source of aromas. Milk proteins degrade and trap fat globules, thus forming an elastic and unctuous curd.

EACH OF THESE OPERATIONS takes place in different locations where the humidity and temperature are pre-determined (re-drying rooms, *haloirs*, ripening cellars). Temperatures range from 5°C (40°F) for blue-veined cheeses, for instance, to 15° C (60°F) for Gruyère and so on. Maximum humidity is often needed, as in the case of Saint-Marcellin. The cheeses are never kept all together. The 'cat's hair' mould, which develops in tufts, is sought-after in the ripening of Tomme de Savoie but detrimental to many other cheeses, especially those made from goat's milk.

IN MY CAPACITY OF RETAILER-*AFFINEUR* I undertake the full ripening process of those cheeses that come to me very young; others, delivered by specialist *affineurs* who have already done the bulk of the work, simply have to be 'finished'. Denis Provent from Chambéry is one of these specialists, Jean-Charles Arnaud, at Poligny, Carlo Fiori from Piedmont, Joseph Paccard, from near Manigod and Bernard Sivignon from the Charolais region are others. It is far better for the great wheels of Comté to be cared for in the sumptuous cellars of Fort des Rousses, near the Swiss border, where they spend at least 18 months. I go there personally and choose them while they are still young, then the *affineur* cossets them to the peak of perfection before sending them on. Goat's milk cheeses, on the other hand, are delivered to me 'white'.

HOW TO AVOID OVER-DOING THE RIPENING PROCESS? It is a question of judgement. The commonly held idea that the longer a cheese is ripened, the stronger and better it becomes, needs knocking firmly on the head. The search for strength often crushes out all the finesse and complexity from the aromas. Just as only great wines are worth laying down, only the best cheeses – those capable of benefiting from it – deserve a prolonged period of ripening.

IN THE FOLLOWING PAGES my six favourites are, precisely, cheeses which give an over-view of the different methods of ripening and the traps to be avoided. One must know how to control the development of the rind, which should be moderately wrinkled (Coeur Téotsky), and not become too thick (Lavort); one must also allow penicillium to develop (Cendré de Champagne), and handle alcohol with moderation (Petit Camembert in Calvados, Saint-Marcellin in Marc de Bourgogne, and so on).

Asiago

Italy (north-east)
Cow's milk

From the high plateau of Asiago, this cheese was originally made with ewe's milk but this has been completely ousted by cow's milk. It comes in two radically different forms, depending on how it is matured. The most usual one, Asiago Pressato, is eaten when it is about one month old. It is often made from pasteurized milk and its flavour is quite mild. Very much a universal cheese, it offends no one. The Asiago d'Allevo is cheese of a very different calibre. It hides beneath a thick brown rind and can be eaten *mezzano* (six months old) or *vecchio* (one year old). At that stage it is, *par excellence,* a candidate for the cheese board. Then, with the passing months, it dries out and shrinks. An Asiago d'Allevo *stravecchio* (two years old) has a dry, almost crumbly texture; when grated it is marvellous for cooking, adding intense flavour to many dishes – risotto in particular. Simply by using different ripening methods, a single cheese gives two very different results.

Cendré de Champagne

France (Champagne-Ardennes)
Cow's milk

These *cendré* cheeses are part of a great Champagne tradition linked to work in the vineyards. They were intended for the vineyard workers, particularly at harvest time. For the local cheesemakers, ash was the best medium for keeping their products over a period of months. The cheeses were rolled and stored in chests filled with ash from burnt vine prunings and other kinds of wood. From Troyes to the Ardennes, one finds numerous variants of this (something similar is produced in the Orléans area). These *Cendrés* have gradually died out with the advent of refrigeration. The basic recipe in those areas bordering the Aube and Chaource resembled that of Coulommiers; in those nearer to Burgundy, that of Epoisses.
Their flavour, it seems, was quite pronounced. One of those that has stood the test of time is Cendré d'Aisy, a cheese of the Epoisses type made to the north of Dijon. Ash is only applied to the cheeses now after they are fully ripened, just to give them the *cendré* appearance.

Coeur Téotski

France (Midi-Pyrénées)
Goat's milk

This little heart-shaped cheese is a real treat, a delicious 'sweetie' to be left to melt on the palate. It was invented by a man who took part in the demonstrations of 1968 and came to the Albigeois plateau looking for a different kind of life, while differentiating himself from a certain tradition (that of the *Cabécou*). Originally from Macedonia and resident in France for 30 years, Dragan Téotski, the 'creator' of this cheese, spent ten years working in industrial design at Mulhouse, before taking up a new trade in the Tarn, birthplace of his wife, Chantal. The farm is about 20 kilometres (12 miles) from Albi, in a hilly, very wooded area – predominantly oak, chestnut and especially hazelnut trees. The acid, shale soil is not very good for arable farming, but ideal for the hundred or so goats raised on the farm. The cheese is made from raw milk and hand-ladled into moulds. Its delicate, broken white bloom forms naturally. Only 1.5 centimetres (½ inch) thick, it ripens quite quickly, starting from the rind, but care must be taken that the rind remains attached to the cheese and doesn't 'wander'. The Coeur Téotski only takes two to three weeks to develop the creamy texture that delights gourmets.

Saint-Marcellin au Marc de Raisin

France (Rhône-Alpes)
Cow's milk

Alcohol has powerful antiseptic qualities capable of preserving products for long periods. This Saint-Marcellin au Marc de Raisin was traditionally made at the time of the grape-harvest. The cheeses were macerated in marc, in a stoneware terrine, which was subsequently sealed. The cheeses, known as *Séchons*, were dry when selected and alcohol brought them to life again. Bernard Gaud, of the Etoile de Vercors, distinguishes between the 'Saint-Marcellin du Pêcheur', which is eaten rather young, and the 'Saint-Marcellin du Vigneron', which is best after two or three months of maceration. Its slightly damp rind has a brownish tinge. The marc is very evident on the palate – this is not a cheese that suits all tastes. In every area where alcohol is produced, macerated cheeses are also found; some are made with brandy, others with marc, others still, with white wine. Here are a few more examples: Arômes à la Gêne de Marc, from the Lyons area; Cabécou des Mineurs from Aveyron; Fromage Fort du Mont Ventoux, from Provence, Confit d'Epoisses from Burgundy; Camembert au Calvados from Normandy; Crottin Repassé from the Berry region … What does the type of alcohol matter, as long as it inebriates?

Lavort

France (Auvergne)
Ewe's milk

Though it is shaped like a cannonball, this cheese could not be more gentle. First made in 1988, it was the fruit of the fertile imagination of former dairy-technician, Patrick Beaumont, who settled in Auvergne at Puy Guillaume, near Thiers. He went to southern Spain in search of suitable moulds, and decided to keep Lacaune sheep – a very rare breed in Auvergne whose milk is used, notably, to make Roquefort. Lavort is a pressed-paste cheese, which develops a quite soft consistency after four months ripening. It should not be matured for longer, because thickening of the rind then becomes unstoppable at the expense of the cheese, reducing it to an insignificant quantity. The rind of Lavort is similar to that of Tomme de Savoie, but there the comparison ends. The character of the raw ewe's milk is revealed here by the very sharp, almost sweet, flavour that lingers interminably. Aided by success, Patrick Beaumont encouraged young stockbreeders to establish herds and provide him with milk. Starting from nothing, this original product has managed, in the space of a few years, to carve out a niche for itself and find an undoubtedly permanent place on the already well-filled cheese boards of Auvergne.

Petit Camembert au Calva

France (Basse-Normandie)
Cow's milk

It was my Auvergne compatriot, Henry Vergnes, from the Au Sauvignon bistro in Paris, who gave me the idea of this miniature Camembert macerated in Calvados. These two great products of the Normandy *terroir* have long been linked. There are also excellent Camemberts macerated in cider. I asked Philippe Meslon, from the Saint-Loup-de-Fribois cheese-dairy, near Cambremer, to make a special batch of Camemberts from raw milk, 5 centimetres (2 inches) in diameter and 2 centimetres (¾ inch) high. He had to have the moulds especially made. Because of its small size, these cheeses ripen more quickly than traditional Camemberts. After three weeks they are ready and are put to macerate for 24 hours in Calvados. Thus impregnated, they are then rolled in fine breadcrumbs (no need to remove the rind), then each one is tied with a little green ribbon and decorated with half a shelled walnut. Result: 60 grams (2 ounces) of pure pleasure which is gone in two mouthfuls. Its size makes it the petit four of the cheese world. Perfect as a midday snack, it is also makes an attractive addition to the cheese-board.

Summer

pears, cones, effigies of people or, more often, rough spheres. This process has now been largely automated and the balls of mozzarella are rarely still made by hand.

NEVERTHELESS, WITH ITS PORCELAIN WHITENESS, its delicately acidic flavour and its very elastic texture, mozzarella is truly unique. The name Mozzarella di Bufala Campana was given the protection of an AOC in 1979. That made with cow's milk (sold under the name of 'fiore di latte'), is produced all over the world – in particular in Canada and the United States, where substantial Italian immigration has created a demand, and as far away as New Zealand. In Italy, the cow's milk version is made over the whole country, whereas Mozzarella di Bufala is produced in Campagna only (at Salerno and Caserta). For the cheesemaker, buffalo's milk is a joy to use; it is three times as rich in protein as cow's milk, which makes it particularly suitable for cheese-making.

Imposing provolone hung in the cellars of the Guffanti Company at Arona. One cheese can weigh up to 100 kilos (220 pounds) and needs ripening for a year. Provolone is largely used in cooking.

Will cheese spoil your figure?

Cheese is often said to be a sinful indulgence we pay dearly for in gained pounds. This impression is further reinforced by stereotypes such as the fat, jovial monks that so often figure on the labels. Cheese does, undeniably, contain fat; but not as much as is popularly believed, and in varying proportions according to the way it is made.
The rule to remember is that the drier the cheese, the more concentrated the nutrients, the lipids in particular.
The fat content, indicated by law on the packaging, is very misleading: a Camembert marked 'fat content, 50 per cent ' is actually lower in fat than a Comté similarly labelled.
The figure indicates the amount of fat as a percentage, not of the whole cheese, but of the total milk solids it contains. Thus a Camembert, with a fairly moist dough, contains only 22 per cent fat against 31 per cent in the Comté, with its much drier pressed dough.

The illusion of low-fat cheeses: insipid and deceptive

Since it is the fat in cheese that puts on the weight, all that is needed is a low-fat product! This kind of thinking gave rise to cheeses 'lightened' by the use of milk skimmed to a greater or lesser degree. Unfortunately they have at least two drawbacks. First of all, their flavour puts them beyond the pale as far as gourmets are concerned. Fat is the element in cheese that carries the aroma and gives the cheese its sensual texture. Without it there is no pleasure in eating them. Secondly, our metabolism does not allow itself to be tricked for long. At each meal it carefully counts the calories consumed in order to regulate the appetite; if it is deceived by a low-fat item in the course of one meal, it will arrange to make up the difference at the next…
For me, low-fat cheeses have half the fat and double the quantity of insipid matter for twice the price.

A WORD OF ADVICE: since it has no rind, only a fine whitish skin, mozzarella must always be kept in its whey, or in salt water, or it risks becoming tough and 'going off'. Only the version smoked over wheat straw, leaves and wood (Mozzarella di Bufala Affumicata), can be exposed to the air without suffering damage.

IS IT POSSIBLE TO FIND DAIRY BUFFALOES IN FRANCE?

It is. To my knowledge there are two herds at least. The best known is the one at La Bergerie Royale at Rambouillet, in the Paris region. It was established about ten years ago by Italian restaurateurs who wanted access to mozzarella made with raw milk. La Bergerie makes mozzarella with buffalo and cow's milk mixed, but hopes, as the size of the herd increases, to make more and more 'pure buffalo'. Their cheese is mainly distributed to restaurants in the Paris area, and to customers of La Bergerie's delicatessen.

MORE RECENTLY another herd of buffaloes has been established in the south of the Cantal region, where 70 animals are kept at Maurs. Their milk is made into two cheeses – a type of Perail and a Tomme weighing a kilogram (just over 2 pounds). Between April and September there is enough milk to make mozzarella as well. For the moment these cheeses are sold from a little regional outlet. As for the male buffaloes, I'm told they make excellent salami.

MOZZARELLA LENDS ITSELF TO A GREAT MANY RECIPES as delicious as they are refreshing. I adore those of Paula Lambert, an American from Dallas, Texas, who fell in love with mozzarella while on holiday in Italy and set up a cheese dairy at the start of the 1980s. Since then she has widened her range to more than 30 cheeses and regularly publishes recipes which are all lightness and subtlety, inspired by Mediterranean cooking If you want a mouth-watering experience, I suggest you investigate her website on the internet (see page 229).

DRAWN-CURD CHEESES – from which I have chosen two delicious examples – are often similar in taste, which is why I have allowed myself to include cheeses that, in my opinion, are veritable little summer miracles of finesse (Chabichou de Poitou), originality (Brousse de Rove) or character (Tomme Capra).

Brousse du Rove is a strange little fresh cheese that is whipped vigorously before being moulded in narrow, elongated strainers, probably modelled on the rams' horns used in earlier times.

75

Chabichou du Poitou
France (Poitou-Charentes)
Goat's milk

Nicknamed 'Chabis', its full title is 'Chabichou du Poitou AOC'. Six centimetres (2½ inches) high, this little goat's milk cheese's truncated cone shape – the diameter decreasing slightly from base to summit – is easily recognized. It is sold in a range of qualities, from the authentic farmhouse products made from raw milk, to the more commonplace pasteurized industrial cheese for which Poitou has become a centre. You can tell the farmhouse ones – those made by the Georgelet company, for example, – by their impeccably smooth texture resulting from very careful moulding by hand. They are really excellent after three to four weeks' *affinage*. A small historical note: 'Chabichou' could be a corruption of the Arab word *chebi*, meaning 'little goat'. Every French schoolchild learns that Charles Martel halted the Arab advance at Poitiers in 732. It was more probably a brief incursion by a war lord intent on pillaging the countryside, but what does it matter as long as the Saracens left behind their recipe for a cheese made from goat's milk? In fact, goats were depicted in local engravings long before the time of Charles Martel, so the mystery of the origins of Chabichou has still to be solved.

Brousse du Rove
France (Provence-Côte d'Azur)
Goat's, cow's or ewe's milk

Brousse du Rove is sold in its curious, elongated plastic mould – sometimes charmingly called a 'fairy's finger'. Taken out, it would collapse completely. This mould is based on the shape of the ram's horn which was used in earlier times and subsequently replaced by tubes made of tin-plate or plaited rushes. Brousse was first made a very long time ago, in areas inland from Marseilles, where there have always been goats of the Rove breed. Nowadays, ewe's milk, and even cow's milk, are used by the three remaining farmers still in production. The recipe uses up a great deal of energy; immediately after milking the milk is heated to 80°C (175°F) then acidified with white vinegar, or acetic acid, to curdle it. The cheesemaker then beats it vigorously with a whisk (*brousser* means 'to whisk') until it forms globules. These are collected with a skimmer and placed in the moulds, where they agglomerate and settle. The process is similar to that used in the making of Brocciu with the difference that Brocciu uses whey rather than full milk. All that remains to be done is to turn the Brousse out onto a plate and enjoy it. Its acidic flavour needs some kind of sweet accompaniment, such as red fruit coulis, honey, sugar or – why not – a few drops of strong alcohol. A delicious pudding!

Burrata
Southern Italy
Cow's or buffalo's milk

Burrata is a colourful speciality that originated in the Apuglia region and has spread throughout the Italian south. It looks how cheeses must have looked in Antiquity, left out in the air to drain on fresh leaves (rushes or asphodel, among others). It is always sold wrapped in leaves and held together by a strand of raffia. The name of the cheese changes according to the various shapes it is made in. In one place it is *Butirri*, in another *Palloni* and in yet another, *Occhio di Bufala* (buffalo's eye). Inside, it is a tasty mixture of fresh cream and pieces of still fresh drawn-curd cheese (mozzarella or provolone). Why include the pieces of cheese? These come from unsaleable broken cheeses, explained Fiori Carlo of the Guffanti Company, important specialists in traditional trans-Alpine cheeses. He regularly supplies me with a Burrata made from whole cow's milk, very delicate and slightly imbued with the scent of its leaf covering. Sometimes I leave a few to mature and they become more compact and develop a more pronounced flavour.

Délice de Pommard

France (Burgundy)
Cow's milk

This is a really original cheese, in shape as well as in flavour. Délice de Pommard was created around 1996, by a Burgundy cheese merchant, Alain Hess, *affineur* and retailer at Beaune. He started with an ordinary fresh triple-cream cheese, which he flavoured with mustard or, more precisely, with mustard-seed bran. Since this has neither the same strength, nor even quite the same taste as mustard, the great majority of consumers were unable to guess the source of its strange and seductive aroma. The cheese is dipped into the mustard bran, then kneaded and hand-moulded with a cloth, which gives it the shape of a fresh fig. It was an immediate success, and a number of restaurants have found a place for it on their cheese board. Imitations were not slow to appear. Délice de Pommard is best eaten still cold, at the end of a meal. Alain Hess, who tried garlic and many different herbs before coming up with the winning idea, tells me he is busy working on a new revolutionary product.

Tomme Capra

France (Rhône-Alpes)
Goat's milk

This little goat's milk Tomme could be a member of the Picodon family, being similarly close-textured. But it is a little thicker and, more especially, has a more pronounced flavour. A colleague from Vincennes, Bruno Collet, introduced me to it after discovering it in a market near Privas. It is made by a farmer in the village of Saint-Bardou. In order to ease the transport costs (prohibitive for such a small cheese), we recommended it to the wholesale market at Rungis. There are excellent cheeses all over France that would never find outlets outside their local market if they were not offered this 'open Sesame'. Only made with raw milk, Tomme Capra is subject to very careful *affinage*, for a good month at least. Right from the start the cheeses are selected and assigned as necessary. Some customers require dry cheeses that need to mature for up to three months and only those Tommes that are not too moist on the surface and have already begun to form a bloom are suitable for this. The cheeses are ventilated at the start of the ripening process (*ressuyage* is the cheesemakers' jargon) to give them an attractive surface. Eventually a fine blue skin appears, not necessary evenly. Like all cheeses of this type, Tomme Capra is at its peak of excellence at the end of spring and beginning of summer.

Provolone

Southern Italy
Cow's milk

King of southern Italian cheeses, provolone has a great affinity for pasta dishes. It is hung up in the kitchen, where it continues to shrink as its moisture evaporates. In specialist Italian grocers' shops, it is suspended from the ceiling among the hams and salamis. Provolone, like mozzarella, belongs to the extensive family of drawn-curd cheeses but, unlike the others, it does have a rind, because it is eaten when more matured, as much as six months and more. Some *affineurs* offer a *picante* (piquant) version, which is matured for a year. It is difficult to define the appearance of provolone; like a potato, its shape is varied and unpredictable – usually at the whim of the cheesemaker – but a great many are roughly pear-shaped. On the scales it can weigh anything from half a kilo (a pound) to almost 100 kilos (220 pounds)! It used to be made from buffalo's milk but cow's milk is almost always used nowadays. Very accommodating, it is just as much at home cut into cubes and served with assorted condiments to accompany an aperitif, as it is at the dinner table, grated over a steaming hot dish of pasta.

There's thunder in the air...

As a living product, cheese reacts to differing climatic conditions, even though dairies are tending more and more to cut themselves off from outside influences.

Summer is a tricky time for cheese producers; if the weather is too dry the quality of the grass deteriorates and milk yields go down. This is a more serious problem in low-lying areas than higher up, where the pastures are less exposed to a lack of moisture. Although there may not be an abundance of milk, the quality itself is quite good; it is particularly high in fat and rich in protein during that phase when the animals are coming to the end of their lactation period.

WHEN THE WEATHER IS STORMY the cheesemaker has a long face. Not only does changeable weather upset the animals but, more importantly, the milk can also react differently; it tends to be more acid, producing closer textured, less unctuous curd and recipes have to be adapted accordingly.

GENERALLY SPEAKING rain and damp weather are a worry for the cheesemaker. Those who face the Mediterranean also have to monitor the prevailing winds and dread the moisture-laden winds from the south. 'The enemy,' a Pélardon producer told me, 'is the wind that comes off the sea. In the scrubland of the Gard, as in the mountains of the Cévennes, when it blows for several days running, the curd drains less well and unwanted mould growths can appear on the ripening cheeses.' The ideal, for this cheesemaker, is the strong, cold, dry wind called the Mistral. 'The cheeses practically make themselves,' he maintains. 'The cows give lots of milk when we get thunder in May.'

I unearthed a proverb from Quebec on an Internet site, which is a variation on the same theme: *Pluie de mai, vache à lait* (Rain in May, cows with milk). This is because rain makes the grass wet and more moisture means more milk. This is quite true but, contrary to what you might think, it does not please the cheesemaker. On the one hand cows hate the damp (they are less upset by extreme cold or heat), on the other, and more importantly, the milk is proportionately poorer in milk solids, especially proteins, which are the vital ingredient of cheese.

Claire Guillemette, of the Bergerette farm at Thiers, in Auvergne, raises 30 goats and is almost self-sufficient. Her cheese, Cabécou, is eaten rather soft.

Cancoilotte or Gaperon, from whey. Proteins, therefore, play an essential role, both in the texture and the taste of the cheese; as they break down they generate a wide variety of aromatic compounds. The richer the milk is in proteins the better its quality and its suitability for making into cheese. Ewe's milk, which contains twice as much protein as milk from cows, is very much to the cheesemaker's taste. These are the reasons why the level of milk solids is an important criterion to be taken into account, and why wet weather does not sit well with cheese dairies.

AMONG THE OTHER COMPONENTS OF MILK, the fats, the main carriers of flavour, have the ability to 'fix' the aromatic content. They also make textures more sensual (unctuous, melting, smooth), which is why low-calorie products are rarely to the taste of gourmets. Lactose (milk sugar), for its part, plays an important role in cheese production; lactic bacteria transform it into lactic acid, the first stage in the coagulation of the milk. Milk also contains various minerals (calcium is one), vitamins and, of course, water.

TO EXPLAIN: proteins, when coagulated by lactic bacteria or rennet, turn a liquid product into a solid. The long chains of molecules come together to create a unified network that is subsequently destroyed by the ripening process which, for example, makes a Camembert runny. The main proteins are caseins. There is also soluble nitrogenous matter, the serous proteins contained in whey; these make it possible to make cheese, such as

Cabécou de Thiers is processed raw with a culture of whey saved from the day before, then ladle moulded.
Opposite, top left: removing the cheeses from the mould.

How to ensure your cheese keeps well

The two enemies of cheese are a dry atmosphere and changes in temperature. Here are two rules to remember in order to avoid problems.

• *Keep them in the 'cellar' compartment of the refrigerator* if it has one. The temperature is a few degrees higher than in the rest of the fridge and will keep the cheese in good condition, away from any airflow. Failing this, you must use the salad compartment, which retains the moisture.

• *Don't take the cheeses out of the refrigerator too often.* That way you will spare them changes in temperature and humidity, which tend to dry them out.

• *Don't stock up* for more than a week ahead. Few cheeses keep well for long periods, especially when they are at their peak. It is better to buy regularly from your cheese merchant, who is far-better equipped to keep them in condition. And buying more often, in smaller quantities, allows you to enjoy a greater variety.

• *Keep the cheeses wrapped,* preferably in their original packaging. Most of them have a characteristic smell that can contaminate other products (butter, cream, liquids and certain fruits). Inversely, the fat in the cheese may well pick up the smells from other items stored with them. In addition, they risk cross-contamination: a Morbier could become covered with the white mould from a Camembert. Finally, an unwrapped cheese in a refrigerator (other than goat's milk cheeses) rapidly dries out. Cover the cut surfaces with cling-film and the cheese will keep its flavour longer.

• *Avoid leaving cheese too long in sealed containers:* the atmosphere is too confined. A cloche serves more for presentation than preservation, other than for short periods, when it will slow down the temperature rise and thus the drying process. But these items are often too large to put in the refrigerator, and also fail to separate the cheeses one from another.

• *Remember to get cheeses out* an hour or two before they are needed – the time to become acclimatized.

A CHEESEMAKER must always keep an eye fixed on two essential levels – the casein content and the fat content. The higher they are, the more cheese is produced. This is taken into consideration throughout the day; the morning milking, generally the most abundant, also has a lower fat content than that of the evening. And so, in certain dairies in the Seine-et-Marne region, the evening's milk, higher in fat, is made into triple-cream cheeses, like Brillat-Savarin, while that milked in the morning is used for cheeses that can be made from partially skimmed milk, like Brie de Melun.

THE SIX CHEESES that follow all come from small cheese-producers and for this reason are sensitive to changing weather conditions. Forgive them, should they occasionally be out of sorts!

Nicole Aigoin making Pélardon on the lower Cevennes slopes. Moulding must be done by ladle, taking care not to break the curd.

81

Bonde de Gâtine
France (Poitou-Charentes)
Goat's milk

This cheese was created to order in the late 1970s. A dairywoman in Saint-Germain-en-Laye was looking for a cheese along the lines of a Selle-sur-Cher, but twice the height. She talked to Louis-Marie Barreau, a small goat-breeder at Verruyes in the Deux-Sévres region, who embarked on a series of trials and came up with Bonde de Gâtine. This has been a registered trademark since 1978. The dairywoman had real flair – the Gâtine region has always been a favoured area for stockbreeding. Let Louis-Marie tell you himself: 'As its name indicates, this region is *gatée* (spoiled or indulged), with its woods and hedges, valleys and chestnut forests – very like Normandy. The land, which is clay, is left permanently to pasture.' At seven centimetres (2¾ inches) high and the same in diameter, Bonde is a stocky little cheese. It is made with less than two litres (3½ pints) of raw milk, which is coagulated immediately after every milking and hand ladled into moulds. A real farmhouse cheese. I heartily agree with Louis-Marie (who now processes the milk from two neighbouring farms), when he says that Bonde is nondescript if eaten fresh. He ripens it for 45 days, after which time its dough has tightened up and developed the sweet flavour typical of goat's milk cheeses.

Cabécou de Thiers
France (Auvergne)
Goat's milk

Try out a different way of living, in near self-sufficiency, cocking a snook at society; these were very much the conditions in which this excellent little goat's milk cheese came into being, at an altitude of 650 metres (2,130 feet). Claire Guillemette, its creator, keeps a tiny herd of about thirty goats on the 35 hectares (85 acres) that surround her farm in the village of Thiers. The countryside, made up of moors, woods and a few hectares (acres) of meadows, is not very fertile, but her goats' needs are few and they seem happy to roam in the open air, gazing over the Puy de Sancy and the Puy de Dôme. For 25 years now Claire has been making this cheese, by a method similar to that used to make Cabécou. The milk is processed raw, with the addition of whey saved from the previous day, and the cheese is ladle-moulded. It is eaten fairly soft after ripening for 15 to 20 days. Its flavour is very balanced, almost sensual.

Claire keeps chickens, makes bread, jams and sorbets, but for all that she finds time to keep herself in the public eye (her cheese was first discovered at the Saint-Maure-de-Touraine fair) and to apply European manufacturing standards.

Pélardon
France (Languedoc-Roussillon)
Goat's milk

This little disk-shaped cheese, covered with a slight white bloom with occasional touches of blue, is a traditional speciality of the Cévenole Mountains, though its appellation also includes a large part of the Languedoc-Roussillon region. For a long time it was subjected to fierce competition from companies who passed off cheeses made with frozen curd, imported from Spain and other countries, under its name. Since the recent granting of an AOC, it has rediscovered its qualities and its roots, with the help of a prolific network of farmhouse cheesemakers who represent three-quarters of the appellation. For farms situated at altitudes of less than 800 metres (2,600 feet), below the limit of the white oaks and the chestnut trees, the goats must be put out to pasture for at least 210 days in the year. For those higher up, among the spruce and pine trees, the figure is at least 180 days. Another good point is the banning of pre-draining; while this speeds up the process and saves on manpower, it spoils the finesse of the cheese. Ripened for two to three weeks, Pélardon has a fine, compact but smooth dough, with a sweet goat's milk cheese flavour.

Rebibes cheeses

Switzerland (Bernese Oberland)
Cow's milk

It is difficult to make one's mark in Gruyère country; the competition is so strong among high-quality small producers that it needs a stroke of imagination. The cheesemakers of the Bernese Oberland, a high mountain region to the east of Lake Léman, had the excellent idea of launching a fashion for *rebibes* (cheese 'shavings'), already long used for Etivaz, a cheese from the high pastures of the pre-Alpine cantons in the Vaud. Before serving, this Gruyère is cut into rolls, as neat as a Russian cigarette, using a plane or a thick-bladed knife. They are excellent, for example, with aperitifs. All it needed was thinking up! But I hasten to assure you that this is much more than a mere marketing ploy, easily imitated elsewhere. The standards required for the producers of *rebibes* cheeses are extremely high in terms of quality: only raw milk is used; seasonal production only, in one of the region's 169 summer mountain pastures; recommended maturing period of two to three years. Each wheel of cheese carries the distinctive mark 'CasAlp' and weighs between 8 and 13 kilos (18 and 29 pounds).

The acme of Swiss quality!

Rotolo

France (Corsica)
Ewe's milk

Rotolo is derived from a traditional Corsican cheese called *Bastelicaccia*, which I, personally, *affine* for much longer than normal. It is named after a village near Porticcio, where I met two people, Jean-François Brunelli and his mother Madeleine, (*La Mamma*) who have been making Brocciu for decades. If you should be in the area, you might be lucky enough to watch her moulding her cheeses beneath the shade of the olive trees. The family have been producing them since 1891! The farm's pastures border on the sea and about 120 ewes roam freely there. The cheeses are made in the morning, with the morning's milk together with that of the night before, which has been kept cool. The milk is made into *Bastelicaccia*, an unpressed, soft-curd cheese, cylindrical in shape (from 12 to 14 centimetres (4.7 to 5.5 inches) in diameter, and four to five centimetres (1.5 to 2 inches) thick), and the whey left from it is turned into *Brocciu*. While Brocciu is sold all over continental France, either fresh or matured, *Bastelicaccia* is hardly known outside Corsica. No doubt this is because it is eaten too fresh and so does not have time to reveal its very original flavour. I have chosen, therefore, with Jean-François' agreement, to *affiner* his *Bastelicaccia* for a minimum of six months and up to a year, and to market it under this name of Rotolo. I think he too was surprised at the resulting flavour.

Pouligny-Saint-Pierre

France (Centre)
Goat's milk

For some obscure reason, the Berry region has given us three goat's milk cheeses shaped like a pyramid, the most famous being this Pouligny-Saint-Pierre, named after a small Berry village. Sometimes called a Tour Eiffel, on account of its pointed shape, its neighbours, Valençay and Levroux – now put together in the same appellation – are truncated pyramids. This is no mere detail, for the surface-to-weight ratio changes the way in which the cheese ripens and acquires its flavour. I have, generally speaking, a penchant for the Pouligny-Saint-Pierre, feeling that the texture and the taste are more delicate. The moulding, during which great care must be taken not to break up the curd, plays an essential part and is the only way to obtain a very fine-grained texture. Pouligny is an authentic farmhouse product (small herds still predominate in the Berry region, unlike that of Poitou), and for this reason it is greatly influenced by the changing seasons. I recommend it to you particularly from the month of May, when it is still slightly soft and creamy. A treasure trove of finesse.

Down they come from the mountains...

Mountainous regions have always produced large cheeses, made in the summer, up on the heights; from dire necessity, not preference. It needed great ingenuity to find a way of producing such gastronomic treasures in these very rigorous conditions.

You have probably noticed that the largest cheeses come from mountainous areas. Look at the display shelves in my shop; the Comtés were made on the slopes of the Jura, the Beauforts and Fribourgs in the heart of the Alps, the *Idiazabal* beneath the summits of the Spanish Pyrenees. 'The higher the bigger' could almost be their catch phrase. Large size unfailingly indicates a cheese of mountain origin, or to be more precise, one originating in an inaccessible area.

THE REASON is easy to understand. Imagine, at the start of the last century, a cowherd from Savoie taking his herd up to the high pastures the moment the fine weather arrives, and remaining there for about 100 days. He had to milk the cows twice a day and right away turn the milk into cheese – the only way to preserve it, since refrigeration would not be available for many years to come. He could not go back down to the valley regularly to sell his produce in the market; this would have involved several days' travel by donkey, and missing many milkings, since metalled roads had not yet come to the mountains and the four-wheeled drive was still to be invented.

THE MOST PRACTICAL SOLUTION lay in making cheese that would keep for a long period; one that matured very slowly and could go through the whole season without spoiling. This gave rise to the many cheeses of the Gruyère family. A wheel of Comté weighs about 40 kilos (90 pounds) and

The countryside at Arèches,
in the region of Beaufortin.
Above right and opposite page:
hand milking on the Salat farm
at Cussac, to make Salers.

A little cheese tourism: the impact of the forts

In the mountains of the Jura there are two magnificent military establishments that have been converted into ripening cellars for Comté cheeses.

• *In the Pontarlier region (in the department of the Doubs)* Fort Saint-Antoine, which belongs to the Petite company has, for a number of years, housed some totally peaceable wheels of Comté within its massive walls. At the present time it contains 40,000 cheeses. Largely hidden away, this fort was built after the defeat of 1870 on the assumption that the Prussians would not respect Swiss neutrality. Kilometres of shelves are swallowed up in dark tunnels and lost in a labyrinth of little cellars that open out in into monumental chambers, where the cheeses on the highest shelves are some six metres (20 feet) from the ground. A positive cathedral!

• *In the heart of the Haut-Jura National Park* in the Rousses region, at an altitude of 1,150 metres (3,800 feet) and two kilometres (just over a mile) from the Swiss border, the Jean-Charles Arnaud cheese dairy took possession, in July 2000, of an ancient fort covering an area of more than 200,000 square metres (2 million square feet), which the army no longer needed after the end of compulsory military service. Built in 1840 and 1860, also out of fear of the Prussians, it was used until fairly recently as a training centre for commandos of the French army. One part of the fort is buried under 12 metres (40 feet) of stone and earth, and the most prestigious tunnel is over 100 metres (330 feet) long. The fort can house up to 20,000 cheeses. A statue of Saint Uguzon, patron of the Guild of Cheesemakers, has an honoured place, watching over two superb vaulted galleries.

In these two exceptional sites, the temperature never varies by more than a few degrees, even though the thermometer outside may rise to 40°C (104°F) in summer and drop to minus 20°C (minus 4°F) in winter. The proprietors, who use these forts for ripening their best products, have arranged tours so that you can plunge into the cool, humid, aroma-filled atmosphere of these temples of traditional cheeses. The experience is well worth the effort.

A riddle

Where does the name Gruyère come from? According to the Swiss, the name came from the coat of arms, adorned with a crane, of the ninth-century Counts of Gruyère in the Canton of Fribourg. The French prefer another version: according to them the term comes from *gruerie*, a word used to designate forests in the Middle Ages. Indeed, heating the milk did require a great deal of wood.

Salting and rubbing the wheels of Beaufort in the cellars of the Guiguet cheese dairy in the Col des Saisies. This cheese can be recognized by its concave rind. *Page opposite:* Salers ripening in the cellar.

uses up 400 litres (700 pints) of milk; one of the largest types of Emmenthal needs up to 1,000 litres (1,800 pints) of milk!

IN CHEESEMAKERS' JARGON we talk of *pâtes pressés cuites* (cooked pressed doughs). These are made by a recipe that requires the milk, once coagulated, to be drained of as much of its moisture as possible; the resulting curd is then chopped quite small and heated, kneaded, and finally pressed into capacious moulds. The drier the curd, the less 'alive' the cheese, with a corresponding reduction in biological activity that slows down the ripening process. And the longer a cheese takes to mature, the longer it will keep.

IT IS HARDLY SURPRISING, THEREFORE, that so many large cheeses have been generated by the immense Alpine Massif: cheeses that can easily keep up to two years, and even longer in the case of the finest. On a visit to Gstaad, in Switzerland, at the invitation of Hanspeter Reust, master cheesemaker and member of the Cheesemakers Guild, I came across a real collector's piece – an Alpine cheese that is more than a hundred years old and still very presentable, though probably no longer edible. A wine of a similar vintage would be rapidly approaching its limit too.

Washing the churns at
the Guiguet cheese dairy.
From the smallest producers
to the most modern dairies,
hygiene has become the
primary concern.

MOUNTAIN REGIONS, such as the slopes of the Massif Central which, while lower down, are scarcely any more accessible, produce large cheeses such as Cantal; cheeses made in low-lying areas are almost always small and fast-ripening.

I LEAVE IT TO HISTORIAN JEAN-ROBERT PITTE to raise a factor other than inaccessibility that caused areas to produce cheeses that keep for long periods. 'To make long-keeping cheeses, one must practise a form of collective farming, keeping the animals as a combined herd during the summer in the high pastures and sharing out the resulting cheeses in the autumn. The cheesemakers of Franche-Comté and Beaufortin adopted this system, unlike their opposite numbers in the Massif Central or the Pyrenees. It is largely a question of culture.' In this respect, there is a project in view which rather bears it out: that of putting all the Swiss and French products together under one name – Gruyère. After all, does Nature recognize frontiers? For decades the two countries have expended a great deal of energy in fruitless discussions over this 'paternity' issue; rather than agree to share the name, they have allowed it to be progressively appropriated by the entire world. History records that, in the seventeenth century, cheesemakers from the Swiss region of Gruyère emigrated to France, taking with them their knowledge and the name of their cheese. This resulted in the formation of a common heritage, and this

would be acknowledged if a common cross-border AOC were established. It would, of course, require terms of reference providing for equal constraints on both parties to be set up and agreed.

WHY NOT CONSIDER a similar set-up for the Vacherin Mont-d'Or? The project could also be of interest to other mountainous regions, such as the Pyrenees: would it not be advantageous for the Spanish Idiazabal and the French Ossau-Iraty to work together? Admittedly the idea is perhaps easier to moot than to put into practice. In the meantime, let me invite you to come with me to breathe the clean air of the mountain summits in the company of various 'big cheeses'…

Beaufort being withdrawn from the vat in a cloth. This ancient practice is tending to disappear, to be replaced more and more by automated methods of collecting the curd.

Emmenthal from Allgäu
Germany (Bavaria)
Cow's milk

Herds decimated; installations destroyed; guardians of vital practical knowledge killed in battle; Germany rebuilt its cheese-making industry out of the debris left by the Second Word War, starting from virtually nothing. In the event, a clean sweep was made of all tradition; German cheese production is today largely industrialized. The mountainous zones in the south of the country, particularly the Black Forest, are where one finds the most interesting cheeses. This imposing Emmenthal is made by co-operatives at Allgäu, one of the most beautiful regions in Germany. I discovered it while attending the huge cheese fair at Lindenberg with the Cheesemakers' Guild in 2001. The mountain that overhangs the town – the Pfänder – offers an unforgettable view of Lake Constance and of Switzerland, from where the cheesemakers brought this recipe, at least two centuries ago. A single one of these cheeses can weigh up to 100 kilos (220 pounds) and use not far from 1,000 litres (1,800 pints) of milk – almost always pasteurized, which explains why this cheese has less flavour than the Swiss version. And why it is generally sold while quite young, although it would be improved by a good period of ripening.

Appenzell
Western Switzerland
Cow's milk

Appenzell has a secret; it is matured with the aid of a mixture of herbs (the composition of which is jealously guarded) that give it a very distinctive flavour. The Appenzell commercial cheese office distributes this aromatic mixture to about a hundred cheesemakers and the ten participating *affineurs*. Some of them personalize it by adding pepper, for example. It's impossible to find out any details. Appenzell is regularly rubbed with this brine, which helps a rind (called *morgée*) to develop. It is already mature after three months but it will not show its full potential until six months have passed and will reach complete maturity at the end of ten months. It is made in the north-east of Switzerland, an area of moderately high mountains. Its texture is similar to that of Raclette, its flavour close to that of the Gruyères. The labels are colour coded: a silver background for the basic cheese, ripened for a minimum of three months; gold for the *surchoix* (prime quality), at least four months, and black for the *extra-vieux* (extra-old), which is at least six months old.

Beaufort
France (Rhône-Alpes)
Cow's milk

Of all the Gruyère cheeses, Beaufort is undoubtedly the most sensual on the palate. Unlike most of that family of cheeses it is made with full-cream milk. This is also the reason why, as it ages, its full-bodied flavour tends to develop more quickly. Another characteristic, shared with Tomme d'Abondance and Italian Fontina, is its inward-curving rim – an infallible way of distinguishing it from so many other Gruyère cheeses. Made in the Tarentaise, Maurienne and Beaufortin regions, it is quite an imposing cheese, ten centimetres (4 inches) thick with a diameter that can reach 75 centimetres (30 inches). It requires no less than 400 litres (700 pints) of milk to make one cheese, which explains why Beaufort is a 'community' cheese, made with milk from several herds, grazing together in a group. The cowman going to high pastures in the summer will take herds belonging to several farmers with him – as many as 200 animals. The appellation's acme of quality, Beaufort Chalet d'Alpage, is made twice a day, exclusively on high pastures at an altitude of more than 1,500 metres (5,000 feet). Produced only by a dozen chalets, it is truly exceptional!

Gruyère

Swiss Romande
Cow's milk

Apart from being a cheese, Gruyère
is also the name of a charming little
medieval-looking town in the
Fribourg Canton in Swiss Romande.
The name, which is not protected,
is used all over the world and the
average consumer uses it
indiscriminately for any large, firm
cheese, from Beaufort to Emmenthal,
via Comté. Traditionally, therefore,
Gruyère is Swiss. There is evidence
of its goes back to the beginning
of the twelfth century. It is made in
the shape of a great wheel, up to 60
or more centimetres (two feet or more)
in diameter. Beneath the rind, the
cheese is quite firm and can have a
scattering of pea-size holes ('eyes',
in cheesemakers' jargon). Any *lainures*
– small horizontal cracks – are an
indication that it is over ripened. Half
of the entire production comes from
the Fribourg Canton, about one-third
being made in the summer on high
pastures. Swiss *affineurs* offer
Gruyère known as 'reserve', which
come from selected cheeses matured
for at least eight months. Gruyère is
generally at its best between 12 and
18 months.

Phébus

France (Midi-Pyrénées
Cow's milk

Perched beneath the Col del Fach,
Philippe Garros, goat-breeder and
producer of an original and very
seductive Cabri Ariégeois, was not
slow to notice the immense cheese-
making potential of the milk produced
by a neighbouring farmer, who raises
30 or so Brunes des Alpes – an Alpine
breed, brown in colour – using
traditional methods, and used to sell
all his milk to a co-operative. The milk
from these cows is highly regarded by
cheese-producers for its rich protein
content and, since 1999, Philippe
now buys a part of the yield and
makes it into this large Tomme,
which is similar to a Bethmale.
A single cheese needs 50 to 55 litres
(88 to 95 pints) of milk. He called
his cheese 'Phébus' in honour of a
local medieval figure, the Chevalier
Gaston Phébus. Philippe Garros has
espoused a tradition and rediscovered
a cheese from the past. The rind is, as
it was then, *cendré* – powdered with
vegetable charcoal – after an ideal
ripening period of four months,
during which time it is washed
regularly. The texture of the cheese
is quite supple, almost melting,
and it exudes rich, very voluptuous
fruity aromas.

Salers

France (Auvergne)
Cow's milk

A clean, dominant acidity and a touch
of bitterness – Salers is not always
very approachable, as its thick, rough
rind indicates. Austere and rugged,
it loses its reserve as it warms up on
the palate, offering rich, very full and
splendidly complex aromas of dried
fruit and butter. A fiery temperament
and well justified! It must be made
only from raw milk, between May 1st
and October 31st, at an altitude of
more than 850 metres (2,800 feet).
It is certainly not a suitable product
to be sold in supermarkets. Its
appellation zone is restricted to
Cantal and a few cantons bordering
it. Thus, it is produced exclusively by
a hundred or so farms. From his
ringside position at Saint-Flour, my
brother Alain, a retailer, always dreads
the period from June to July, when he
finds it difficult to bridge the gap
between the previous summer's
excellent cheeses, which have spent
the winter in the cellars, and those of
the new season, which only reach
their best at the end of July. Contrary
to popular belief, Salers is rarely
made from cows of the Salers breed,
recognizable by their lyre-shaped
horns and their mahogany colour;
these animals are mainly bred for
their famous beef.

On the road to the chalets in the high summer pastures

One day, on a bend in a mountain path, you may come across a little stone house with a few milk churns standing outside. Come back early in the morning and you could catch a glimpse of some of the farmhouse cheesemaker's secrets.

There is a little hut, like those I sometimes see on my mountain hikes, containing only the bare rudiments of home comforts: a single room huddled within thick stone walls and floored with tiles and wooden planks; a granary that serves as a bedroom and a copper cauldron on the hearth; a radio on the shelf, but no telephone or television; a few books and a ham hanging from a joist. Twice a week an off-road vehicle comes to collect the cheeses to take them down to the ripening cellars. The hut is situated in the Ossau valley, in the Bearne region, in the heart of the Pyrenees, at an altitude of 900 metres (3,000 feet). Over the door, engraved in the stone, is the date it was built: 6th May 1846. The shepherd will only stay there a month before going on up to the high pastures at 2,000 metres (6,500 feet), where he will remain for about two months. From there, the cheeses will be brought down once or twice a week on the backs of donkeys. When there is no more grass

In the Pyrenees, the tradition of taking the flocks to high pastures in summer is a very ancient one. Here a flock of sheep grazes on the higher slopes above Saint-Jean-Pied-de-Port.

93

(the summer heat scorches it in the end), and the ewes' milk supply dries up, it will be time for them to come back down again.

HUTS LIKE THIS ONE, *cajassous* in the local *patois*, are becoming fewer all the time. In the neighbouring Basque country they are called *cayolars* and in the mountains of Cantal, where Cantals and Salers are traditionally made, *burons*. Known as *jasseries* in the Forez Mountains, they are where the first Fourmes were made. In all the mountain regions devoted to stock rearing, the one thing these practical shepherd's huts have in common, apart from their design and the materials used, is the solid way they are constructed to withstand any conditions. They are all small, easily heated, all-purpose buildings – cowshed, barn, dairy and living quarters all rolled into one – built straight on the ground, generally on a mountain slope, and empty for most of the year.

IN THE SPACE OF HALF A CENTURY many of them have disappeared through lack of use. The combining of the herds, the disappearance of small farms and numerous farmhouse producers, the shifting of cheese production to the valleys and the rural exodus to the towns have all played a part. Those huts that have survived the rigours of the weather have been converted into holiday homes for people from the cities. As for

those that are still in use, the frontage is all that remains of the original building; inside, the need to comply with hygiene regulations have meant installing tiling and nonporous plastics, at a cost that is too high for mere seasonal occupation.

FOR THAT REASON, THE SHEPHERD'S HUT HAS LARGELY BEEN REPLACED BY A MOBILE HOME: a converted caravan or old refrigerated truck that is taken up at the beginning of the season – if necessary by helicopter – and brought down three months later. Automated milking machines are not left behind, either. Often, too, the cheeses do not remain up in the mountains. An off-road vehicle passes every two or three days to collect them and take them to ripening cellars in the valleys and the shepherd takes the opportunity to spend a night in the comfort of his home. For many, the stay in high pastures is no longer a lengthy period of isolation from the world.

Opposite page: the countryside near Joursac in Auvergne. The profusion of wild flowers guarantees the quality and diversity of cheeses from the area.
Above: Claudia and Wolfgang Reuss, goat-breeders in the neighbourhood.

95

ON THE ROUTES TO THE SUMMER MOUNTAIN RESORTS there are at least two signs that denote the presence of a small cheesemaker – milk churns drying in front of a building or the presence of a mobile workshop, recognizable by its white paint-work. Generally the animals are some distance away, in the pastures up on the higher slopes. If by chance on your travels you should come across one of these workshops, bear in mind that one of the cheeses I describe in this chapter may well have been made under its roof. They are all six made in the summer.

IN FRANCHE-COMTÉ, a region of gentle slopes, the cheeses are made, summer and winter, in workplaces at village centres. There are about 200 of these cheese dairies remaining. Until recently, milk for the ritual 'pouring' was delivered by farmers, but now, more and more, it is collected by tankers that do the rounds of the farms. There is no farmhouse cheese-making here – the milk is pooled, the cheeses made, and everyone paid on the basis of the milk contributed.

IN THE FRANCHE-COMTÉ REGION, and also in Switzerland, the cheese dairies are called *fruitières* (from the word 'fruit'); making cheese is the smartest way yet devised for preserving milk and making it 'fructify'. Pooling the

Coating the Ossau-Iraty at the Agian cheese dairy at Helette.
Opposite page: what an effort! Denis Provent, *affineur* at Chambéry, cuts a Bleu de Termignon, a seasonal cheese produced in quite small quantities.

Do not confuse DLUO with DLC!

These two indications on a label have very different functions: DLUO is the acronym for *date limite d'utilisation optimale* – in other words, the 'best before' date; DLC (*date limite de consommation*) represents the 'use by' date. Some customers find these confusing.

• **The 'use by' date,** as the name implies, means the date after which there is a risk to health if the product is eaten. While it is the responsibility of the manufacturer to ensure that his product can safely be consumed up to that date, the date itself is often defined by regulations.

• **The 'best before' date** is set by the manufacturer. There is no danger in eating the product after that date, but its quality and flavour are no longer guaranteed. The 'use by' date is a legal requirement and many manufacturers err on the side of prudence. Many cheeses can be ripened well beyond it without risk to health – and give great pleasure to the discriminating gourmet.

The 'girolle', and how to use it

The girolle, an indispensable tool for serving Tête de Moine (see page 100), is made up of a round wooden tray furnished with a central vertical axis and metal stops to prevent the cheese from rotating. The technique for using it consists of removing the top rind from the cheese before threading it over the vertical axis, then fixing the blade in place at the top of the axis and turning it round and round. When the cheese is soft, the girolle forms elegant little rosettes; a more mature or drier cheese produces shavings. When it is finished with, the rind is placed back on the top of the cheese, to stop it from drying.

milk means sharing in the 'fruits' of the sale. These dairies are big buildings with wide frontages, sometimes decorated with magnificent frescoes. In front of some of them – the rare ones where automatic pumps have not been installed – the big linen cloths the cheesemaker uses to 'pull' the curd out of the vat before moulding it are hung out to dry. Legend has it that long, long ago, the cheesemaker was nomadic and went from hamlet to hamlet with his cauldron. He would make one or two cheeses which the villagers shared for their own consumption. Commerce was yet to be invented…

Bleu de Termignon: the mould appears in a haphazard way in this authentic product of summer mountain pastures, made within the confines of the Vanoise National Park.

Bleu de Termignon

France (Rhône-Alpes)
Cow's milk

Bleu de Termignon is unlike any other cheese. Produced in high mountain pastures at the end of the Vanoise valley, it is made from 're-cooked' curd, in which the blue appears spontaneously, in the form of veining and marbling. High in fat, its texture is crumbly and granular. The very unusual method by which it is made gives the flavour a little hint of cooked whey, and sometimes it resembles Salers. Difficult and unpredictable, this cheese presents a unique profile. The five cheese dairies that still produce it are largely run by women, several of them young ones, whose presence is a reassurance that this very sought-after cheese will be with us for a long time to come. Denis Provent told me that it took him five years to master the technique of ripening it to perfection. He pricks the cheeses to help foster the blue veining. The cows graze on pastures at an altitude of 2,000 metres (6,500 feet), and their milk is particularly rich. There were already cows there, it seems, at the time of the Dukes of Savoie. Bleu de Termignon is very prized on the other side of the frontier; the Italians from the Val d'Aosta, who used to bring their cows to pasture in France, became absolutely besotted by it, and still continue to eat it regularly.

Briquette d'Allanche

France (Auvergne)
Goat's milk

This goat's milk Briquette is a curiosity for the mountains of Cantal, where the cows – pride of the region – leave little room for nanny goats. It is made from raw milk by a stockbreeder who keeps 60 goats in the Allanche region (Cézallier), in the north of the department. The farm is perched on a plateau 1,000 metres (3,300 feet) up, set aside essentially for summer pasturing. The cows are taken up there in May, staying until autumn. The goats, however, stay up there all the year round. They are dry during December and January   no Briquette during that time! The ripening of this delicate cheese, which tends to become acidic if kept for long periods, is fairly short – from two to three weeks. The skin becomes very slightly knobbly, while the inside remains smooth, becoming more or less creamy according to season. A real treat! My brother Alain, in whose Saint-Flour shop Briquette sells like hot cakes, stocks the fairly young ones that are to his local customers' taste. For those cheeses that are more mature and full flavoured, he has another use; they are cut into small slices, placed on a slice of toast together with a slice of local ham, grilled, and eaten with a salad. Whenever I visit Cantal to see my family, I never fail to avail myself of this simple piece of pure pleasure!

Chevrotin

France (Rhône-Alpes)
Goat's milk

In the Alps there are undoubtedly as many valleys as there are ways of making cheese. When one mentions Chevrotin to someone from Savoie, they immediately demand which one. On the shelves of Daniel Boujon's shop in Thonon-les-Bains, or that of Denis Provent, at Chambéry, Chevrotins form a widely assorted family group. There are cheeses to suit every taste: tall ones, small ones, big ones, creamy ones, dry ones. And from all over: the Morzine and Bellevaux valleys, from Maurienne, the Tarentaise, Châtel, the Massif des Bauges, and so on. Chevrotin has always swung between the two local types: Reblochon, with its orange-tinged, washed rind, covered with a very fine, white bloom, and Tomme, which has an anthracite-grey, brushed rind. While the texture of the first is supple, the second is closer and firmer. When it comes to creating an AOC, therefore, this is a real headache. The consensus seems more inclined towards the Reblochon model, with washed rind and creamy texture.

The best Chevrotins are made towards the end of summer, when the goats are still on the high pastures and coming to the end of their lactation period. The fat content of the milk is particularly high at that time.

Tête-de-Moine
Switzerland
Cow's milk

Only 10 to 15 centimetres (4 to 6 inches) in diameter, Tête-de-Moine (Monk's head) is a semi-hard lightweight, a stocky little cheese in the country that makes imposing wheels of Gruyère; but this doesn't mean it lacks character. It owes its name to Napoleon who renamed it at the end of an advance during his invasion of Switzerland. With its top removed, it reminded him of a monk's shaved crown. The fairly small production zone (the districts of Franches-Montagnes, Moutier and Courtelay) covers an area at the relatively modest altitude of 1,000 to 1,200 metres (3,300 to 3,900 feet). A dozen or so dairies produce this supple-textured cheese with a taste like that of Gruyère. It owes much of its success to a clever little gadget called a *girolle* (see page 98), which scrapes the cheese and forms it into rosettes, curls and shavings, useful for serving with an aperitif or as a garnish for a dish. This invention dates from the beginning of the 1980s and has made sales go through the roof. Tête-de-Moine is usually matured for three or four months, but it can easily take a good two months more.

Persillé de la Tarentaise
France (Rhône-Alpes)
Goat's milk

Persillé de la Tarentaise is a rare product made only in the summer, at between 1,800 and 2,000 metres (5,900 and 6,600 feet) on the road to Val d'Isère. Rustic in appearance, it comes in the form of a little cylinder, its rind liberally covered with grey, yellow or white mould. On the inside, it seems somewhat coarse and crumbly in parts, showing occasional signs of blue mould. This is a good sign, despite the consumer's apparent preference for white-centred cheeses. Persillé de la Tarentaise owes its characteristics to the unusual way it is made with 're-cooked' curd. The curd is first drained, then kneaded with hot milk before being salted and moulded. Denis Provent, one of the few who know where to find these cheeses, leaves them undisturbed for at least two to three months in a cold cellar. When the quality of the cheese allows it, he extends the *affinage* to as much as five months. The number of producers of this little Alpine jewel can be counted on the fingers of one hand, but there is little risk of it disappearing, as a family of young cheesemakers has decided to ensure its survival.

Ossau-Iraty
France (Midi-Pyrénées)
Ewe's milk

Sheep have grazed in the Pyrenean Mountains since time immemorial. Shepherds go up and spend the summer with their animals, making the cheeses in situ. Each valley has its own version of ewe's milk Tomme, all reflecting their local area and methods. Traditionally, the dough of the Bernese cheeses is more supple with a more marked flavour than the Basque cheeses, which are drier and of smaller size. Having only recently been granted an AOC, Ossau-Iraty would like to think itself the product that sums up this long tradition. Together with Jean Etcheleku and his son Peyo, cheesemakers at Hellette, in the Basque country, I devised a 'made to measure' one. Made with raw milk from Mannech ewes, this cheese is matured for at least nine months and coated with Espelette peppers. An absolute delight with a thousand aromas! Each Tomme weighs from 4 to 4.5 kilos (8¾ to 10 pounds) and requires not less than 25 to 30 litres (44 to 53 pints) of milk. Jean and Peyo, who collect the milk from more than 90 farmers, select the choicest for me. At one time ewe's milk cheeses had a tendency to turn piquant, which is why the Basques drank very powerfully structured wines, such as Irouléguy, with them, or ate them with black cherry jam – *itxassou* – so that the sweetness masked this defect. They are no longer piquant but the combinations are still pleasant.

The taste of the turf

You know those advertising slogans: 'To eat Livarot is to swallow a piece of Normandy'; 'The taste of Roquefort transports you to the Causses in Aveyron'; 'Taste Appenzell and treat yourself to a piece of Switzerland'. Praising the terroir *is the fashion nowadays, but it is often overdone.*

I am in the habit of offering my customers three different kinds of Camembert: one from the Paye d'Auge, another from the Bocage Ornais, a third from Cotentin. Each one has a style of its own, more or less pronounced but easily recognizable. To what should we attribute these different characters? The *terroirs*? The skill of the worker in the cheese dairy who adapted the basic recipe? The subject is complex, touching on both myth and reality.

THE OFTEN-DRAWN PARALLEL with wine is far from convincing. The roots of the vines go deep into the soil but cheese comes from the udders of ruminants and not from the pastures they graze on. Wine comes from crushed grapes, but grass and hay are merely the fuel that contributes indirectly to filling the udders. How much is left of the land after that transformation is complete?

FORGET THE POETIC NONSENSE about the 'scent of *garrigue*' that emanates from the cheeses of Provence, or the 'perfume of gentian' clinging to a Cantal. Such scents are far too subtle to survive the animals' digestive systems! Only extremely strong aspects of milk – generally unpleasant, such as the strong, bitter tastes of silage, cabbage or beet – manage to get over this hurdle. Only the wild garlic present in certain pastures on the Cotentin peninsula can perhaps leave a pleasant trace in the Camembert. While wine experts can show evidence in wines of primary aromas linked to grape variety, cheesemakers have no such recourse.

Cows of the Normandy breed are recognizable by the brown markings on their coats. They are very much in evidence in the whole of western France.

101

WHY THEN, despite everything, do cheesemakers claim differences in milk based on where it came from? 'Milk is the reflection of the soil,' explains Pierre Le Bouc, former director of the Lanquetot manufacturing company. 'The Paye d'Auge is a Burgundy; the Bessin is a Bordeaux.' Experimental studies carried out here and there show that the botanical composition of the pastures where the cows graze can have a certain effect on the flavour of a product and, above all, on its texture. It happens in the mountains, for example, depending on whether the cows graze on a northern or southern aspect. But we are talking of fairly subtle differences, too small to constitute a real 'terroir effect'.

THE AROMAS OF A CHEESE are actually produced by the degradation of the raw material, particularly the proteins and fats, which are transformed into smaller, more volatile molecules. The flavour and aroma do not appear right away, they develop slowly and never stop changing. Gruyère can go from buttery, vegetable notes to aromas of fresh walnuts and of being toasted.

Camembert being made: it needs five ladles of curd to fill a mould. The whey drains off little by little. *Opposite page:* breaking the curd in a Normandy cheese dairy.

What the labels don't tell you

• *Unavowed pasteurization.* In France, home of gastronomy, pasteurization is generally taken as a portent of insipidness, while in Anglo-Saxon countries it is regarded as a guarantee that the product is safe to eat. In France, those cheeses that are lacking in colour are generally made from pasteurized milk.

• *Fraudulent 'raw milk' products.* Taking advantage of a loophole in the law, some cheese producers sell cheeses labelled 'made from raw milk' that have, in fact, undergone a lesser degree of pasteurization. The more a product is heated the greater the loss of its natural flora and therefore of its richness and complexity. It is a questionable practice to profit from the inferred quality of flavour by wrongly claiming that a cheese is made from raw milk. The consumer should ask his supplier for more details.

• *Borrowed names.* In the past, some regions have been unable to protect their local cheeses from imitators. The name has escaped their custody. This has happened with Brie, Gruyère, Cheddar and Camembert, for example, which are made all over the world. When this happens, the only recourse available is to use a geographically precise name – 'Sainte-Maure-de Touraine' instead of 'Sainte-Maure' or 'Camembert de Normandie' rather than 'Camembert made in Normandy'. But these are subtleties that may well go unnoticed by the consumer.

• *The invention of place names* is as old as commerce itself. One need only choose a name that gives the impression of being firmly rooted in a particular area. These places exist nowhere except on the label, of course, and nobody is really taken in by them.

• *Deep freezing.* While demand is constant, production is seasonal, since milk is much more abundant in spring. A current practice that the consumer is completely unaware of, is that of using frozen curd – particularly in the making of goat's milk cheese – or even of freezing already moulded cheeses, such as Saint-Nectaire. Both the flavour and the texture of these cheeses can be affected by this practice, but no mention is made of it on the label. In a way, this is deceit by omission.

Semantic subtlety

Every word on a label is significant. Take Camembert, for example.

• *'Camembert de Normandie'* indicates a true Camembert that comes under an AOC granted in 1983. It must be made within the designated area, from raw milk produced in Normandy, and be ladle-moulded. It is made by 11 cheese producers.

• *'Camembert fabriqué en Normandie'* may be made from raw or pasteurized milk and, while the cheese dairy where it is made must be actually in Normandy, the milk need not necessarily be produced there. This product can often be perfectly worthy, but it is far from offering all the intensity of raw Normandy milk. It is consistent, but never excels itself.

• *Finally, the simple 'Camembert',* with no other details on the label, comes nowhere near the original in quality. The only reason for buying it is its very affordable price.

THESE CHANGES IN THE RAW MATERIAL do not happen spontaneously but are brought about by the *ferments* and enzymes, which can also be specific to the local land. In cheese, therefore, there is an assortment of micro-organisms that have not been intentionally added by the cheesemaker but are present in the animal, the farm, the materials used in transport and the dairy. Milk micro-organisms certainly play a more or less important role in the biochemistry of the milk, depending on the kind of cheese involved.

IN THE OLD DAYS, cheesemakers used micro-organisms that were naturally present in the environment through practical experience, without really understanding them, but nowadays they can draw on a whole list of *ferments* offered by specialists. There is a risk, therefore, of cheeses becoming standardized.

MODERN CHEESE DAIRIES leave less and less room for the land to find an expression, even though the claims they make for it are constantly on the increase. By its very nature, the process of mixing milk from different producers (whether or not they use local breeds and fodder from their farms), the subtleties linked to the individual small *terroirs* are eliminated. Also, with the drastic hygiene measures they employ, from refrigerating the milk to pasteurization, cheese dairies today destroy locally specific flora and replace them with selected agents. Nothing is left of the *terroir* but the style the recipe produces.

THE *TERROIR*, given the opportunity, can still find an expression in the cheeses – by using raw milk, making and ripening the cheeses in situ, with *ferments* taken from the previous day's milk. The real taste of the *terroir* is to be found, for example, in a mountain chalet where you could buy a farmhouse Reblochon on your way to the ski slopes. Or you could go in search of the six cheeses that follow – all of them proud of their regional connections.

After a determined change of occupation, Cragan Téotski, originally from Macedonia, now farms in the Tarn region, near Albi. He and his wife, Chantal, keep almost 150 goats. *Above:* Camemberts in the course of ripening.

Caerphilly

United Kingdom (Wales)
Cow's milk

Lands that have a strong Celtic influence – Brittany, Ireland, Wales – have no real cheese tradition. Local usage has always favoured butter and fresh milk over fermented products. Brittany and Ireland were cheese 'deserts' until quite recently but Wales took to cheese-making much earlier on; Caerphilly, the most famous Welsh cheese, with its soft curd, goes back more than a century and a half, to 1830. Welsh miners gave it its success (Caerphilly is also the name of the mining village where it was originally made). The Second World War brought production of it to an abrupt halt when milk was requisitioned to make Cheddar. Wales, which had allowed England to monopolize the production of its national cheese, often making it with pasteurized milk, has now renewed the tradition. Farmhouse Caerphilly, made with raw milk, is again available, and no one will complain about this return to its roots.

Camembert de Normandie

France (Basse-Normandie)
Cow's milk

There is Camembert and Camembert: the universal Camembert, made everywhere, with pasteurized milk, white as snow and without depth, and Camembert de Normandie AOC, made from raw milk, ladle-moulded and now produced only by 11 workshops retained by 6 dairy companies.
This Camembert derives its generous nature from its place of origin, the lush Normandy meadows. It dates officially from 1791; an abbot from Meaux, the home of Brie, was fleeing to England to escape the Revolution when he stopped in Camembert, at the farm of Marie Harel, and talked her into modifying her cheese recipe. In fact, Camembert would seem to date from before that, but Marie Harel and her descendants were excellent business people and took full advantage of the arrival of the railway, which, around 1850, brought Normandy within six hours' travel from Paris. It really took off in the trenches in 1914 to 1918; included in the rations of the French soldiers – the *poilus* – Camembert became a symbol of the nation. Red-brown streaks show through the slight, velvety white growth on the rind. The texture should be supple but not too firm. On the palate the flavour should be clean and strong, with notes of garlic and sulphur – but not strong enough to evoke the smells of the stable. Irreplaceable!

Saulxurois

France (Champagne-Ardenne)
Cow's milk

The Meuse, that great region of meadowland, is where, over the years, Brie de Meaux came to be made when sufficient milk could no longer be produced in the area to the east of the Ile-de-France. The region is known for Carré de l'Est, a soft-curd cheese that comes in two types: one with a white rind, like a Camembert; the other with an orange washed rind, something like a Pont l'Évêque. Saulxurois belongs in the second category. Its name comes from the small village of Saulxures, situated on the edge of the Langres plateau. Very popular locally at the beginning of the last century, this cheese is now only produced by the Schertenleib dairy, an old Champagne dynasty specializing in making Langres cheeses. Milk is collected from about ten farms and made into cheese right there in the village. It requires about two litres (3½ pints) of milk to make a Saulxurois. The flavour of the cheese develops gently over two months of ripening, during which time the inside becomes creamy. I particularly recommend the version matured in *eau de vie de mirabelles* (wild plum brandy), created a decade ago and called 'Mirabellois'.

Crayeux de Roncq

France (North)
Cow's milk

Crayeux de Roncq (or Carré du Vinage when less *affiné*) gets its name from a little town about 30 kilometres (20 miles) from Lille. A farmhouse product made from raw milk, it was created in 1985 by Thérèse-Marie Couvreur, in collusion with Philippe Olivier, retailer at Boulogne. This energetic farmer's daughter, who strayed into office work for a while, hoped to produce a 'Maroilles that was more delicate than the farmhouse products of the time, but with more flavour than the industrially made ones'. After two or three years of trying, she got off the mark and found the right formula in the end, as is proved by the success her Crayeux enjoys far beyond the boundaries of its northern home. This thick cheese, with its orange rind and strong smell, needs to be ripened for six weeks before its initial chalky texture merges and softens. It needs frequent washing in salt water and beer (unpasteurized, de l'Angelus). Thérèse is happy to welcome visitors to her workshop, specially fitted with a gallery and a shop selling products from the local area.

Tomme des Grand Causses

France (Midi-Pyrénées)
Ewe's milk

The Causses, arid lands in the south of the Massif Central, are among the best areas for the Lacaune breed of sheep. At Séverac, Simone Seguin and her son Rémi raise two flocks totalling 700 ewes. One flock gives milk during the first part of the year which goes to the makers of Roquefort; the other – the autumn flock – numbers just 200 and gives milk until Christmas that is sent to be made into Perail. Since the beginning of the 1990s, Simone and Rémi have been using a little of their milk to make cheeses on their own account. Thus we have the Bleu de Séverac and this full-flavoured Tomme des Grand Causses, made almost entirely in the month of August, when the dairies specializing in Roquefort are closed. Weighing five kilos (11 pounds), it uses 25 to 28 litres (45 to 50 pints) of milk. Its slow development (six to eight months on pine boards) means it is ready for the spring fairs. It can be recognized by its thick, reddish rind and the quite supple texture of its interior. Its fruity flavour is splendidly complemented by red grapes, as an accompaniment to an aperitif. It also comes in a version weighing 800 grams (28 ounces) – the Tommette des Grands Causses, which needs only three months ripening and graces the end-of-year festivities. You can run it to earth at its 'birthplace' every Thursday during the summer, when Simone and Rémi open the farm to visitors.

Pavé de la Ginestarie

France (Midi-Pyrénées)
Ewe's milk

This thick Pavé (from 2.5 to 3 centimetres (1 to 1¼ inches)) makes no attempt to hide its origins; the goat taste is very pronounced. It is made in the Tarn region by Dragan and Chantal Téotski, who also produce Coeur Téotski. On their 45 hectares (110 acres) they practise organic farming. Apart from a short period in winter, the 150 goats roam outside almost all year round. Fond of hazelnuts and acorns, they like to graze in the areas bordering the woods and undergrowth. This diet inevitably influences the aromas of the cheese in the end. Pavé de la Ginestarie (the name of the area) is ripened for three to four weeks. Day by day it shrinks, losing a good centimetre (⅜ inch) of its original size. The cheese is particularly fine-grained – both the quality of milk produced by the flock and ladle moulding play their part. This Pavé is particularly good with white wine. Dragan recommends a Gaillac.

107

Autumn

The leaves are gathered up by the shovelful

Leaves, especially vine or chestnut, were the first form of wrapping for cheese. And why not? Some cheesemakers still make good use of them.

Yarg, from Cornwall, is dressed in fresh nettles. In Italy, pecorino is often decorated with a walnut leaf, Ubriaco is hidden beneath a vine leaf and Seirass nestles in hay. All that has a certain style. Having long rendered a valuable service to producers of small cheeses, leaves and other plants used by cheesemakers are now largely relegated to a decorative role. In the past, they served to preserve the surplus produced during periods of abundant milk yield, for use in the weeks, or even months, to come.

THE MOST PICTURESQUE OF THE LEAF-WRAPPED CHEESES is Banon, made in the *guarrigues* (scrubland) of the Alps and Haute-Provence. For a very long time this modest little cheese was wrapped in vine leaves, but when the source of these dried up during the phylloxera epidemic, it threw in its lot with those from the chestnut trees.

Each of these little Provençal cheeses needs at least four, and up to six or seven of them, first softened in vinegar and water, then steeped in eau-de-vie and tied with raffia. Formerly, the cheese was coated with various spices (pepper, cloves, thyme or bay leaf) before being immersed in eau-de-vie in an earthenware jar, and left to macerate slowly. The subsequent flavour was admittedly particularly spicy. The leaves stopped the Banons from drying and made a useful contribution to the unctuousness of the cheese. Wrapped in that way, the cheese was sealed from the air and would easily keep for use when the goats had gone dry.

COLLECTING THE PRECIOUS CHESTNUT LEAVES is no hit-and-miss affair. It is done in autumn, either before the leaves have fallen, or just afterwards, as happens in the case of Banon-maker, Noël Auxetier. To the best of my knowledge he collects them almost every day for three months, if possible between 11 a.m. and 2 p.m., when they are neither too dry nor too damp. A tedious job.

Wrapping Banons in chestnut leaves at the Chabot cheese dairy. The leaves are collected daily in the autumn. A trained operator can wrap a hundred Banons an hour.
Pages 108–109: a flock of sheep in the French Basque country in the area of Ossau-Iraty.

On the autumn market stalls

For cheese, autumn is a second spring, shorter but just as beneficial from the point of view of quality. The exhausted pastures, dried by the summer heat, are revived when rain returns and produce a second growth of grass. This rejuvenation coincides with the final few weeks of the animals' lactation period, a time when they normally produce richer milk. All this has an effect on the flavour and texture of the cheeses; thanks to the higher fat content they recover their supple texture. Some goat's milk cheeses, such as Sainte-Maure-de-Touraine, lose their lactic and grassy aromas and take on those of dried fruit and of roasting.

• *Cheeses produced by this 'second growth'*. From October onwards, cheeses made after the grass has grown again in the pastures, and requiring only a short ripening period, begin to appear on the market stalls. The bloom-rinded ones are the first: Camemberts, Bries, and so on. After that, allow yourself to be carried away by the stronger smells of the washed-rind Reblochon, Saint-Nectaire, Livarot or Maroilles. But don't hang about – by November they will begin to be past their best. As for goat's milk cheeses, many stockmen have now altered the breeding cycle so that the young are born in July to August and the milk yield is at its most abundant in September.

• *Spring cheeses.* Also at their best are cheeses produced four or five months earlier, during the prosperous spring period, and now reaching maturity: blue cheeses such as Fourmes, Roquefort, Ossau-Iraty, and so on.

• *Long-lasting cheeses.* Made in the summer of the previous year, cheeses such as Comté, Beaufort and Gruyère are coming to full maturity. Time has improved them, developed the flavours deep within them.

• *The Mont-d'Ors* are back, but the start of the season is not the best time for them. Wait until the first frosts before dipping your spoon into their little spruce boxes.

THE LEAVES ARE THEN LEFT TO DRY. Green leaves are never used because of their acrid tannins, which are transmitted to the cheese during ripening. Banon is one of the few remaining cheeses that really does make use of the properties of leaves. For many others, Fougeru, for instance, they are really just a decorative legacy; these habits are kept up long after they have no further purpose. The cheese world offers many examples.

THE RUSHES (OF SEDGE) WRAPPED AROUND LIVAROT are no longer there to prevent the cheese from collapsing. When they were made for the farm labourers to take to the fields, these cheeses, which were 5 centimetres (2 inches) or more thick, tended to sink and lose their shape. To reinforce them the Normandy farmers used leaves stripped from the rushes that grow in the marshes. Gathered at the end of summer and dried for several months in the loft, they were bound around the cheeses as soon as these were taken from the moulds. Today their function is performed by a paper wrapper, which has the disadvantage of sticking to the rind and being difficult to remove.

In the Haute-Provence Alps, at Valensole, in Banon country, man and beast look for some shade.

Preparing the water-reeds for
moulding Jonchée Niortaise.
Sewing machine essential.

IN CENTRAL FRANCE, Sainte-Maure-de-Touraine, a goat's milk cheese made in the form of a long, truncated cone, is pierced by a straw from end to end. Originally this served as a support because the cheeses were delicate and liable to break during production. There again, improvements in cheese-making methods and better control over the vagaries of nature have made it redundant, but it continues to be an abiding characteristic of this cheese, though it is not required by the rules of the appellation.

ANOTHER KNOWN EXAMPLE of 'decorative heritage', found in Franche-Comté, is the black line which runs around the edge of a Morbier; this is a distant echo of the layer of soot with which cheesemakers protected the curd from insects and rodents while it waited to be mixed with the next batch. Adding it today is an extra chore that serves no purpose, since it contributes nothing to the flavour of the cheese but without it Morbier would be indistinguishable from many other cheeses. It is that part of folklore that tradition may not discard.

IT WAS THIS SAME NEED FOR PROTECTION AGAINST BACTERIA that gave rise to *cendré* cheeses. The practice was formerly all the rage among the makers of soft-curd cow's milk cheeses, which kept less well than those with a rind. In wine-making regions, vine clippings were burned to make the ash. Many cheeses are still *cendré*, though the ash, like the soot used for Morbier, has been replaced by organic charcoal.

IF WE TOOK THE LOGIC of this argument to its ultimate conclusion, we would be forced to admit that, since the invention of refrigeration gave mankind complete control over the regulation of temperature, cheese – which, after all, is merely a cunning way of preserving milk – is, like the leaves, no more than the continuation of an outmoded tradition.

Eric Jamans' Jonchée Niortaise.
It is a very short-lived cheese
best eaten the day it is made.

A somewhat sugar-coated legend

A shepherd was tending his flock when he spotted a young girl passing by in the distance and ran off after her, leaving a piece of bread and some milk curd in a crack in the rocks. When he came back, several weeks later, fate had smiled upon him: the bread had gone mouldy and the blue growth had been transferred to the curd, giving it a strange, but appealing flavour. And there, high up in the Causses mountains, Roquefort was born!

When an idea is planted by fate

Cheese undoubtedly was happened upon by accident. Milk curdles spontaneously under the action of bacteria, which come from the air around or, as in the case of Roquefort, from a piece of bread. Man soon grasped the advantage that he could derive from this. Cheese is a sophisticated version of the process, an astute way of preserving milk. No doubt this began in the Middle East, some 7,500 years before our time, when the hunter–gatherer turned farmer and stockbreeder. Various methods were used to coagulate the milk. Poured into the belly or the rennet stomach of a dead animal, the milk was curdled by the enzymes that form part of the digestive process. Later, coagulation was produced by adding small strips of the rennet-producing tissue, or even the sap of certain plants. Finally people learned to drain the curd so that it kept for longer. At first this was done on mats of plaited plants (traces have been found in Sumer), then in proper clay strainers. Perforated pots dating from at least 3000 BC have been found in the south of France and also near Lake Neufchâtel, in Switzerland.

that any moulds contained in the flour are destroyed. Each loaf, made with rye and wheat flour mixed, weighs 6 kilos (13 pounds). Once cooled, they are taken to the cellars and seeded, using a syringe.

INSIDE THE LOAVES the speed at which the mould develops depends on the year. It needs between 60 and 80 days for the bread to become completely mouldy. The loaves, which by then are very light, are cut in half and the soft crumb taken out, spread out on tables and left to dry for a week at about 37°C (98°F). The whole is then pounded and sieved and the resulting powder is put in hermetically sealed jars and stored in a cool place for use throughout the year as required. About half a gram (1/64 ounce) is needed to seed a cheese.

The Roquefort Papillon cellars: the correct distribution of the blue is tested with a probe. *Above:* loaves of bread used to cultivate *Penicillium roqueforti*. *Opposite page:* Roquefort cheeses ripening.

Cabrales is the most famous of the Spanish blue cheeses. *Opposite page:* Cabrales fresh from the mould.

THIS METHOD IS NO LONGER WIDELY PRACTISED. Nowadays the mould spores usually come in liquid form from specialist laboratories. Each cheesemaker uses a specific colony of penicillium that contributes the characteristics peculiar to that cheese. The producers of Roquefort today have a choice of five well-documented colonies that they can obtain from INRA, the National Institute for Agronomic Research. A similar system applies also to blue-veined cheeses as far-flung as Australian Meredith, American Blue, Spanish Cabrales and Bavarian Blue.

THE PENICILLIUM can either be sifted over the curd, like icing sugar over pastry (the more traditional way) or added to the milk in liquid form before coagulation. Each colony exerts its own particular influence on the colour of the 'blue' (which can be green or blue-grey), the colour of the curd (from white to ivory), on its unctuousness, its flavour and its strength.

THE PENICILLIUM MUST BE ALLOWED TO BREATHE because it needs oxygen to develop. This is why cheesemakers also add gas-producing ferments, another kind of micro-organism which, in giving off carbonic gas, allows the grains of curd to remain separate and to form crevices in the heart of the cheese. Mechanical prickers pierce

the cheeses with their needles and finish the job of allowing air to circulate and the blue to thrive.

YEARS AGO ON FARMS, all manner of items were used to aid the cheeses to 'breathe': hatpins, umbrella ribs, knitting needles (not made of stainless steel in those days), etc. The various colonies of penicillium fought amongst themselves for supremacy, leaving man powerless to intervene. Some years one colony would triumph, only to retreat, beaten by another invading colony. The cheesemakers had to stand by and let Nature alone decide what their cheeses would be like. Since that time, the consumer who demands reliable standards rarely has any reason to complain of the unreliability of the penicillium moulds. The cheeses that follow are, in general, abundantly garnished. Penicillium comes in numerous varieties: *Penicillium roqueforti*, *Penicillium candidum*, *Penicillium glaucum* or *Penicillium camemberti* among others. They are the cheesemaker's best adjutants.

Cabrales is unusual in that it is made principally from goat's milk.

Bleu des Causses

France (Midi-Pyrénées)
Cow's milk

Bleu des Causses is a cow's milk version of Roquefort. My impassioned colleague Jean Puig, from Montpellier, tells me that not all that long ago some farmers still mixed ewe's milk with cow's milk. Bleu des Causses has undoubtedly been in existence for several centuries. Made in an area of poor and stony soil, it was ripened in the caves that abound on these rough, chalky plateaux. It has retained its well-structured nature and its straightforward, lively flavour. A few cheese dairies – there are no longer any farmhouse producers – continue to produce it. It needs to ripen in a damp, cool cellar for at least three months. The curd is pricked at the start of production to help oxygenate it and allow the blue to develop. Jean Puig assures me, from his own experience, that Bleu des Causses is rounder on the palate, finer, less rustic and less salty than the much better-known Blue d'Auvergne. The old tradition of drinking a robust wine of the region with it no longer holds good; Bleu des Causses has been promoted and now goes well with sweet wines, the sugar content softening its temperament. Jean Puig recommends further accompanying it with dried figs, cut into fine strips, and a piece of rye bread. A feast fit for a king!

Bleu de Séverac

France (Midi-Pyrénées)
Ewe's milk

Traditionally the cheese dairies that produce Roquefort only work during the first half of the year, when the yield from the ewes is abundant. They close their doors on 27th July and stop collecting the milk. For some time now, while waiting for lactation to cease in mid-September the farmers of the region have made either Pérail, or this blue cheese. Bleu de Séverac, its name taken from that of the village 30 kilometres (18½ miles) from Millau, is thus a kind of Roquefort, though it cannot be called that because it is not ripened at Roquefort-sur-Soulzon. Simone Séguin launched it more than 20 years ago, following in the footsteps of her mother and her mother-in-law, who made a ewe's milk blue-veined cheese at the end of the season. There is no question of competing with Roquefort on its own terms; Bleu de Séverac is smaller, with a more supple texture, yellower in colour and less strong on the palate. Simone, helped by her son Remi, ripens it for as much as two months or more, in an old vaulted wine cellar, but I like to extend that for up to two months more. Perhaps we are assisting at the birth of a future farmhouse Roquefort. But for that, Simone and Remi would have to acquire a disused cellar in the village of Roquefort. Watch this space…

Bleu du Col Bayard

France (Provence-Côte d'Azur)
Goat's milk

The cheese dairy at Col Bayard, in the Hautes-Alpes, lies in a quite steep valley high up in the Champsaur region. There is not a great deal of pasturage there, but the grass is of excellent quality. The farms have always produced blue cheese made with goat's milk – an unusual recipe. The dairy revitalized the tradition in 1978 with this cheese, which is like a firmer, rather smaller version of Bleu de Sassenage, or the Bleu de Queyras that is made in the next valley. It is made entirely with 'mountain milk', collected at an altitude of more than 1,000 metres (3,300 feet), and processed raw or after undergoing a scaled-down version of pasteurization. It weighs about 200 grams (7 ounces) and has a distinctive character, combining the taste of goat's milk cheese with the strength of blue cheese. Eminently suitable for the cheese board, it can also be used in sauces to accompany meat. If you wish, you can taste it in the dairy's own restaurant. There, in addition to a cheese museum, you will find other products made by the dairy, such as Chaudun – an original soft-curd cheese made from 25% goat's milk, 25% ewe's milk and 50% cow's milk – or the Tommette de Brebis, ripened with Alpine yarrow. The Tommette is macerated for 40 days in alcohol with a few sprigs of the yarrow and 40 lumps of sugar. And that is (almost) all there is to know about it!

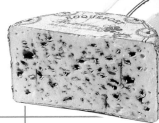

Cabrales
Northern Spain
Cow's, ewe's or goat's milk

This is the best known of the Spanish blue cheeses. Originating in the Asturias, Cabrales is a characteristically strong cheese that doesn't have to be produced to a rigidly precise recipe. Whether it is made with cow's milk, ewe's milk or goat's milk, or all three mixed together makes absolutely no difference. It is a matter of season and opportunity. In summer, when farmers take their animals up to the chalky heights of the Picos de Europa, Cabrales is made with three kinds of milk. In winter, down in the lowlands when the ewes and goats have gone dry, it loses a little of its originality and its piquancy. At times it is very virile, at others perfectly balanced, but it never leaves you indifferent. Traditionally, Cabrales was wrapped in large maple or chestnut leaves but the practice has been largely discontinued on account of hygiene regulations. It is a great shame, because aluminium or tinfoil leaves do not serve the same purpose. In the old days the blue mould appeared spontaneously and settled in cracks in the cheese, which is still crumbly, even today. The cheeses were ripened in natural caves, open to Atlantic winds that gave perfect ventilation. Nowadays, development of the blue mould is fostered by pricking the cheeses.

Gorgonzola
Northern Italy
Cow's or goat's milk

The most famous of Italian blue cheeses bears the name of the village where it was first made, at the foot of the Alps in the Po valley. In the past, it was a halt for herds returning from summer pastures; some of them over-wintered there. At the beginning of autumn, nearing the end of lactation, the milk was particularly rich in fats, thick and unctuous but still quite abundant. Apparently it needed the milk from both the morning and evening's milking to make one cheese. Mixing two curds at different stages, one of them already beginning to ripen, undoubtedly encouraged the spontaneous appearance of moulds in the heart of the cheese. Nowadays, the Italian cheese dairies (60 in all, from the most industrialized to the smallest) seed the cheese with moulds carefully selected from a rich and varied range. There are three types of Gorgonzola: Gorgonzola Cremificato, which is very creamy and with no very pronounced flavour; Gorgonzola Piccante, which is more like a *persillé* cheese, with a stronger taste (a cheese enjoyed by few connoisseurs outside Italy), and Gorgonzola Naturale, which is between the two. Italian consumers like their Gorgonzola very creamy – as my colleague, Edouard Céneri of Cannes discovers every day – while the French look for more firmness. In Paris, Italian chef Rocco Arfuso makes a real dessert of it, heating it slightly in the oven and serving it runny on the plate with a hot, crusty roll and a glass of sweet white wine.

Roquefort
France (Midi-Pyrénées)
Ewe's milk

This one is the absolute benchmark of blue cheeses! Known the world over for its powerful flavour, Roquefort was a cheese born out of chaos. It acquired its character from the bedrock of the village of Roquefort-sur-Soulzon, built at the foot of a cliff, on the scree-covered rocks of a chalky plateau. The crumbling rock-face is veined with *fleurines*, natural chimneys that offer perfect ventilation to the cellars. Only cheeses that have been ripened there may be called Roquefort, even though they may be made in the Grands Causses mountains where the ewes are pastured, and even further afield (Aveyron, Tarn, Lozère, Gard, Hérault and Aude). The blue mould is either dissolved in the milk or mixed with the curd. Some cheesemakers cultivate it using mouldy bread, like the Papillon cheese dairy or, yet again, the Carles companies, of which I particularly appreciate the sharp style and perfectly controlled strength. The first of the French cheeses to have been granted an AOC in 1925, Roquefort is a seasonal product. The lactation period of the ewes (of the Lacaune breed) runs only from December to July, so no Roquefort is produced by the cheese dairies during the second half of the year. Young, soft Roquefort cheese goes well with sweet white wines. For stronger Roquefort nothing less than Port or Banyuls of a certain age will do. They make flamboyant marriages!

The return to the cowsheds

Winter is coming. Soon it will be time to go back to the cowsheds: lactation is coming to an end. Yesterday, we required the cows to give greater and greater quantities and many breeds were sacrificed on the altar of productivity; today, we prefer them to produce better quality.

Can you recognize the different species? The Normande breed, which holds pride of place in the whole of western France, is covered in big brown patches on a white background. The Montbéliard has a white head and coat, with big patches varying from dark red to mahogany, and is most favoured in central France, Auvergne and the Rhône-Alpes region. As for the piebald Friesians, with their black patches on a white background, they were originally Dutch but have been the subject of genetic engineering programmes in the United States. In less than a century this species has become common all over France. These three breeds of dairy cattle account for nine-tenths of French milk production. The same applies in other countries.

The cows enjoy fresh air and lush grass, but they adapt to the confined space of the cowsheds without too much difficulty.

Laguiole's thick, rough rind
serves as a shell for the cheese,
but must be removed before the
cheese is eaten.

What to do with the rind?

The rind is the protector of the cheese; it has its
own texture and its own flavour, often much stronger
than that of the rest of the cheese (it is always salty).
A bloomy rind (Camembert, Brie and many goat's
milk cheeses), generally gives off agreeable aromas
of mushrooms. The washed rinds (regularly
moistened in ripening cellars) are the site of intense
fermentation and delight lovers of strong smells and
flavours. Brushed rinds (Tomme de Savoie) smell of
the cellar and damp stone, and also have their
followers. On the other hand, very thick rinds (Comté
or Laguiole), or those coated in paraffin wax, are
unfit to eat. One must refrain from giving too much
advice in this matter – it is a question of personal
preference. Some people maintain that the strong
flavours of the rind can spoil one's perception of the
subtler aromas of the cheese and, for that reason,
should not be eaten. Others, on the contrary, think
that it is an integral part of the cheese's character.
There is a risk that poor *affinage* may generate
unpleasant tastes (ammonia, soap, bitterness and
acrid flavours). The best way is simply to taste the
rind and find out what it is like before deciding
whether to eat it or not.

BEFORE 1914 there were about 50 different local breeds
in France. At the end of the Second World War, when the
watchword was increased production, it was decided at
national level to give priority to three breeds of dairy cows
and three breeds of beef cattle. The race for productivity –
it was essential to achieve self-sufficiency in food – meant
losing the less productive strains. That is how the Friesian
which, as the saying goes, 'pisses in the pot' (it can give
10,000 litres/2,200 gallons of milk in a year), came to be
the primary dairy breed in France, to the extent that, in
Normandy for example, there are as many Friesians as
there are people.

THE TIME IS LONG GONE when each area had its own
specific breed, evolved to suit local conditions, like the
native Vosges cattle and those from Limousin, Maroilles
and Villard-de Lans – small, robust mountain cows, like
the tawny Tarentaise (also called Tarine) from the high
valleys of Savoie, which was sure-footed in the
inescapably difficult terrain of the Beaufort mountains.
And those more rustic, larger animals in the lowlands
– the first crossbreeds would appear to go back a century
and a half, at least.

FOR THE CHEESEMAKER, it is a matter of judging whether
the Saint-Nectaire is as good and as typical when made
with milk from Dutch cows. The answer is not a foregone
conclusion. Unlike grape varieties, which give a
characteristic taste to wine, the breed of cow does
not seem to leave an equivalent imprint on the milk.

Roland Barthélemy at
Isigny-sur-Mer, checking
the progress of the specially
selected spheres of Mimolette
(ripened for 24 months).
The cheeses are brushed
regularly.

129

The type of fodder they receive plays a much more important part in the quality of the end product. It would seem that it is the cheese's texture that is more influenced by the breed. The presence of certain specific types of casein can have a marked effect on the coagulation of the milk and the retention of fat content. From there to bringing out the flavour in the end product is something that has yet to be demonstrated.

THE FACT REMAINS THAT, IN THE CONTEXT OF ESTABLISHING AN AOC and attempting to produce a faithful reflection of the *terroir*, the exploitation of local breeds would seem to be the way to go. The time has come to bring them back; producers of Salers want to reinstate the Salers cow, with its beautiful mahogany coat, black-rimmed eyes and lyre-shaped horns. And there are the blue cattle from Vercors-Sassenage, the Villard-de-Lans, those from Munster and the small ones from the Vosges mountains.

IN PARALLEL WITH THAT, THE WELFARE OF THESE ANIMALS becomes a priority. All stockbreeders agree that an animal that is comfortable and not stressed gives higher-quality milk. Modern methods of rearing have so far paid little attention to the well-being of the animals. The general public is becoming so much more aware of this that the European authorities have brought relevant standards to bear.

Making Laguiole in a *buron* (Auvergne name for a hut) at Carmejane. Cutting, crushing, pressing – many processes are needed to make the treasure of the Aubrac plateaux.

DID YOU KNOW THAT COWS ARE SOCIAL ANIMALS? That they appreciate the company of other cows and make friends? They eat their food more readily when there are cows around them, even if only on the other side of a fence. When their neighbours are stressed their appetite suffers. They communicate their 'feelings' and their uncertainties (notably via the smell of their urine).

THE STOCKMAN also plays a determining role in the well-being of his animals. A French researcher told me of an experiment carried out on several farms in Australia; milk production varied by up to 20% according to the way the stockmen behaved. Friendly pats, they way they spoke to the animals – a general attitude rather than specific gestures can bring about an increase in milk yield. Cows that feel secure produce more; the stockman, therefore, is a comfort factor! I always find a little visit on the ground very instructive.

131

Cheshire (known in France as 'le chester')

United Kingdom (north-west England)
Cow's milk

Cheshire – better known in France as *le chester* – is said to be one of the oldest British cheeses and a monument to Britain's cheese-making heritage. It was known in Roman times, as was Cantal, the French cheese it most resembles. On the Continent it is often confused with its co-national, Cheddar, which is made to a similar recipe. Cheshire cheese is made in the form of a cylinder of equal height and diameter. Its texture is granular with a number of small cracks running through it – a characteristic linked to the way it is made. The curd is crushed and therefore irregular. The pressing it subsequently undergoes is not sufficient to eliminate all these little 'openings'. In farmhouse production the cheese can even have a tendency to crumble. Formerly, a blue mould occasionally developed (one referred to 'Blue Cheshire' or 'Green Fade'), but this version seems to have disappeared in recent years. Traditional Cheshire, made with raw milk, has become something of a rarity and is only produced by a handful of cheesemakers. This is a pity, because a good farmhouse Cheshire cheese, ripened for six months or more, was really worth seeking out.

Laguiole

France (Auvergne)
Cow's milk

The high basalt plateaux of Aubrac, where this cheese is made, have imbued Laguiole with a primitive, mineral character, somewhat brusque in the first instance. But as it melts on the tongue it releases warm aromas of dried fruit, of roasting and of butter. Originally it was only made in summer, when the cows – of the Aubrac breed – were up in the high pastures. Wars and the rural exodus almost sounded the death-knell of this magnificent cheese, but it was saved in 1960 by the cheese co-operative, Jeune Montagne. André Valadier, chairman of the company for the last 40 years, was one of the principal architects of its rebirth. Since 1976, thanks to its commercial viability, Laguiole can now be made the whole year round. The area where it is produced goes from an altitude of 600 metres (2,000 feet) to 1,400 metres (4,700 feet). The abundant permanent grassland guarantees the presence of the very specific micro-organisms that undoubtedly contribute to the unique nature of this cheese. One Laguiole cheese needs 300 to 400 litres (500 to 700 pints) of milk. It must be ripened for at least four months, but this can be extended to a year or more. This is why one can find excellent Laguiole at any time of year, including winter. Its irregular curds gradually take on a slightly melting texture. A programme is under way to bring back the attractive local Aubrac breed of cows, with their almost flirtatious black-rimmed eyes.

Chaource

France (Champagne-Ardenne)
Cow's milk

This cheese has not been well served by the vicissitudes of history. While Camembert is the symbol of Normandy and Comté that of the Jura, Chaource is having to struggle to attain the rank of gastronomic ambassador. The fault lies not with its quality but the fact that the area where it is made straddles two regions – Champagne and Burgundy. To make matters worse, both these regions produce excellent wines that amply suffice as symbols reflecting their image. Chaource belongs to the prolific category of bloomy rind cheeses that describes a virtually unbroken arc on the map of France stretching from Normandy (Camembert, Neufchâtel) right to the east (Carré de Lorraine), making a small detour via Ile de France (Brie, Feuille de Dreux). Distinguished by their downy white rind, these cheeses develop reddish streaks when they reach an advanced state of ripeness. One characteristic of Chaource is the high degree of acidity, which prevents it ripening right to the centre. The texture always remains slightly granular, with a more or less fine grain. The acidity is very evident when the cheese is eaten fresh; at that time it has a slightly sour taste that counteracts its fairly salty flavour. Indeed, that is the way it always used to be eaten. There are only five cheesemakers still producing Chaource, and only one of those – a recently-established young farmer – uses raw milk; he deserves every encouragement.

132

Neufchâtel

France (Haute-Normandie)
Cow's milk

While not the most famous of the Normandy cheeses, Neufchâtel is certainly the oldest. Generally heart-shaped, it can also come in the form of a plug, a square or a briquette. Covered with a fine white bloom, this cheese is dominated by a distinct salty taste that is an integral part of its character, especially when the salt has been added directly into the curd rather than to the surface. The area in which the milk is collected and the cheese made is limited to the small region of Bray, contained within a radius of 30 kilometres (20 miles) from the town of Neufchâtel-en-Bray. There are three unusual aspects to the making of Neufchâtel: crumbled pieces of matured cheese are sometimes added to the curd, a practice carried over from the old days when no one knew how to isolate and handle the ferments; it is kneaded, either by hand or machine (a baker's dough-mixer), to make it more homogenous; finally, the cheese is lightly pressed, giving it a drier, more compact texture than most bloomy rind cheeses, such as Camembert or Brie. It can be eaten after ten days of ripening, and up to three months.

Mimolette

France and the Netherlands
Cow's milk

Beware of misconceptions! Mimolette is almost unknown among the Dutch, who prefer to export it. Its adopted home, perhaps even where it originated, is France. It is possible that the French were inspired by Dutch cheeses (egged on notably by Colbert, advisor to Louis XIV), but the cheese could have come into being much earlier, in the vast region of Flanders, which was neither French nor Dutch, but Spanish. But what does it matter? French Mimolette, like the Special Reserve one I get from the co-operative at Isigny, when ripened for up to two years gives off an irresistible smell of hazelnuts. By that time its texture is hard and crumbly. The *affineurs* regularly sound the cheeses with a mallet to keep track of any irregularities in their make-up, and brush them about once a month so that mites – that abound on the surface without posing any danger to human health – do not nibble at the cheese. The Dutch prefer to coat the cheeses in protective paraffin wax. The colour of the cheese came originally from a Mexican plant called *rocou* but nowadays cheesemakers use carotene. A little historical note: Mimolettes from Isigny are made with milk from mixed herds containing equal numbers of French cows (Normandes) and Dutch (Holsteins).

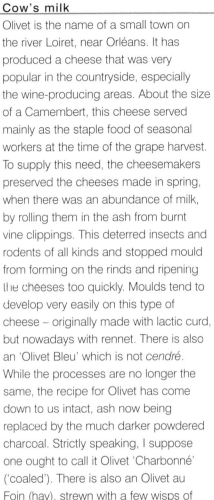

Olivet Cendré

France (Centre)
Cow's milk

Olivet is the name of a small town on the river Loiret, near Orléans. It has produced a cheese that was very popular in the countryside, especially the wine-producing areas. About the size of a Camembert, this cheese served mainly as the staple food of seasonal workers at the time of the grape harvest. To supply this need, the cheesemakers preserved the cheeses made in spring, when there was an abundance of milk, by rolling them in the ash from burnt vine clippings. This deterred insects and rodents of all kinds and stopped mould from forming on the rinds and ripening the cheeses too quickly. Moulds tend to develop very easily on this type of cheese – originally made with lactic curd, but nowadays with rennet. There is also an 'Olivet Bleu' which is not *cendré*. While the processes are no longer the same, the recipe for Olivet has come down to us intact, ash now being replaced by the much darker powdered charcoal. Strictly speaking, I suppose one ought to call it Olivet 'Charbonné' ('coaled'). There is also an Olivet au Foin (hay), strewn with a few wisps of straw. This cheese, made with partially skimmed milk, needs a proper ripening period of about a month to bring out its flavour; cow's milk cheeses always need a little time to develop their full potential.

'Stolen' cheeses

Some gastronomic delights owe their existence to practices which, it must be admitted, are of dubious morality. But don't let's deprive ourselves of these pleasures on account of what is now ancient history...

If the peasants had been above perpetrating the occasional crafty move, our cheese heritage would undoubtedly lack several of its treasures. In this context, Reblochon is one of the best known because of its name, which betrays the depravity of its origins. In the Savoie *patois* (dialect), *reblosser* means to re-milk and *reblasser* to pilfer or to glean. The story began in the Aravis mountain chain, more than five centuries ago, when farmers were obliged to rent their pastures from the local nobleman or from abbeys, such as the abbey at Tarnié. The rent they paid, either in cash or in cheeses, was calculated on the amount of milk the cows gave.

IT IS NOT DIFFICULT to cheat someone who has never milked a cow in his life, as was undoubtedly the case with the majority of controllers sent to collect the rents. The farmers would milk the cows of only a part of their yield, then wait until the controller had turned his back before finishing the job. This subterfuge yielded a double benefit for the farmer: he was charged a proportionately lower rent and kept the second, richer milking for his own use. As you know, cream rises to the top, and the milk remaining in the udder was, therefore, creamier than that at the start of milking.

FROM THIS 'GLEANED' MILK the farmer made Reblochon, a little cheese with a particularly rich and unctuous texture. The fact that it is still made from full-cream milk accounts for its quality. Reblochon remained a 'contraband' cheese – one that didn't exist officially – for a long time before seeing the light of day a few centuries later in the markets of the Thônes valley and well beyond.

FURTHER TO THE EAST, ON THE OTHER SIDE OF THE RHÔNE VALLEY, in the Bourbon region, another cheese was also made well away from indiscreet eyes. Chambérat only merited a very brief mention in certain writings from the eighteenth century onwards, and rightly so. Right from its earliest origins this cheese was cloaked in secrecy.

The slopes of the Col des Aravis (*above*), where they were first made, and at Manigod, (*opposite page:*) in Joseph Paccard's ripening cellars, where the Reblochon cheeses give off a delicate scent of cream. To reach their best they need up to six weeks of care in the cellar.

Its existence, and the way it was made, were closely bound up with the system of tenant farming, then widely practised, which involved sharing the produce. Kept in abject poverty, the peasants did what they could to lighten the yoke. They diverted part of the milk and surreptitiously turned it into cheese with which to supplement their income and make a little extra. Chambérat was originally made in spring, when milk was abundant and the calves did not completely empty the udders – or were prevented by the farmer from doing so. The earliest examples of Chambérat were made with this 'drained-off' milk.

THE ENTIRE RECIPE was devised to enable the cheese to disappear into the cellars as soon as possible. The curd was made quickly by heating the milk and adding rennet, which took only an hour, whereas coagulation with lactic mould cultures alone takes 24 hours. It was moulded and pressed by hand to remove the whey, then the cheeses were put into wooden chests in the cellar. The warm, humid climate of the region, which encouraged the growth of moulds, made it necessary to wash the cheeses daily. This task, which traditionally fell to

Opposite page: making farmhouse Gaperons at Montgaçon; the curd is kneaded then drained in big cloths suspended from the ceiling.
Picture right: cheesemaker Patricia Ribier hand-moulding the garlic-flavoured cheese.

How to teach children to appreciate cheese

Children's preference for soft, insipid cheeses often reflects their parents' prejudices, influenced by the 'gastronomes in short trousers' school of advertising. But no biological factor exists that will automatically lead children to appreciate cheeses of character – they need to be shown the way. Children acquire their taste for different foods by imitating others; they copy their parents, their brothers and sisters and their friends at the nursery, which demonstrates the importance of the role-models that are held up to them. Sometimes they rebel, in a sudden show of defiance (usually between two and three years of age), even refusing food they ate happily before. This 'neo-phobia' reaches its peak when they are about five or six years old, and girls are more susceptible than boys. Just remember – never force children; give them time to get used to new ideas.

These are a few suggestions for helping children to become accustomed to the various flavours and textures of cheese.

• *Organize tasting games.* You could put different cheeses on pieces of toast: blue cheese made with raw milk, Gruyère, Roquefort, etc. and invite them to smell and taste them, and question them about what they have been eating. They will tell you their impressions, in their own words, and will eventually finish by being able to tell the difference between ewe's milk and cow's milk cheeses – especially if you explain the nature of these animals.

• *Why not make them responsible* for choosing the cheeses for a cheese-board? Teach them about the different shapes and colours.

• *Put the cheeses* that you teach them about in a geographical context, giving preference to those regions the child has already discovered.

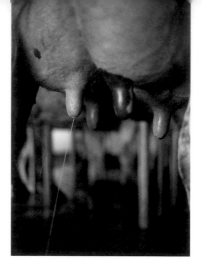

the farmers' wives, caused the appearance of the 'red mould', characteristic of all washed-rind cheeses and guarantor of a lively flavour. At the end of three months of ripening, the Chambérats were ready to be sold at the very ancient and famous horse fair at Chambérat while waiting for the new production cycle to begin in the following spring.

ONE LAST, FAMOUS EXAMPLE, that of Saint-Félicien. According to Bernard Gaud, of the Étoile du Vercors, a cheesemaker established in the Croix-Rousse quarter of Lyons formed the habit of collecting the unsold cream, or skimming it off the top of the milk, and mixing it with cheeses of the Saint-Marcellin type. The fruit of this 'recuperation' was the Saint-Félicien cheese. The story

Opposite page: crinkly Gaperons packed in wooden boxes, awaiting delivery to the shops.

is not entirely confirmed; another version maintains that it was a cheesemaker from Villeurbanne who invented the recipe in the 1930s, but either way, the process was much the same.

IF ONE IS TO BELIEVE ITEMS RECENTLY IN THE NEWS, pilfering still happens, but no longer on the part of the stockbreeders. An internationally reputed French dairy group has recently been accused of cheating almost 200 dairy farmers by systematically understating the fat content of the milk collected. White gold can give rise to terrible greed…

THE CHEESES that follow are more or less all 'contraband' cheeses, though amongst them I have slipped in Gaperon and Cancoillotte. While the origins of these two are above reproach, they still qualify as 'recuperated' cheeses since they are made from whey – an alternative method of making cheese out of virtually nothing.

Cows on their way back to the cowsheds for the afternoon milking.

Herve

Belgium
Cow's milk

Sandwiched between two big exporters of cheese – France and the Netherlands – Belgium is hard put to establish a foothold in the cheese community. Herve is its best-known product. It belongs in the wide category of soft-curd, washed-rind cheeses, which abound in the whole of north-west France. It is made in French-speaking Belgium and its origins go back at least to the time of Charles V. It was then called Remoudou, from *remoudre*, which is to say 're-milk', as in the case of Reblochon. The farmer waited until the proprietor had gone away before finishing milking. The very rich milk that resulted served to make small cheeses for domestic consumption. Herve is now made in a rectangular shape coated in a damp, orange rind. Washed regularly in beer, it has quite a strong flavour after two to three months of ripening, especially if it is made with raw milk, which is not always the case. It must not be confused with Plateau-de-Herve, a cylindrical cheese of the Saint-Paulin type, made in the same region, which is softer. The milk spirited away to make Herve was very probably originally ear-marked for making this cheese.

Reblochon

France (Rhône-Alpes)
Cow's milk

Centred on the Thônes valley in the Aravis chain, the Reblochon region covers the east of Haute-Savoie and the north of Savoie. The altitude is never less than 500 metres (1600 feet). More than 200 farmers, together with numerous cheese dairies, ensure the continued vitality of this 'stolen' cheese (see page 134), a delicious treat once it has become creamy, glossy and very aromatic. I recommend a visit to the market at Grand-Bornand, which is held every Wednesday; at the edge of the traditional market, 30 or so people sell their wares along the side of the church, from capacious pine chests inside which are 'white' Reblochons, pale and slightly frothy, from one to two weeks old; the *affineurs* take weekly delivery of the cheeses produced by farmers in the area. Among them is Joseph Paccard for Manigod, who knows just how to bring out the aromatic potential of these cheeses without rushing them, simply by washing them in salt water (which causes the rind to turn pinkish orange). Look at the rind; if it is flat the cheese will still be quite firm, whereas if it is domed then the texture will be soft and creamy. It needs five or six weeks of ripening to make a really good Reblochon. It is quite fragile and, once opened, should be eaten fairly quickly.

Saint-Félicien

France (Rhône-Alpes)
Cow's milk

This is an enriched version of Saint-Marcellin, in a slightly larger format. Two cheese merchants are both credited with having created it, one at Lyons and the other at Villeurbanne (see page 138). This absolutely delightful cheese comes in a raw version, a pasteurized version, and a third one made from raw milk and pasteurized cream. In the absence of a blueprint giving a precise definition of this cheese, everyone makes it in their own way. Its delicious smell of cream, its creamy texture and its slightly ridged rind, tinged with blue mould, really make the mouth water. It is particularly full flavoured in spring, when its fresh cream smell is very pronounced. Great care must be taken when ripening this type of cheese; it can quickly get out of hand and develop defects, of which the most usual is a soapy taste under the rind. Because of the success of their product, and in the face of competition from industrial copies, the eleven makers of this cheese, almost all of whom produce Saint-Marcellin also, are beginning to look for some sort of official recognition. Be warned: there is also a Saint-Félicien made in the Ardèche from goat's milk and not enriched.

Cancoillotte
France (Franche-Comté)
Cow's milk whey

Cancoillotte, pronounced con-coy-otte, is a cheese dating back to ancient times that is very popular in its place of origin, Franche-Comté. It is wonderful mixed into scrambled eggs, as a coating for roasted potatoes, or spread on lightly toasted bread. It is made from partially skimmed milk set to coagulate at ambient temperature. The whey drains slowly away, leaving a whitish block called the *méton*. What follows is most extraordinary. The *méton* is then crumbled and left to ferment – to rot, as an old, traditional song puts it, somewhat baldly:

'So that the *méton* will be well rotted, Leave it a while at the foot of your bed, Under the eiderdown, beside the hot-water bottle.'

Once it is ripened – the smell is unmistakable – the *méton* is heated over a low fire with salted water and some butter. It is ready once it has become yellow and sticky – at which time a little kirsch or white wine will do it no harm at all. Formerly made at home by housewives, Cancoillotte is nowadays made commercially and marketed in plastic or earthenware pots or preserving jars. It had a more pronounced flavour in the past, if the names it was called then are anything to go by – 'Strong cheese', 'Tempest' and 'Devil's Droppings'…

Gaperon
France (Auvergne)
Buttermilk and whey from cow's milk

No part of milk is wasted. After the cheese is made, the remaining whey can be used to feed pigs or calves, or made into another, less calorific form of cheese (ricotta or Cancoillotte, for example). The buttermilk left after churning butter can also be made into cheese. Gaperon, a product that originated in Limagne, is one of these. This white, dome-shaped cheese is made from *gaspe* or *gape*, which is Auvergne *patois* for buttermilk. To give it a little flavour the peasants used to add salt, pepper and, above all, garlic (Billom, in Auvergne, is the garlic capital). The ingredients are chopped and added to the buttermilk, and if necessary, a little curdled cow's milk and some whey are added. The whole thing, after being carefully kneaded and drained in a large cloth, is hung from the ceiling or near the fireplace, where it takes on a smoky flavour. Gaperon can then be ripened on rye straw. In days gone by, the amount of cheeses thus produced was considered to be an external indication of wealth, and was taken into consideration when discussing a young girl's dowry. Today, Gaperon is enriched and its texture is not so dry, but the flavour is still very pronounced.

Chambérat
France (Auvergne)
Cow's milk

Made in the Bourbonnais region, this cheese disappeared in the 1960s, when the last woman farmer gave up production. It was re-launched in 1989 by Yves Adrian, of the Du Chalet cheese dairy at Domérat. Based on information gleaned from the local people, he set about exhuming this quite distinctive, chunky, creamy cheese. Its reddish rind, covered with a fine white film, is reminiscent of Reblochon but its inside is more like that of a Saint-Nectaire. The dairy has since encouraged four farmhouse producers to join in the Chambérat venture by supplying them with materials, advice on making the cheese and technical assistance. These farmers now account for more than half of the cheeses produced. This is sufficient to arouse hopes for an AOC, the area of which would correspond to the historic Combraille – a region of plateaux and deep coombs taking in Puy-de-Dôme, Allier and Creuse. Chambérat could then consider aiming at larger markets than its own immediate area, where it seems to be greatly appreciated.

141

Wines and cheeses: let's play go-between!

Autumn, season of the grape harvest… Wine, together with bread, is the best companion to cheese. However, beware of lapses of taste and dubious combinations! Here are a few suggestions to surprise and tickle your taste buds.

Despite being common practice, serving red wine with cheese as a matter of course often does a disservice to both. How many good bottles have been sacrificed to the cheese platter in this way, unable to express themselves and make themselves heard? It is true that cheese comes at the end of the meal and that in France, they like to build to a climax, starting with younger wines and working their way up to the oldest and most prestigious – generally reds. However, this can often lead to the finest wines being mishandled.

AND YET WHITE WINES, WITH THEIR FRESHNESS AND LIVELINESS are, on the whole, better with cheese: Sauvignon with the goat's milk cheeses from Touraine and Berry; Gewurtztraminer with Munster; Vin Jaune with Comté; Jurançon with Pyrenean ewe's milk cheeses; Marc de Bourgogne with Epoisse, etc. Equally, it is possible to break away from the usual idea of marrying products from the same area and allow oneself to be seduced by some very unusual, but sumptuous combinations.

Did you know that Champagne is perfect with Parmesan and that Port enhances the quality of Beaufort? Or that the sweetness of Sauternes envelops and smoothes the rough edges of Roquefort, Banyuls gives nobility to a Bleu d'Auvergne and a delicate Vouvray adds structure to a Fourme d'Ambert?

DON'T TRY to stick to rigid rules. To quote Jacques Puisais, cheese expert and founder of France's *Institut du goût* (Institute of Taste): 'All that exists are a few milestones, or points of reference that, from the very start of our personal "apprenticeship", let us embark on the marvellous adventure

Traditional practices are an inseparable part of the cheesemaker's art.
opposite: wrapping Livarots in natural sedge (Thébault cheese dairy).
opposite page: in the *Parmigiano Reggiano* cellars: detaching slivers of cheese.
Above: strips of sedge.

of marrying wines with cheeses. There are simple moments, exquisite moments, emotional, lively or fickle moments, but in every case the combination has to be right.'

YOU DON'T INTEND GIVING UP RED WINE? In that case choose a Burgundy rather than a Bordeaux. It's primarily a question of style; while Bordeaux wines are generally balanced and harmonious, Burgundies tend to be more straightforward, rougher, more voluptuous. Faced with cheese, the finesse of a Bordeaux is often overshadowed by the lactic tones, whereas the tonic quality of Burgundy gives it greater control over the dominant acids.

APART FROM THESE QUESTIONS OF CHARACTER, it is the presence of tannin that makes the difference: derived from the stalks, skins and pips of the grape, these complex molecules build the wine's structure and give it its keeping qualities. Until they have completely dissolved into the wine they can be very astringent and drying to the palate, and leave a bitter note at the end. While Cabernet Sauvignon, frequently used in the making of Bordeaux, is one of the very tannic grape varieties, the Pinot Noir of Burgundy is much less so, giving more

View of *Parmeggiano Reggiano* being made. The cheesemaker has taken two lumps of curd from the vat and hung them up to drain before moulding them. Each vat produces two Parmesan cheeses.

Champagne with cheese!

As an aperitif or dessert wine, Champagne is synonymous with refinement. Yet, people hardly ever think of serving it with cheese, which is a pity! Champagne enjoys travelling more rustic routes, especially when it is young and lively. It goes wonderfully well with goat's milk cheese. And its slightly fruity aromas (notably apple and peach) will give warmth to a Sainte-Maure from Touraine. Its liveliness and sparkle lend volume and vitality to close-textured Charolais. Teamed with a Pouligny-Saint-Pierre, it willingly releases its 'brioche' notes, so in tune with the delicate, buttery flavours of the cheese. Generally speaking, Champagne likes to be matched with cheeses with a lactic and acidic character. Neufchatel and Brillat-Savarin are also worthy of its company. And continuing along the same lines, its encounters with Parmesan – a cheese with a dominant lactic content – are very successful. For yet more surprises, serve Champagne with very old Mimolette, or cheeses redolent of the countryside: Camembert, Coulommier, even Epoisses or Maroilles.

The precious role played by salt

Salt is the characteristic flavour of all cheese but, for the cheesemaker, it is much more than mere flavouring. Salt is, first and foremost, a wonderful means of regulating the appearance and longevity of cheese.

• *In the initial stages, it improves the straining* of the curdled milk. Depending on the process used, the curd is either plunged into a brine bath (this is the system always used for large cheeses) or sprinkled with dry salt, either manually or automatically.

• *It allows a crust to form* by encouraging the action of certain micro-organisms. Each of the mould families has its own particular sensitivity to salt; from the moulds present in the cellar where it is matured, the cheesemaker, thanks to salt, is able to select the ones he needs (a ferment of 'red' organisms for cheeses with washed crusts, or from the penicillin family for the flowery-crusted ones) and inhibit the others.

• *Finally, salt brings out the flavour of cheese.* During maturation, salt effectively 'migrates', little by little, to the centre of the paste. But this is a two-edged sword. If there was too much salt in the brine it will drain to excess, leaving a dry, over-salted paste. Some cheesemakers cannot resist the temptation to over-salt because this masks the defects in their product and, above all, allows it to keep for longer. Salting is sometimes the easy way out.

flowing, supple wines. Thus, when they come into contact with cheese, the fruity aromas of Bordeaux tend to be eclipsed, leaving only the taste of tannin. Literally stripped of all its finery, the wine firms up, shrivels, hardens. In the end only the 'skeleton' is left.

TO HELP YOU CHOOSE, bear in mind that the better a wine's origin and vintage, the more tannic it will be and, in consequence, the more unsuitable to accompany cheese. Grape variety is another important indicator of tannin content. Wines made from the Gamay grape are generally less tannic. Beaujolais is produced from this variety, as are the Gamays from Touraine and, in part, Passe-Tout-Grain. These, together with other red wines from Touraine, such as Chinon and Bourgeuil (though not the very top quality ones), are the best red wines to drink with cheese.

WHAT IF, DESPITE EVERYTHING, you really do want to open a good Bordeaux? Simply follow the example of the people of that region: serve hard cheeses with a fairly neutral flavour, such as Gouda. Generally speaking, the round, generous Merlot grape variety – a major component of Saint-Emilion and Pomerol – offers a satisfactory combination. Wines from the Rhône Valley also work very well because their tannins are well coated. And with Camembert? Try dry cider…

A PRACTICAL SUGGESTION: when choosing the make-up of your cheeseboard, take into account the wine you intend serving (it is quite likely to be the one you opened for the main course); to do otherwise is risky. If you don't want to serve alcohol, there are other drinks that stand up well to cheese: green tea, for example, which smoothes the passage of cloying, soft-paste varieties; or coffee, which miners in northern France drink with strong cheese. Unsweetened fruit juices, too, go well with fresh cheeses.

Opposite page: Parmesan cheeses being plunged into their brine bath.

146

Boulamour

France
Cow's milk

This most original cheese has already gone all around the world. It was created by Adèle Forteau, my predecessor at Rue de Grenelle, in Paris. When I took over from her in 1971, my wife Nicole developed the recipe further by perfecting the basic principles. She starts by macerating sultanas and currants in kirsch for a month then, when they are thoroughly impregnated with the alcohol, she mixes them into a triple-cream cheese from Burgundy to which she adds a little extra salt. Everything is done by hand; the texture has to be fairly malleable to lend itself to this treatment. The result is an astonishing dessert cheese, which combines the sweet flavours of the fruit with the salty taste of the cheese, the whole titillated by the alcohol. Boulamour has been most successful across the Atlantic, where it even has its imitators, largely because of its name. Marilyn Monroe was infatuated by the word *amour*, and the sensuous way she pronounced it gave it such a cachet in Anglo-Saxon countries that the ground was already laid for Boulamour. I recommend it at aperitif time, with a glass of Champagne.

Gratte-Paille

France (Ile-de-France)
Cow's milk

This cheese was created in the 1960s by the Rouzaire Company of Seine-et-Marne. It is a triple-cream cheese enriched with fresh cream, which gives it a particularly generous and delicate texture and, when young, a very distinct flavour of cream and butter. It is a variant of Brillat-Savarin – a similar cheese created between the two World Wars by Henri Androuët. Very knowledgeable about this type of cheese, my colleague, Sylvie Boubrit – a cheese retailer in Paris – is one of the people for whom Gratte-Paille holds no secrets. She never tires of saying that this is a cheese that deserves rediscovering. In her opinion it has more flavour than a Brillat-Savarin or a Pierre-Robert, on condition that it is ripened for up to ten weeks – but not more, for the cheese becomes too strong after that. In the cellar, you have to be careful not to let it 'turn', which would leave it with a predominantly salty or bitter flavour. Though it is available all year round, it is in spring and during end-of-year festivities that this generous cheese finds its most devoted following. Sylvie cordially recommends a white wine from Quercy to drink with it. Can you guess where the name *gratte-paille* (scratch-straw) comes from? It is that of a bush that grows at the side of lanes and catches on the straw piled on passing carts.

Langres

France (Champagne-Ardenne)
Cow's milk

Small in stature but with a big character! Langres is a cheese from the Champagne region; the AOC is centred on the Langres plateau, a big grazing area. It has a curious hollow in the centre of its rind – the 'fountain' – that deepens as the whey drains from the cheese, which is never turned over. This feature is the best indicator of ripeness in a Langres; the deeper the hollow the more *affiné* the cheese. It is at its best when the hollow is five millimetres (⅕ inch) deep, by which time the cheese is dense and has a melting quality, and the flavour is expansive without being strong.

It is regularly rubbed with salted water, every two days or so, to help foster the growth of the 'red mould' that gives it its orange colour and encourages the flavour to develop. Langres goes back a long way; it almost disappeared in the 1950s but now four producers are working towards its re-establishment, including enterprising farmer Claudine Gillet, from the Modia farm who, with the help of her family, raises about a hundred dairy cows. She tells me that in the past Langres was simply a fresh white cheese, drained in earthenware moulds and ripened no more than a few days. It became dry and yellowed. Nowadays consumers prefer it ripe and very creamy. Before eating it, I suggest you pour a few drops of Champagne, or Marc de Bourgogne into its hollow.

Livarot

France (Basse-Normandie)
Cow's milk

Livarot was the premier Normandy cheese for a long time, before being dethroned by Camembert, which travels better. The area where it is produced is restricted to a very small zone within a radius of about 20 kilometres (12 miles) of the town of Livarot. It corresponds to the hills of the Pays d'Auge, the famous wooded landscape that typifies the countryside all the way from Epinal to Normandy, with its dovecotes by the houses and its apple trees in flower. You can recognize Livarot by the band of natural reeds (sedge) bound around its edge or, in their absence, paper bands. There are five of these bands around each Livarot, hence its nickname of 'Colonel' – alluding to the five rings worn on the uniform of a French army colonel – but nowadays these are merely decorative (see page 113). This member of the washed-rind cheese family has quite a clean-cut character when it is correctly ripened (about two months). Apart from its very definite flavour, this rich, full cheese is delicate and supple and – when made from the milk of cows fed on fresh grass – a beautiful bright yellow in colour. A matured Calvados would go wonderfully well with it. Its flavour is so distinctive that cheeses that – for whatever reason – have developed a flavour that resembles it, are often said to be 'Livaroted'.

Parmigiano Reggiano

Northern Italy
Cow's milk

In the kitchens of Italy, from Parma to Modena, from Bologna to Mantua, a gentle rain of Parmesan cheese never ceases to fall. It is almost like a miracle. Parmegiano Reggiano is an institution in the Po valley and even more so in Emilia-Romagna, the area where a large part of its consumption is concentrated. Produced only in the Modena, Parma and Reggio Emilia provinces, and a part of Bologna and Mantua, this cheese, with its very distinctive texture, really should be allowed to leave the kitchen for the cheese board much more often. It has all the potential and quality needed to make the transition. Made in more than 600 cheese dairies, now mostly in low-lying areas rather than the mountains, its reputation is based on the solid principles by which it is made: milk from cows fed on silage is strictly prohibited; only raw milk to be used; a ripening period worthy of the name (two years, generally). At 12 months the texture is still smooth. Only after 15 or 16 months does it become granular, and then sandy, at which time the cheese has finally acquired its real character. At this stage it is delicious with a lively, fruity Champagne. In the course of two years it loses a quarter of its original weight, which explains why it is fairly expensive.

Pétafine

France (Rhône-Alpes)
Cow's milk whey

In the Lyons region they have a veritable passion for gastronomy in liquid form; wine, of course – the Rhône valley is richly endowed with that – and also cheeses that lend themselves to ripening to a very creamy, runny consistency that can be easily spread on bread. On the western slopes of the valley one finds different sorts of Brique, including Brique du Forez; on the eastern slopes there is Saint-Marcellin, which *La Mère Richard* made fashionable in the markets of Lyons, ancient capital of Roman Gaul. Pétafine is in the same category; also, it recaptures another Lyons tradition: that of macerated cheeses. It is made to an old local domestic recipe for a cheese made from whey – *pâte fine* (fine paste), which became Pétafine. The local cooks used to mix raisins and leftover grated cheese into this little whey cheese and put it to macerate in the local 'gut-rot' alcohol. The result, formed into a ball and rolled in breadcrumbs, was a light brown paste that was spread on stale bread or toast to accompany the *vin du patron* – the house wine. This is one of the things cheese was used for in Lyons – to make people thirsty. I used to deliver Pétafines to the Elysée Palace when Georges Pompidou was President of the Republic. He was very fond of them. The hygiene regulations have now put an end to the marketing of this 'shepherd's pie of the cheese world' and it only survives in domestic kitchens. If you wish to maintain the custom, it should be accompanied, naturally, by strong alcohol.

Cheese made from raw milk, or nothing!

In the space of half a century, cheese made with pasteurized milk has become the norm. Cheeses made from raw milk have difficulty complying with the excessively harsh hygiene regulations which, if nothing is done to restrain them, will one day put an end to all live produce.

I am a stout defender of cheeses made from raw milk and sell little else in my shop. I have chosen to describe some of my favourites at the end of this chapter. Full of rich and varied micro-organisms, these cheeses have quality and character and are truly distinctive. Milk, when used in its raw state, is a reflection of the area where the animals grazed and of an environment consisting of the specific moulds and ferments naturally present in the local ecosystem. It applies to cheese and to all foods; pasteurization robs them of their means of expression. The addition of a few ferments, however well chosen, cannot restore fullness and complexity to cheese made with pasteurized milk. With a small number of molecules one could perhaps manage to reproduce some approximation of the original aroma, but that complexity and depth would still be lacking.

WHEN IT WAS RUMOURED in 1992, that the European authorities intended banning the making of cheese from raw milk, it caused a sensation among all cheese lovers. It was a close shave, and cheesemakers accepted some draconian hygiene regulations in return for safeguarding this heritage. The matter re-surfaces from time to time; it has been hived off to the international authorities that regulate world trade in foodstuffs (Codex Alimentarius), where cheese seems perpetually to be under suspended sentence. In Europe itself, someone has dreamed up a way of making cheese from raw milk that would simply be a sham; the name would remain but the milk would be micro-filtered – an operation which gives much the same result as pasteurization.

WHY IS IT THAT NATURAL PRODUCTS that have been made for countless generations, have now been singled out for straitjacketing? Why should one wish to pasteurize, or partially pasteurize milk? The reason given is that of

Jeff Rémond's Rouelles du Tarn are *cendré* with organic charcoal as soon as they are out of the mould. The great majority of producers of farmhouse goat's milk cheeses work with raw milk.

hygiene: these procedures, which consist of subjecting the milk to high temperatures, destroy harmful bacteria and allow products to keep for longer. But heat robs the aromas of their subtlety and destroys the natural microbiological flora, blindly eliminating the good with the bad. Milk that is fully or partially pasteurized loses its identity; the flavour of the region floats away on the steam that rises from it.

IN PRACTICE, PASTEURIZED MILK is heated to between 72 and 85°C (160 and 185°F) for a few seconds; partial pasteurization requires a temperature of around 65°C (150°F) for 20 to 30 seconds. The milk is then easier to handle and less likely to cause problems during cheese-making, but it has neither the finesse nor the character of raw milk.

Milk heated in this way has to be 'reinforced' with a few well-chosen and well-monitored cultures to give it back the typical flavour of cheese. This allows for the manufacture of cheeses that taste the same all year round, with no unpleasant – or pleasant – surprises, but never produces the rich flavours of those made with raw milk.

IT IS OBVIOUSLY IN THE INTERESTS of industrial producers to collect vast quantities of milk from various sources: heating allows them to make more homogeneous products and the public to become accustomed to a regular, recognizable flavour. Cheese made from raw milk is much less predictable; its flavour changes with the seasons. The debate reveals a profound cultural divide within Europe. In Protestant countries, food tends to be judged on its nutritional value; in traditionally Catholic countries it is seen more as a source of pleasure. The priorities are different; in the north the taste is for clean food – a cheese, to be good, must also be

Cheeses on Marthe Pégourié's stalls at Gramat at different stages of ripeness. As the weeks go by they shrivel until they become totally dry.

The safety of cheeses made from raw milk

The notion that cheeses made from raw milk carry a greater health risk than those made from pasteurised milk – especially that of contracting listeriosis – is firmly anchored in the minds of the consumer. However, this condemnation is totally unjustified; available epidemiological studies show that they are both equally open to question. Listeria, a bacterium omnipresent in the environment, is harmless to the great majority of the population. It only presents a danger to certain, well-targeted 'at-risk' groups: pregnant women, who run the risk of spontaneous abortion, and people with weakened immune systems. For everyone else, listeria either has no effect or, at worst, causes passing tiredness and perhaps a slight fever. In addition, listeriosis only occurs if there is an abnormally high presence of the listeria bacterium. Pasteurization is no solution; a cheese in which the original microbiological content has been destroyed by this procedure is not immune to subsequent contamination. In this case, and unlike that of cheese made from raw milk in which there is a microbiological balance, the way is clear for the noxious bacteria to thrive.

Real epidemics are rare. Listeriosis is a notifiable illness, which means that if several people are struck down by the same strain of listeria, the product which caused it can quickly be identified simply by questioning the sufferers about what they have eaten in the course of the previous weeks. Once identified, the product is withdrawn from sale. In the past, it required the occurrence of numerous cases of listeriosis before the alert was given. The most susceptible cheeses are the soft-paste ones with bloomy or washed rinds, that are ripened only for a short period, (Camembert, Brie, Chaource, Époisses, Pont-l'Èvêque, Livarot, Munster, etc.) Products that are ripened for long periods, such a Roquefort, or the various Gruyères, pose absolutely no risk whatsoever, and neither do goat's milk cheeses, which have the protection of acidity.

wholesome and safe. In the south, where the taste of the *terroir* is important, it must have 'roots'. These different approaches condition our expectations. For an Anglo-Saxon, Cheddar, whether produced in England or New Zealand, is still Cheddar. What does it matter if they are exactly alike? For a Latin, a goat's milk cheese that does not evoke its origins is of no interest. Does it come from Apuglia, La Mancha or the *garrigues* of Haute-Provence?

THIS IS A FUNDAMENTAL CULTURAL DIFFERENCE. It explains the numerous divisions that arise during international discussions. On the one hand is the 'zero microbes in the final product' approach; on the other, that of maintaining the balance between microbiology and hygiene 'from pitchfork to table fork'. The first method, which turns cheese dairies into hospital wards, seems to be making inexorable headway. It is far from conclusively proved that the combination of nonporous plastics, stainless steel and chlorine-based chemicals is necessarily the most effective and the most pragmatic safeguard in terms of public health. At times, hygiene ends where hygiene-fixation begins; a pathogenic microbe penetrating a sterile environment has a clear field in which to develop. Some industrialists are beginning to look seriously into 'ecologically-controlled workplaces', and the role played by microbiological balance. In a word, they are seeking an ecological solution… which is precisely what has prevailed in agriculture for thousands of years.

Cheddar

United Kingdom (England)
Cow's milk

Before the First World War in Great
Britain, there were thousands of farms
producing Cheddar. After the Second
World War these were reduced to
fifteen hundred and now there are
barely half a dozen. Cheddar has
become an industrial cheese, made
all over the planet from pasteurized
milk; Americans, Australians and New
Zealanders have even made a
speciality of it. In Cheddar itself, a little
village in Somerset, in south-west
England, there is only one remaining
cheese dairy, and that is only open in
the summer, for the benefit of tourists.
A minute part of the British production
is made from raw milk. This cheese
goes back to ancient times. Cheddar
seems to have been a favoured halt for
the Romans during their conquest of
Britain. Was it they who brought the
recipe for Cantal to Auvergne? Cantal
is made in much the same way as
Cheddar. The curd is crushed before
being pressed into moulds, which
accounts for the numerous irregularities
in the texture. Each cheese weighs
about 25 kilos (55 pounds). Cheddar
may be eaten 'mature', when it has a
characteristic flavour of fresh hazelnuts,
but personally I prefer the 'extra
mature', ripened for more than a year,
with a much more pronounced taste.

Gramat

France (Midi-Pyrénées)
Goat's milk

Big brother of Rocamadour, Gramat
is the only child of Marthe Pégourié,
a prominent figure in the department
of the Lot. This energetic cheese
merchant, established in the village of
Gramat, has appointed herself the
mouthpiece of the traditional local
cheese, and has made an important
contribution to its increased popularity.
For 30 years she has collected cheeses
from the neighbouring Causses region
and ripened them in her cellars. She
considers the Cabécous from
Rocamadour too niggardly for her
customers' taste and dismisses them
as mere 'medallions' or 'disks'; the
eight centimetre (three inch) diameter
Gramat is much more acceptable to
her. The methods she uses, on the
other hand, are exactly the same as
those of Rocamadour. This cheese also
has the advantage of keeping better.
Like the little Cabécou, Gramat
becomes blue at the end of ripening.
Marthe is at pains to explain to her
customers – especially to the many
tourists who stop at her shop
convinced they are visiting a national
monument – that Gramat is at its best
once it has turned blue. Whatever you
do, don't complain that the rinds of
her cheeses have gone mouldy!

Fleur du Maquis

France (Corsica)
Ewe's milk

Fleur du Maquis – flower of the Corsican
scrubland – is the most famous of the
Corsican cheeses, also known under
the commercial name of Brin d'Amour.
I particularly like the recipe concocted
by Claudine Vigier, retailer-*affineur* at
Carpentras. She perfected it after
experimenting for four years. She starts
with fresh Tommes, which are delivered
from Corsica. She ties each cheese in a
little cloth, knotting it to give it the desired
shape, and leaves it overnight to drain.
The next day she removes the cloth and
sets the curd on a plank in a draught of
air. She turns it regularly for several days,
then she moistens the surface and rolls
it in a skilfully chosen mixture of herbs:
oregano, savory, rosemary, a touch of
pimento, juniper and a few grains of
pepper. The cheeses are then covered
with film and left in the cellar for three
days, after which the film is removed
and they are put in a wooden chest with
more herbs for another ten days to a
fortnight. At the end of that time, beneath
the herbs and spices is a creamy paste
with the good, honeyed taste of ewe's
milk. Claudine only makes Fleur du
Maquis from November to the end of
June – the ewes' lactation period.

Gris de Lille
Northern France
Cow's milk

Its nickname is 'stinking macerated' and making it is quite a procedure! Gris de Lille is not recommended for sensitive nostrils or delicate palates. It is a Maroilles that has been ripened for three to four months. During that time it is washed regularly with salt water, which makes its rind sticky and develops the flavour. It can undoubtedly be described as a 'sturdy character'. Its texture, fairly chalky in the first weeks, softens in the end. The colour of its rind swings between cream and the grey shades that give it its name. Philippe Olivier, famous *affineur* in northern France, who supplies me with them regularly, tells me it is also called 'Maroilles Gris'. This cheese, however, has never been made in Lille, but in Hainaut. It was the miners who made it popular. They enjoy it for breakfast with black coffee and a glass (or more) of gin. It appears that Nikita Khrushchev too, on a visit to Lille in 1960, was not indifferent to its charm. Unfortunately, its somewhat overwhelming presence does not make it easy to market.

Rouelle du Tarn
France (Midi-Pyrénées)
Goat's milk

This could be called a goat's milk Murol; with the hole in its centre it is very much like the cheese from Auvergne. But the comparison ends there. Rouelle du Tarn is made, from goat's milk, by a veteran of the student demonstrations in 1960 now established on the edge of the Quercy Causses. Jeff Rémond started 25 years ago with about 40 goats and today has 500, which are put out to pasture whenever the weather permits – that being any time it is neither raining nor snowing. The rest of the time they are fed cereals and forage made on the farm. Rouelle du Tarn is made by the most typical of farmhouse methods: with raw milk, using lactic ferments (saved from the whey of the day before), ladle moulded. Most of the cheeses he produces are *cendré* with organic charcoal; initially black, the rind is made progressively greyer by the formation of a fine yeast mould (Geotrichum). The cheese is about 10 centimetres (4 inches) in diameter and weighs about 250 grams (9 ounces). The central hole is made with a pastry cutter after 24 hours of drainage in the mould. Jeff, whose products range from Cabécou to a large Tomme weighing 2 kilos (4¼ pounds), is himself surprised by the success of his Rouelle, which has become a leading product. The idea was suggested to him by my colleague Robert Céneri. His French pun goes: *Il suffit d'un trou pour faire son trou* – all you need is a hole to make a breakthrough.

Mâconnais
France (Burgundy)
Goat's milk

Smaller than its neighbour Charolais, which is made in much the same way, Mâconnais only weighs between 50 and 60 grams (1¾ and 2 ounces), according to how long it has been ripened. Like Crottin de Chavignol, its small size is due to it having been originally made in the vineyards, where the vine growers' plots were often very small. Each of them kept a goat or two, which fed on grass along the roadsides. The quantity of milk they gave was only enough to make small cheeses, which went to feed the workers. Today, more than 400 farmers produce this little cheese, and it can only be a question of time before it is given an AOC. Locally it is eaten fairly fresh, six days after it is taken out of the moulds. After two or three weeks it begins to develop a fine growth speckled with blue. It is quite fine and very slightly acidic. In the Mâcon vineyards it is often eaten as a snack at ten in the morning, with a little glass of white wine – a Mâcon-Village, for example, or a Pouilly-Fuissé.

Winter

The pallor of
winter cheeses

Check the dough (interior) of a cheese. Is it a pronounced colour? Does it have bronze-yellow tones? If so, it was undoubtedly made in spring. Does it look a bit pallid? Has it got a bluish tinge? Then it is most certainly a cheese that was made in winter.

Like everyone, I have a natural affinity for things that look healthy and in good shape; rich and glossy cheeses with gold glints rarely fail to arouse my interest. There is always a touch of excitement about cutting into a wheel of Brie de Meaux, a farmhouse Saint-Nectaire or a big slab of Beaufort. What treasures lurk beneath their rinds? What flavourful delights are promised by the mere appearance of the cheese? In actual fact, the reaction of the dough when pressed with a thumb to test its suppleness and the way it behaved in the cellar during ripening, have already given me a pretty clear indication.

I EVEN HAVE A QUITE PRECISE IDEA of the colour the interior will be, based on when it was made, but no great expertise is needed for that. Spring milk produces cheeses of superb appearance, both yellow and golden in colour. This natural 'tan', a most attractive effect, really gets the taste buds going. In winter, however, the colours lack brightness; the cheeses look pale, even lacklustre. The six cheeses I will introduce you to at the end of this chapter are all, to different degrees, subject to these variations.

THE SIMPLE EXPLANATION is found in the fodder; the yellow colour of the dough is linked to carotene, a pigment present in the plants the animals are fed on. This substance is fairly fragile and easily destroyed by heat and oxidization. It doesn't survive the process of turning fresh grass into hay or silage (fresh grass sprayed with a serum and stored under canvas). Since grass only grows in spring and summer, these glowing colours disappear in autumn and winter. The colour of a cheese is, therefore, a good indication

Les Villedieu, a village in the Doubs region. In the past the snow prevented milk being taken to the village cheese dairies. The cheeses had to be made on the farms.

Page opposite: making Comté in the Chapelle-du-Bois cheese dairy.
Pages 156–157: a herd of cows at Rochejean.

The best of winter

Weather you wouldn't turn a cow or a goat out in…
Winter, when the pastures are denuded of grass
and swamped by rain, is not the best time to make
cheese. Many of the animals have gone dry and all
are being fed on hay or, even worse, silage
(fermented grass). For many cheeses it is a
transitional period.

• *Without meaning to belittle them* those
cheeses needing only short or medium ripening
times (from two weeks to two months), which is
to say the bulk of the soft-curd ones, never quite
manage to reach their peak. This is equally true of
the bloomy-rinded cheeses (Camembert, Brie) and
the washed rinds (Pont l'Évêque, Livarot, Langres).
As for goat's milk cheeses, there are none on the
market stalls at this time.

• *Be on your guard during this period* against
cheeses made from frozen curd. They are inferior
in quality and are easily recognizable by the fact
that their rinds can be removed without effort.

• *On the other hand, cheeses made in the
mountain regions* in summer are presented in
a very favourable light. You can throw in your lot
with Ossau-Iraty, Salers, Laguiole or Appenzell
without fear of disappointment. The long-lasting
cheeses made the year before have had 18 months
of ripening. They should really be at their best.
Sumptuous Beauforts, Gruyères and Comtés are
at their most inviting. In the French language, winter
(*hiver*) rhymes with Gruyère! And don't forget the
Mont d'Or, which is perfect from the end of
December to mid-April.

THE DIFFERENCES IN THE COLOUR OF THE INTERIOR only
applies to cheeses made from cow's milk; goats and
ewes cannot assimilate carotene, which is why cheeses
made from their milk, whether in autumn or spring, are
always a pale colour. A more precise indication of when
they were made lies in the quality of their texture – how
rich and unctuous it is – and the flavour, which is fresher
in spring and more nutty in autumn.

THIS PHENOMENON of seasonal colour can cause
difficulties for cheesemakers and retailers. Take
the example of Comté, a French cheese produced
in the Jura Mountains according to traditional methods.
The regulations of the AOC specifically forbid (more
power to them) the use of added colouring matter

of when it was made. At the production stage milk
is always white, even after coagulation. It is only in
the following weeks that the carotene present in the milk
will appear as colour in the dough.

and therefore the colour of this jewel in the crown of the Franche-Comté cheeses varies with the seasons. From November to April, when the cows are fed on hay, the dough is pale, while those made in the summer months are an enticing, strong yellow.

IN CONSEQUENCE, retailers and consumers are inclined to leave aside the pale cheeses and over-value those made in summer, thus complicating the supply chain. For all that, there is no question of lifting the ban on artificial colouring.

REGIONAL DIFFERENCES, due to differing plant species and variations in their carotene content, have to be taken into account; as a general rule, vegetation in the regions of eastern France is less rich in carotene than in that of the west. The salt-laden air in coastal areas can favour the presence of carotene, either by stimulating the growth of certain types of grass, or by acting as a catalyst.

FINALLY, BACTERIA can influence the colour of the cheese, particularly in washed-rind products (Maroilles, Livarot) in which ripening progresses from the outside towards the centre. On the other hand, it can be necessary to remove some of the colour (using chlorophyll) from those cheeses that are too rich in carotene. This is done in the case of Fourme, to give its interior an

ivory-whiteness that enhances the brightness of the blue. These little tricks-of-the-trade – arrangements with nature – have gone on since the beginning of time, and are perfectly acceptable as long as they are not used to deceive the consumer.

ARE PALE CHEESES inferior? It is difficult to answer that question with any degree of certainty; so many factors contribute to the flavour of a cheese and the fat and protein content, both indicators of quality, reach their highest levels towards the end of lactation in the autumn.

SO LET'S NOT BE TOO HASTY. We should judge products by their taste rather than just their appearance, and accept that even the pale ones can have golden qualities. Otherwise, artificial colouring could one day become an automatic addition, and then we won't know which colour cheese to rely on.

Making Comté: the cheesemaker slips a casein plaque onto the side of the rind which serves to authenticate the cheese.
Page opposite: salting and checking the ripeness of Comté with a probe, in the cellars at the Arnaud cheese dairy.

Bleu de Vercors-Sassenage
France (Rhône-Alpes)
Cow's milk

Bleu de Vercors-Sassenage is the most 'Italian' of the French blue cheeses, with its milder and slightly less creamy texture that bears some resemblance to certain types of Gorgonzola. Quite different from its close relatives of the Massif Central, it is all delicacy and balance, almost discretion. Not much given to extremes, its mould is a fairly pale blue and its soft, melt-in-the-mouth interior tends to be supple and elastic. It is excellent for cooking – delicious as raclette or fondue. This is a fairly atypical cheese, made by mixing the evening's milk, which is pasteurized, with the raw product of the next morning's milking – a technique that harks back to ancient times when the Vercors peasants would boil the evening's milk to keep it from turning sour. Pasteurization before its time! The cheese originated on the Vercors plateau (formerly known as 'Monts de Sassenage'), a true natural fort amid extensive farming land. All of the farmhouse producers gave up in the 1950s and for half a century only one cheese dairy continued to make this blue cheese. When Vercors was declared a nature reserve, the influx of tourists created a demand that resulted in a dozen farmers taking up the trade.

Brie de Malesherbes
France (Ile-de-France)
Cow's milk

In 1982, when I acquired the former town milk depot at Fontainebleau, I found old documents and heard local old people's accounts of a technique for ripening Brie des Moissons – a cheese I undertook to resuscitate. Its origins – on the sandy Montereau plain, in the Seine-et-Marne region – go back to the nineteenth century. This is a poorer area for cattle-farming than the rich dairy areas of Brie further to the north, and since there was less milk, the farmers made their cheeses smaller – 800 grams (1¾ pounds) against about 2.6 kilos (5¾ pounds) for a Brie de Meaux, for example. There was one notable cheesemaker at a place called Ville-Saint-Jacques, near Montereau. This little cheese, which the men took when they went fishing, or to work in the fields, was rolled in ash to preserve it and had a very pronounced flavour. The one we recreated, using organic charcoal, is more to modern taste. I couldn't call it Brie de Ville-Saint-Jacques as that name was already in use for a commercial product, so I opted for Brie de Malesherbes, the name of the milk depot in Fontainebleau, which was subsequently taken over by Gilles and Odile Goursat, nephew and niece of my wife Nicole. The Brie de Malesherbes is in good hands.

Comté
France (Franche-Comté)
Cow's milk

Comté is a typical mountain cheese that takes up huge quantities of milk. One large round cheese – 65 centimetres (2 feet) in diameter and weighing 50 kilos (110 pounds) – is made with between 500 and 600 litres (110 to 132 gallons) of milk. The AOC zone is restricted to the Jura Mountains and each cheesemaker is only allowed to collect milk within a 25 kilometre (15 mile) radius. In France and in Switzerland, these cheese dairies are known in the profession as *fruitières* (literally, places where the milk is 'fructified'). They number more than 200, producing Comté according to very strict specifications as to quality. The cheese is made from raw milk, from cows fed on fresh grass or hay (not silage, since this may contain bacteria that cause the cheeses to split) and additives and colourings are forbidden. A traditional method of cheese-making involved the use of a big linen cloth. The cheesemakers used the cloth to collect the grains of curd – suspended in whey – from the vat, plunging their arms deep into the steaming liquid. Unfortunately, this spectacular method has almost disappeared. Like good wine, Comté's most precious ally is time. The minimum ripening period is four months but it needs at least 18 months to develop all its aromas. Impatience can do it irreparable harm.

Coulommiers
France (Ile-de-France)
Cow's milk

This cheese is something between a Camembert and a Brie. Coulommiers certainly originated in the Brie area, to the east of Paris and home of the present-day Brie de Meaux and Brie de Melun. Like them, its texture is perfectly unctuous, but its size – only about 13 centimetres (5 inches) in diameter – and its greater thickness give it the appearance of a large, flattened Camembert. This format, easier to transport to the Paris markets than the larger, fragile and difficult-to-handle Brie, was responsible for its rapid development and great success in the nineteenth century. Coulommiers has copied Camembert's chunky format, but does not quite match its Norman relative's fulsome flavour. This is hardly surprising since, for the most part, it is now produced from pasteurized milk. Not covered by an AOC, it can be made anywhere in France, though in fact it is mostly made by the producers of Brie de Meaux or Brie de Melun, established in a wide area running from the Seine-et-Marne region to the Meuse. Ideally Coulommiers should be ripened for up to two months. The reddish streaks that may appear on the white rind during this time are a reliable indication of a more pronounced flavour and a very creamy texture. Watch out for them.

Dunlop
United Kingdom (Scotland)
Cow's milk

Dunlop is a Scottish version of Cheddar – more sensual, softer and more civilized. Its curd is not so pressed and its dough is richer and more moist and therefore ripens more quickly. A well-ripened Dunlop (up to six months) may be covered with a bloom that wavers between green and grey tones. This ancient cheese is named after the town of Dunlop, south-west of Glasgow in the extreme north of Ayrshire. Its origin is well documented; around 1660, during a period of Scottish unrest, farmer's wife, Barbara Gilmour, fled to Ireland where she learned the recipe for a cheese made with full-cream milk. She began making it when she returned to Scotland in 1668 and it was soon imitated by others. Barbara Gilmour's cheese press is still on display in Dunlop. The arrival of the railway in the little town at the end of the nineteenth century encouraged trade with Glasgow and carried the fame of the local cheese far beyond the region's frontiers. It came close to disappearing in the 1950s and was reintroduced by cheesemaker Anne Dorward, who began making it with surplus raw milk in the 1980s. A real success story.

Pavé d'Auge
France (Basse-Normandie)
Cow's milk

Pavé d'Auge was defined by Thierry Graindorge, *affineur* at Livarot, as a double Pont l'Eveque – not twice as big but twice as thick. Five litres (9 pints) of milk go to make this square cheese, produced in fairly small quantities for local markets and cheese merchants. It needs at least six weeks to ripen to perfection. The ripening takes place from the rind inwards, under the action of surface moulds stimulated in the first week by regular washing with salt water. It is then brushed regularly in the cellar; its rind gradually becomes covered with a fine pale mould and takes on pinkish-grey tints with reddish streaks. The cheese, with its quite characteristic flavour of hazelnut, was originally made in the Moyaux region. In the local markets it sometimes goes under the name of Pavé de Moyaux. I enjoy it when it is very creamy but not necessarily unctuous. Above all, don't miss out on the ones made from the excellent spring milk and those from the late summer re-growth period.

163

Cold-weather cheeses

In the absence of Gruyère we can make do with Tomme. When cold and snow prevented production of the prestigious big wheels, cheesemakers invented smaller, secondary cheeses. Many cheeses born out of this necessity have since become acclaimed in their own right.

Only artists allow their imagination to carry them away. For working farmers, imagination and luck are a luxury they can rarely afford, for in rugged rural areas everything comes at a price. When ice, snow and freezing temperatures spread across mountains and down valleys, everyone's cooped up indoors and the animals stay under cover. Pooling the milk from several farms to make fine, long-lasting cheeses becomes impossible, but the animals must still be milked twice daily and the milk, even in small amounts, is too precious to waste.

TAKE THE EXAMPLE OF THE JURA, where the flagship cheese is Comté, formerly made in every village in the cauldrons of the communal *fruitière* (cheese dairy). Although the Jura plateaux are not all that high – 1,400 metres (4,600 feet) at the most – the continental winds that sweep over the Franche-Comté make it one of the coldest regions in France. In winter, each farm would find itself isolated, with no means of reaching the nearest village. Many dairies had to close. The peasants learned to make a smaller cheese, weighing from 8 to 10 kilos (18 to 22 pounds), in their own homes. They coagulated the milk from one milking and covered the curd with ash to protect it from insects while it waited for that of the evening – or following morning. It was a rudimentary system but it worked and gave rise to Morbier, with its famous black stripe (see pages 114 and 170).

Making Morbier in the workroom of La Chapelle-du-Bois. The curd, taken from the vat and put into the mould, is a shapeless mass.

A recipe suggestion – fondue made with Vacherin

In Franche-Comté they are in the habit of making fondue with Mont d'Or. This succulent recipe consists of soaking a Mont d'Or, still in its box, in cold water for 15 minutes; the wooden box becomes thoroughly wet, and cold hardens the dough. Next, a hole a few centimetres across is hollowed out from the centre of the cheese and filled with white wine from the Jura, then the whole thing is put to warm through in a slow oven. The cheese melts before the wet box dries out enough to start to burn. The cheese is then poured over hot potatoes and eaten with *charcuterie* (ham, salamis and so on).

A specialist job: 'cheese binder'

The strips of spruce used to bind around the Mont d'Or cheeses are gathered all the year round, other than in exceptional circumstances, like those of the great storm of Christmas 1999, which blocked access to them for several months. Collecting them forms part of a specialist job – that of the *sanglier* ('binder') – a trade followed by about 20 people in the Jura mountains. The task begins as soon as a tree has been felled. Only spruce is suitable (pine bark, for example, tends to break). The bands are stripped from the layer immediately below the bark (the sapwood). They must be 47 centimetres (18½ inches) long for the small Mont d'Ors, 55 centimetres (22 inches) for the medium size and a metre (39 inches) for the largest format. The bands are then left to dry in attics, where they gradually harden, in which state they will last almost indefinitely. Later, in the cheese dairy, they will be plunged into boiling salted water, to soften and sterilize them. Some cheesemakers buy them in Switzerland and even as far away as Poland, where they are much cheaper.

Only after moulding and pressing does Morbier take on its definitive shape.

This process of alternating Comté made in the cheese dairies with Morbier made on the farms went on for a very long time. Nowadays both products are made all the year round. Communications have been greatly improved, while the two products are made in separate workplaces.

ALONG THE SWISS FRONTIER, in the south of the Jura, Mont d'Or is another product of similar circumstances. Here the farmers chose to make a smaller cheese which, unlike Morbier, is made with full-cream milk. As you know, at the end of the lactation period the milk is particularly rich and high in fat and the resulting cheese is especially unctuous, so the peasant farmers had to bind their cheeses with strips of sedge before putting them in boxes. Since its origins, possibly because the mountainous Doubs region is still more isolated than the Jura, Mont d'Or has remained seasonal, though its production now carries on well into the summer period. Personally, I wait for the first frosts before offering it to my customers.

A VERY SIMILAR PHENOMENON occurred in the Alps. When prevented from making their splendid Beaufort wheels, the farmers of Savoie made do with a mundane domestic form

Wood is the natural ally of cheese. For example, it forms a belt around a Vacherin Mont-d'Or, and helps ripen any number of products through its role of thermal regulator.
Page opposite: a Morbier cellar.

Making Morbier: after cutting the block of curd, the cheesemaker smears it with organic charcoal, which forms the black streak that is a characteristic of the cheese.

of Tomme, called *Boudane* in the Haute Tarantaise dialect but not to be confused with a cheese of that name launched by an industrial concern in Haute-Savoie. This somewhat rustic cheese was not made for sale and, since it was for home consumption, was made with skimmed milk, leaving the cream for making butter. The peasants never ate Beaufort, which was made strictly for market.

IN THE NEIGHBOURING BAUGES MOUNTAINS, when there was insufficient milk to make Tomes (not Tommes – in this area they have retained the archaic spelling), Vacherin was produced instead. This weighs 700 to 800 grams (25 to 28 ounces), while Tome is double or triple that. An identical situation occurred in the Abondance valley; peasant life there used to be regulated by the alternate making of Tommes (about 10 kilos/22 pounds) in summer and Vacherin (1 kilo/just over 2 pounds) in winter. Come south with me, over the frontier to northern Italy, where Taleggio lived for a long time in the shade of Parmigiano Reggiano, serving it as a kind of 'variable adjustment'. In Switzerland, too, they have traditionally alternated the hard-pressed Gruyère of the summer with the winter Raclette or Vacherin.

THESE INTERWOVEN CYCLES are not confined to cow's milk products; in the Aveyron Causses, kingdom of the ewe, the lordly Roquefort – only made during the first part of the year – leaves the stage to Perail in summer and at the end of the lactation period. This humble little

disc-shaped cheese was intended for home and local consumption only. Today it has made a name for itself and there are now cheesemakers dedicated solely to producing it. When I visit the Millau area I can see from their confident bearing just how proud the farmers are of their little cheese.

CONCEIVED IN THE WAKE OF MORE PRESTIGIOUS CHEESES, as a source of basic income in rural areas, these 'by-products' have become extraordinarily emancipated. Mont d'Or obtained its AOC quite some time ago; Morbier has just been granted one and it is hoped that Tomme de Savoie will soon gain Europe-wide recognition. These little cheeses – these 'also-rans', produced for the most part in the dead of winter, in the shadow of their renowned elders, have gained their independence and are now claiming their share of the limelight.

Taleggio
Northern Italy
Cow's milk

Taleggio gets its name from a little town in Lombardy not far from Bergamo in the Taleggio valley. It is made in a wide area surrounding the Italian Alps: Lombardy (the provinces of Bergamo, Brescia, Como, Cremona, Milan and Pavia), the Veneto (Treviso) and Piedmont (Novarra), principally in the Po valley. Its history is linked with that of transhumance – the summer exodus of animals to the high mountain pastures. It undoubtedly began at the foot of the Alps, where the herds assembled before ascending the mountains. Cheeses such as Gruyère and Parmesan were made up on the higher slopes. The cheesemakers in the valley waited for the animals' return to start making their cheeses again. The cheeses I get from the great Italian *affineur* Carlo Fiori are made from raw milk and are remarkable for the sensuality of their almost soft texture. The light brown, bordering on pink, rind of Taleggio is imprinted with the letters CTT, acronym of the consortium that links all the producers covered by the appellation. It is quite the best example of the square Lombardy cheese family known as Stracchino, from *stracche*, which means 'limp' or 'tired' in the Lombard dialect.

Vacherin des Bauges
France (Rhône-Alpes)
Cow's milk

Watch out, this is a rare and elusive product. Vacherin des Bauges is very popular in the areas around Annecy, Chambéry and Albertville, where it is eagerly awaited and ordered in advance. At one time it was traditionally made in winter on all the farms in the Bauges; today there are only three farmhouse cheesemakers still producing it, possibly because it requires a lot of effort, vigilance and care. The milk must be coagulated immediately after each milking, and ripening the cheese requires any number of procedures – binding, turning, washing, packing in boxes. This Vacherin is only made in December and January, and sometimes up to mid-February. The winter milk, coming at the end of the lactation period, is particularly rich in fat, which means that the texture quickly turns creamy then unctuous after three weeks' ripening – the length of time recommended by Denis Provent, who has a real passion for this product. The bindings and the box are essential to stop the cheese from overflowing. Vacherin des Bauges always retains a little taste of sour milk and its flavour is strongly reminiscent of the rustic notes of the Tome des Bauges.

Vacherin Fribourgeois
Switzerland
Cow's milk

Originally from the Fribourg canton in Swiss Romande, Vacherin Fribourgeois owes its reputation to its combination of very soft texture and strong flavour. Always made from raw milk, it comes in the form of a wheel, 30 to 40 centimetres (12 to 16 inches) in diameter. In the past there were two kinds of Vacherin: one used in fondue, a hard-pressed one made in winter and a handmade Vacherin – a softer product of autumn. This is no longer the case and the most prestigious cheeses are now made in mountain chalets. They are sold under the name of Vacherin Fribourgeois Alpage. According to how long they have been ripened, they may also be marked 'Select' (12 weeks) or 'Extra' (17 weeks). Vacherin Fribourgeois can be used equally well on the cheese board (the Swiss say they eat it 'with their fingers') or made into a fondue, where it will greatly enhance the flavour. Vacherin Fribourgeois is traditionally used in the so-called 'half-and-half' recipe for fondue, together with Gruyère de Fribourg. The very mature ones can be used to make the 'shavings' popularly served with an aperitif.

169

Morbier
France (Franche-Comté)
Cow's milk

Would this cheese be as successful without its characteristic black stripe? In the old days it smelled deliciously of ash; when the milk was cooked in a cauldron hung over a wood fire, the cheesemakers used to rub their hands around its blackened sides and coat the curd with soot to protect it (see page 114). When wood fires were replaced by gas, they collected soot from the chimney and sifted it over the curd. Nowadays organic charcoal (sold in all chemists' shops) is used instead of soot. The dark stripe, ranging from black to blue-grey, is now merely a decorative reminder of the cheese's origins and imparts no particular flavour. Made throughout the Jura, generally in the Comté dairies, Morbier begins to acquire real character after three to four months of ripening. Recently covered by an AOC, it will never have the strength and richness of Comté, which is made from the same milk, but it is notable for the very agreeable creaminess of its texture and its delicate, fruity aromas.

Saint-Niklauss
Switzerland (Valais)
Cow's milk

Originally from the Rhône valley, Raclette dates back to the Middle Ages. It was the people of Valais who first thought of heating a cheese in front of the fire and scraping off the top layer as it melted. Nowadays we have small pans heated by electric elements to facilitate making it. Undoubtedly the best Raclette is that made with Bagnes – known as Raclette Cheese in Switzerland. Sadly, it is a rare product – almost a limited edition – made on the summer mountain pastures, and hardly ever exported. The ones from the Anniviers, Conches and Ornières regions are very well known. As for Saint-Niklauss, it is a very well-reputed commercial brand; personally I extend the *affinage* period to almost five months. The cheese needs to retain a certain firmness. Raclette has been widely promoted in France in winter sports resorts. Traditionally it is eaten with baked potatoes and small pickled onions and gherkins. Dried meats from the Graubünden canton or raw ham also go well with it. Like all upmarket cheeses, products from the Valais have given rise to many imitations made with pasteurized milk. It is hoped that a projected AOC will put an end to this.

Mont d'Or
France (Franche-Comté)
Cow's milk

Each autumn, the return of Mont d'Or (or Vacherin in the high areas of the Doubs) celebrates the affinity of wood for cheese. This is no mere coincidence. Direct contact with its restricting box, and the spruce bands that encircle it, impregnate Mont d'Or with a soft, balsamic aroma. This is, above all, a winter cheese, and only in demand when the temperature plummets. Indeed, originally it was only made from All Saints' Day to Easter. Nowadays it makes its appearance around the middle of August, gives generously of itself throughout winter and bows out at the beginning of spring (March 30th). A dozen cheese dairies make Mont d'Or but, since seasonal production is uneconomic, they all make Comté as well, and even Morbier and Raclette. However, for all of them the Mont d'Or is the most demanding and the most delicate. It is very labour intensive, needing binding, brushing, washing, turning and boxing. The cheeses stay in the cellar for at least three weeks. I keep mine for twice that length of time; by then the rind has crinkled and the interior is creamy. To my customers I recommend removing the top rind and eating the cheese with a spoon. Such a treat! I can well understand why it is so widely copied.

Those warming dishes made with cheese

Cooking with cheese is, above all, a winter speciality. Its warming qualities are amply illustrated by the two flagship cheese dishes: fondue and raclette. They both celebrate simple fare and the pleasure of sharing it.

It is true that 'lightness', in the low-calorie sense, is not a feature of cheese cookery, which has its origins in the poorest areas. In farming communities, the finer, expensive foodstuffs, like meat, were not everyday items but reserved for special occasions. These people were content with little: eggs, milk (which was made into cheese) and starchy foods (potatoes and bread). The need to combine these products resulted in a whole host of nourishing and inexpensive dishes that have long constituted the staple, daily fare in the country.

ALL GOOD, TRADITIONAL FRENCH COOKERY BOOKS give a recipe for 'truffade' (sliced potatoes fried in lard and covered with strips of fresh Cantal) and 'aligot' (an unctuous purée made with one-third Cantal and two-thirds potatoes) from Auvergne, and also 'tartiflette' from Savoie. This latter involves a Reblochon, sliced in half and put to *gratiner* on a bed of potatoes. When funds

allowed, the addition of a glass of white wine or eau-de-vie didn't come amiss, the acidity helping the solubility of the fat content and aiding the digestion. As for cheese soufflé, it is universal, as are the numerous *gratins*, tarts and coating sauces of which cheese is the main ingredient.

CHEESE HAS DIFFICULTY IN BREAKING FREE of this association with things rustic. Alain Dutournier's *Mille-feuilles au Roquefort*, or Bernard Roux's *Craquelin au Bleu* with compote of figs are most original. The recipes of Emmanuel Laporte, an inventive Parisian chef, are truly

Bleu de Gex in its mould in the abbey's cheese dairy at Chezery. The word 'Gex' will be imprinted into the rind.

171

flavour is very invasive – some people consider that steak with Roquefort is a waste, neither of the ingredients being enhanced by the presence of the other. Secondly, it may give off fairly strong aromas in the course of cooking, but this results in its most subtle perfumes disappearing for good.

THE ALTERNATIVE WAY OF COOKING WITH CHEESE is … not to cook it. It is preferable to combine it with other foods that will leave its flavour intact. Think of the exquisite combination of tomatoes with mozzarella, balls of Bleu d'Auvergne rolled in chopped walnuts, Chaource flanked with mirabelles – delicious little wild plums – or Ossau-Iraty and Morello cherries. Think of rich combinations of cheese and wine, like the sumptuous marriage of Roquefort with port, or the ethereal union of Sainte-Maure and sparkling Vouvray. Cookery it may not be, but gastronomy it most certainly is.

mouth watering: steamed oysters with spinach and a light sauce made with Fourme d'Ambert; a creamy chestnut soup with Vacherin; a crunchy crème brulée made with Brillat Savarin; chocolate *ganache* with crystallized peeled oranges, pistachio nuts and creams made with Beaufort and vanilla. But these are just marginal instances and, for the most part, cheese fails to stir the imagination of great chefs and rarely finds a place on their menus. Cheese cookery is the poor relation of gastronomy.

ONE COULD LEGITIMATELY SAY – and this is my personal opinion – that cheese has more to lose than to gain in the kitchen, other than in dishes like fondue and raclette of which it is the major ingredient. First of all because its

At the moulding stage the interior of the cheese is still pristine white.
Above: the 'blue' appears progressively in the heart of the cheese, in the form of speckles.

Making raclette

• *To stand up to the heat of the stove* you need a relatively dry cheese that holds its shape and, above all, does not melt too quickly. Check the elasticity of the dough – generally speaking that is the test of a cheese that will behave correctly under the influence of heat. The Valais cheeses are ideal but Appenzell, which is more readily available in France, is a good substitute. Certain of the raclette cheeses from Franche-Comté or Savoie are not without merit, on condition that they are make from raw milk (absolutely essential) and are sufficiently matured. One could even try an Abondance. My colleague, Daniel Boujon, established at Thonon-les-Bains, recommends a raclette made with a very mature Vacherin Fribourgeois.

• *Use about 200 grams (7 ounces)* of cheese per person.

• *Add potatoes cooked in their skins* (300 grams (10 ounces) per person), gherkins, small pickled onions and pepper. And why not include some *viande des Grisons* (a form of dried meat eaten in Switzerland) or ham?

• *To drink with your raclette:* a Fendant du Valais or a dry white wine from Savoie are heartily recommended. You could also drink tea with it, but never water, which hardens the cheese in the stomach and makes it difficult to digest.

Attenshun! Presenting fondue dishes!

• *When making fondue* the Swiss often add cornflour or potato flour (once the cheese is completely melted). Not generally included in French recipes, both these ingredients produce a smooth and unctuous texture. They prevent the mixture from becoming elastic and sticky, especially if using less mature cheese. On the other hand, they can make it expand and turn frothy.

• *Mixing cheeses from different sources* is an innovation thought up by imaginative, 'lowland' cooks. For purists of the classical school, a real fondue needs only one type of cheese (and no cornflour!).

• *A successful mixture* depends on the taste and texture you are aiming at. The first requirement is a good basic cheese with a fairly bland flavour (French Gruyère, Emmenthal). The other cheeses should contribute flavour and bind the mixture (Appenzell, Comté or Fribourg). Be sparing in the use of cheeses with a very high fat content – they give plenty of flavour but are difficult to digest.

• *For a perfect consistency* the hard-pressed cheeses should be grated or cut into small cubes. More supple cheeses can be cubed or cut into strips.

• *A fondue that is too liquid* can be thickened by the addition of a little cornflour mixed with eau-de-vie or white wine. If too thick, add white wine to slacken it.

• *When choosing the wine* to accompany it, this should be fairly dry and with a good acidity. Matching cheeses and wines from the same area is considered a smart thing to do.

• *It is essential to serve bread that was made the previous day,* or it will break down in the hot mixture and swell in the stomach.

Bleu de Gex needs a good two months' ripening. More than that and it tends to dry out and lose its soft texture.

Brie de Meaux
France (Ile de France)
Cow's milk

Its creamy texture, which has always delighted gourmets, is linked to the recipe (natural drainage, which retains a great deal of moisture) and to its lack of depth (this cheese ripens from the rind inwards under the action of moulds on the surface). It is quite different from all other cheeses, with a brilliance that makes it exceptional. In the corridors of the Congress of Vienna, in 1815, the 143 delegates present declared the Brie contributed by Talleyrand to be the 'prince of cheese and the foremost of desserts'. Unanimously! It is also recalled that Louis XVI, in his flight from the revolutionaries, committed the imprudent act of stopping at Varennes-en-Argonne to eat a piece of Brie. Initially made on the Brie plateau, the area where it is produced has widened progressively towards the west. The AOC zone extends as far as the Meuse. Brie de Meaux should not be over ripened: from six to ten weeks, according to the season, is sufficient. Being rather delicate to keep, especially in summer, it is better to buy it at its peak and eat it as soon as possible. The one from Madeleine Dongé, at Triconville, always delights me. Did you know that *Bouchées à la Reine* were originally made with Brie de Meaux? These days cheese is often used in such rustic dishes as *Croque-Briard* (a form of toasted cheese made with Brie).

Bleu de Gex
France (Franche-Comté)
Cow's milk

This fairly dry, blue-speckled cheese was first made by monks, but the medical profession extended its popularity beyond the Jura, where it is made. Starting in the twelfth century the monks of the Sainte-Claude Abbey undertook the clearance of the higher land, opening the way, first to sheep and goat farming and then to cattle. Two centuries later a 'grey cheese' made its appearance – the forerunner of the Bleu de Gex. The establishment of coal mines in the Stephanoise region opened up new markets for it. The doctors who looked after the miners recommended this cheese to them because it contained penicillium – or so I am told by Isabelle Seingemartin, reputed cheese-*affineur* specializing in Bleu de Gex. The Saint-Étienne region, where they prefer chalky textures, is still a major market for it. My customers like them ripened for about two-and-a-half to three months, when they develop a softer dough and more pronounced blue colour. In the Jura they are used to make raclette and soufflés. Always made with raw milk, the tiny hint of bitterness is an integral part of its flavour. Isabelle's grandfather used to collect the milk from 65 farms. Today it is made by only three cheese dairies, but the future of Bleu de Gex gives no cause for alarm.

Feuille de Dreux
France (Centre)
Cow's milk

Right up to the end of the Second World War, Feuille de Dreux, also called Dreux á la Feuille, did duty as a midday snack for the agricultural workers employed by cereal producers at Beauce. It was a domestic cheese, disc-shaped and made from skimmed milk, often with a greyish rind and a sometimes very strong flavour. An unpretentious, rustic cheese, it was surmounted by a leaf. Today only one cheesemaker makes Feuille de Dreux and the cheese has gone upmarket; it now resembles a larger but thinner Coulommier with a white rind. In Chartres it is known simply as Le Dreux or Le Marsauceux – the name of a little town in Eure-et-Loire that used to produce a famous cheese. The chestnut leaf laid on the rind, now purely for decoration, was traditionally used to separate the cheeses and prevent them sticking to each other during ripening. In the country the peasants use Dreux for a very unusual concoction called *fromagée*. This consists of strips of cheese layered with pepper, moistened with cider or alcohol and macerated for two weeks hermetically sealed in an earthenware dish. A way of resuscitating cheeses that are past their best that results in a pretty strong flavour!

Soumaintrain

France (Burgundy)
Cow's milk

Soumaintrain is an ancient cheese that was relaunched about 15 years ago after almost disappearing. Farm production, quite considerable in the last century, practically closed down. The project was finally given a boost by the milk quotas that incited three young farmers to make a more profitable use of their milk (it takes 3 litres/5 pints to make one Soumaintrain). I followed with great interest the efforts of Claude Leroux, *affineur* at Brion, who actively encouraged the resurrection of this rustic-looking cheese, largely sold locally, and who now collects the produce of five farms. This very characteristic cheese is made in a similar way to Epoisses – the same fairly fine-grained interior, the same ochre, sometimes sticky rind, frequent washing (two or three times a week) to encourage the appearance of 'red mould', clear evidence of quality. The basic difference is that Soumaintrain is not macerated in alcohol. Claude Leroux keeps it for a minimum of 18 days – there are those who prefer it young – and up to two months for lovers of strong flavours. It can need boxing when it is very mature (some people put it in the oven before eating it with potatoes). The Soumaintrain that is made in springtime is really excellent. Claude advises eating it as an early snack in the morning, with a glass of Chablis.

Sbrinz

Central Switzerland
Cow's milk

Sbrinz (the z is pronounced like an s) is thought to be one of the oldest Swiss cheeses; it is known to have existed in the fifteenth century. It is very like the Parmigiano Reggiano made on the Italian side of the Alps, sharing with it the same need for a long ripening period (as much as four years) and the same crumbly, very dry interior which consigns it to the kitchen. One cheese weighs on average about 40 kilos (88 pounds). The cheese is ripened in a fairly warm cellar. Its intense, concentrated, very aromatic flavour goes marvellously with any dish; sprinkled on in grated form, it brings out all the flavour. Jacques-Alain Dufaux, retailer and *affineur* at Morges, recommends serving it with an aperitif in the form of small cubes or shavings, and letting it melt on the tongue in company with a dry white wine made from the Chasselas grape, which is grown in the same region. Three years ago its producers undertook to redefine the *terroir* where it originated, centred at the foot of the summit of Mont Rigi, in the Lucerne region of central Switzerland. It is the third most exported Swiss cheese, after Gruyère and Emmenthal.

Tilsit

Eastern Switzerland
Cow's milk

Don't look for Tilsit on the map of Switzerland; it is the name of an ancient region in east Prussia – now a part of Lithuania – where Dutch immigrants perfected the recipe for a Gouda-type cheese. In 1893 the product found considerable favour with a passing Swiss cheesemaker – a certain Wemüller – who in his turn took it to his home canton, Thurgau, in eastern Switzerland, on the banks of Lake Constance. Tilsit, also made in the Saint-Gall and Zurich cantons, should soon be granted an AOC. The Swiss like to use it to prepare *gratin* dishes, to which its supple and close texture lends itself to perfection. Its semi-hard dough is very smooth and unblemished, unlike that of the German cheese of the same name, which shows many fermentation holes. Its rind, which is rubbed regularly in the ripening cellars, is reddish-brown in appearance. It starts to be at its best after six months of ripening, by which time it has developed quite a refined flavour.

Cheeses for special occasions: the whole world on a cheese board

A cheese board should be like a fashion show: it should appeal to the eye, arouse cravings, stimulate the imagination. It must be choreographed so that each item plays its part to perfection.

Whether or not to serve cheese? This question always arises when one is planning the menu for festive meals at Christmas and New Year. Coming between a main course that is rarely frugal and a hopefully grandiose pudding, cheese is sometimes felt to be an unnecessary charge on the stomach. Only very careful selection of the menu can resolve this problem. A cheese board should be put together like a dessert; it should have subtlety, freshness and, above all, appeal. A great deal of thought needs to go into its composition and presentation if it is to have originality and style – something this course often lacks.

IT MUST CONTINUE THE THEME OF THE MEAL, otherwise it risks sounding a false note in an otherwise harmonious occasion. The most sophisticated dishes need to be followed by light, subtle cheeses (young goat's milk cheeses, fresh cheeses, Comté ripened for a few months). More robust dishes will stand up to cheeses of a more forceful character (blue cheeses, ewe's milk cheeses,

Maroilles). And a certain order needs to be observed when eating the cheeses; unless those with the strongest flavour are kept until last, the more delicate ones will seem insipid by comparison.

A MIDDLE-OF-THE-ROAD SOLUTION is to serve a single, well-chosen cheese; a Brie de Meaux, for example, a nice large piece of Gruyère (Beaufort, Comté, Fribourg) or a creamy, perfectly-ripened Vacherin – any of these could be the star of a 'one-cheese show'. As a solution, however, it does present one major difficulty – it must be a cheese that will appeal to all the guests.

ORGANIZING A SUCCESSFUL CHEESE BOARD is, as you can see, a delicate task that requires a lot of thought. Small mistakes can ruin an otherwise praiseworthy effort: damp salad leaves that stick to the cheese; an over-exuberant Camembert that merges with a Pouligny-Saint-Pierre, or an unbalanced choice that leaves a piece of Roquefort marooned in a sea of fresh cheeses.

A cheese board prepared in a rustic manner by my colleague from Boulogne, Philippe Olivier. A carefully studied arrangement that makes the mouth water.

The art of cutting and serving cheeses

The way cheeses are cut is governed by a combination of etiquette (respect for both the cheese and the other diners) and practical considerations both for using it and keeping it in good condition. A typical example of bad cheese manners is to cut yourself the piece from the centre of the Roquefort, where the 'blue' is most concentrated, and leaving the paler, blander outer part for the other diners. The rule is that each helping of cheese should include a little of the rind – firstly so that everyone has a fair share, and secondly because the flavour of a cheese is never uniform throughout; it is usually more pronounced near the rind. These nuances form part of the pleasure of eating it. There are a number of special tools for cutting cheese correctly. The *Roquefortaise*, made for cutting Roquefort, resembles the wire used for slicing butter and slices through the delicate interior without crumbling it. As for the *girolle*, this allows one to cut shavings from the Swiss Tête-de-Moine. Some hard-pressed cheeses need a double-handed knife, while for soft cheeses the little curved, two-pronged knife is perfect. Don't hesitate to dip the knives into hot water before cutting blue cheeses, for instance. If you have none of these implements, then use a long knife with a rigid blade, augmented by a fork.

A few tips about the cheese board

• *The surface of the cheese board can be wood,* wicker, or marble, but never plastic or metal. It can be covered with straw before setting out the cheeses. The cheeses should be presented as simply as possible, without their boxes or wrappings (except in the case of Saint-Félicien, Vacherin and so on).
• *To make your cheese board look even more appetizing,* you could add cherry tomatoes, grapes, slices of apple, walnuts or raisins. Whatever takes your fancy.
• *Butter has its supporters* and its detractors. Whatever your opinion, let those who favour it succumb to the pleasure.

How much per person?

One way is to count the number of diners and divide by two, offering five cheeses for a table of ten people, for instance. But remember that it is imprudent to exceed ten cheeses on the board.

Cheeses that are attractive to the eye: an appetizing display at the Goursat cheese dairy at Fontainebleau.

CHEESES like plenty of elbowroom. They should not touch each other, so your board must be large enough to leave them room to breathe and the guests room to cut into them easily (cheese boards with rims are impractical and not recommended). If space is a problem, use two cheese boards.

EYE-APPEAL IS THE FACTOR THAT MAKES US CRAVE CERTAIN FOODS. Diversity and contrast are a part of this appeal, and cheeses offer both. The truncated pyramid of Pouligny-Saint-Pierre, the small wheel-like Murol, the log-shaped Sainte-Maure-de-Touraine, conical Spanish Tetilla, cylindrical Lancashire or spherical Mimolette, they complement and contrast with each other. The small size of Cabécous enhances the slender slice of Beaufort, the stocky Maroilles looks down its nose at the puny ewe's milk Pérail, the compact little Crottins de Chavignol sneer at the fragile fromage frais. The variety of colours, too, provides the scope for attractive combinations; think of grey-green Roquefort, alabaster Provolone, yellow-gold Cantal or the orange rind of Herve.

BUT BE CAREFUL NOT TO OVERDO IT. 'I hate the terrible promiscuity of a cheese board where the aromas merge together, not blending amicably but in indescribable cacophony', said Curnonsky. The sight of an abundantly garnished cheese board gives one the urge to taste each and every one, and causes the confusion of the senses described above by the 'prince of gastronomes'. In this instance quantity is not what is required; something to arouse the curiosity is more appropriate. Along with the classic choices, slip in a few relatively unknowns, like the Corsican Niolo, a Chevrotin des Aravis or an English Stilton.

WHEN SHOULD ONE SET UP THE CHEESE BOARD? Above all, not more than two hours before it is needed, otherwise there is a risk of cut surfaces discolouring, rinds sweating, cheeses collapsing. If you have to do it in advance, leave it in the bottom of the refrigerator and bring it out half an hour before it comes to the table, remembering to trim any of the cut cheeses that have discoloured to restore their fresh appearance.

A successful cheese board is a fantastic symphony of shapes, colours, aromas and flavours. A work of art that appeals resolutely to all the senses.

SHOULD IT BE OFFERED MORE THAN ONCE? The notion, firmly anchored in people's minds, that the cheese board should not be passed round a second time, and that it is not done to take a second helping, is not entirely unjustified; the lingering flavour of the strong cheeses would overshadow that of the milder ones the second time around.

ON THE FOLLOWING PAGES YOU WILL FIND a few cheeses that are always an attractive addition to the cheese board, either because of their shape (Bouton de Culotte, Coeur d'Arras), their generous flavour (Explorateur) or their curiosity value (Corsican Venaco).

Dauphin
Northern France
Cow's milk

A derivative of Maroilles, Dauphin (dolphin) is made in a region which has nothing of the maritime about it. Its shape is a nod in the direction of history. When Louis XIV went to the Hainaut province to claim the territories that went to him under the terms of the Treaty of Nijmegen, his hosts prepared a very out-of-the-ordinary cheese for him. It was a Maroilles – the pride of the locality– flavoured with fresh herbs. It was greatly enjoyed by the royal cortège, which included the king's heir – the Dauphin. This occasion made the cheese's reputation and it was duly given the name – and the shape – of a dolphin. It is made from Maroilles that have been damaged in production and not presentable enough to be sold. The dough is kneaded with different herbs and spices (tarragon, parsley, cloves, pepper), and coloured with *rocou* (a Mexican plant used as a vegetable dye). Its composition is much the same as that of Boulette d'Avesnes. Dauphin is ripened for two to four months, long enough for the aromas and flavours of the different ingredients to merge perfectly.

Coeur d'Arras
Northern France
Cow's milk

Philippe Olivier, my fellow-*affineur* from Boulogne, told me the following anecdote. When the town of Arras was under Spanish rule, the occupying forces put notices up on the town gates saying: 'When the French take Arras, the mice will eat the cats.' The town was finally taken by Turenne in 1654, after a century and a half of occupation. The people of Arras, with wry humour, posted the response: 'When the French give up Arras, the mice will eat the cats.' Every year at Whitsuntide, the Feast of the Rats is held to commemorate these historic events. The name of the festival probably comes from a bad pun (*à rats* for Arras – both pronounced the same way in French), but it could equally refer to the claim that the Spaniards let rats loose in the town. But be that as it may, on this occasion the local specialities are on show and, traditionally, they are all – chocolate, gingerbread and so on – made in the form of a heart. It was inevitable that a cheese should also be produced in that shaped, something that happened recently. When tasted blind, Coeur d'Arras can easily be mistaken for Maroilles, the recipes are so close. Its interior is closer-textured, because, being smaller, it ripens more quickly. This little heart is as meltingly soft as you could possibly wish and utterly irresistible.

Bouton de Culotte (trouser button)
France (North)
Cow's milk

The largest goat farm in Europe also produces the smallest cheese: Bouton de Culotte weighs only about 15 grams (half an ounce) when *affiné*, and twice as much in its fresh state. For Thierry Chévenet, the project grew out of a whim; in 1966, when he was still a small child, he asked his farmer parents for a goat. Since then, in the space of 25 years, he has built up a herd of 1,700 goats in the Saone-et-Loire region. His farm combines the most up-to-date, sophisticated equipment (his goats carry electronic implants so they can be traced) and traditional methods: no silage; no vaccination or treatment for parasites, no skimming, animals put out to pasture whenever possible. The very few Bouton de Culotte that are produced are only offered to famous names. One of the first customers was Paul Bocuse, followed by his colleague Georges Blanc. It is one of those rare cheeses that can drain without being turned, thanks to its truncated cone shape. This is not due to mere chance; in this wine-making region the women were in the vineyards all day and only returned in the evening, which meant they were not able to turn the cheeses during the day. Bouton de Culotte is eaten very fresh – for breakfast, for example – if not, then almost dry after ripening for three to four weeks.

Explorateur
France (Ile de France)
Cow's milk

Explorateur was first made in the 1950s in a cheese dairy in the Seine-et-Marne region and later named in honour of the space shuttle Explorer. It is a commercial brand name. It is one in a long line of cheeses enriched with fresh cream, starting in 1890 with Excelsior, popularized by Brillat-Savarin (relaunched in 1930 by Henri Androuët), then given a boost in the post-war years. With the rigours of rationing over, these cheeses, with their satiny texture and their good aroma of cream, were synonymous with abundance and regained prosperity. There have been any number of imitations, mostly in Normandy and Ile de France – home of this 'explorer', which only needs to be ripened for two or three weeks. Is it as rich in fat as one would suppose from reading the 75 per cent on the label? This figure is misleading, because it refers to the percentage of the total milk solids in the cheese made up by fat – in other words, 75 per cent of the weight of the cheese without its water content. Since a product like Explorateur contains almost 80 per cent water, especially when fresh, this puts a different perspective on the fat-content figure.

Venaco
France (Ile de France)
Goat's or ewe's milk

Venaco is one of Corsica's most famous cheeses. It bears the name of a village in the centre of the island and is square shaped with rounded corners. Originally it was a goat's milk cheese but, like Niolo, it is now made either with ewe's or goat's milk. More and more cheeses are being made from ewe's milk in Corsica these days, partly because it is cheaper than goat's milk and partly because consumers prefer the less pronounced flavours produced by the much milder ewe's milk. Venaco is part of a pastoral tradition that is still very strong in this 'Isle of Beauty', as the French call it. The cheese used to be made exclusively up in the high summer pastures and has a characteristically strong, piquant flavour partly because the rinds are frequently washed in salt water. Everything depends on the degree to which it is ripened: fresh, *fattu* (from six to eight weeks) or *vecchiu* (three or four months or more). The colour of its rind swings between grey and orange tints. Its off-white centre tends to become unctuous and never lacks character. The ripening of this cheese demands a high degree of know-how as the flavour can easily become too strong.

Laruns
France (Aquitaine)
Ewe's milk

Laruns – also the name of a town in the Ossau valley, in the Béarne region – is one of the main ewe's milk cheeses produced in the Pyrenees. In the past it was made largely on the high mountain pastures from the end of spring to the beginning of autumn, in huts with the local name of *cajulas*. Hardly any was produced in winter. Nowadays, cheese dairies in the valley collect the milk from several sheep farms and keep up production all the year round. This cheese is a good introduction to the more ambitious cheeses that are made exclusively up in the mountains. Laruns, which weighs on average about five kilos (11 pounds), has a quite supple dough, with hardly any holes, protected by a thick rind – the product of regular washing and drying. It can easily spend six months ripening in the cellar. Shepherds engrave their names on the rinds of the farmhouse Laruns, so that they can identify their own products when they collect them from the *affineur* entrusted with their ripening… and paid in cheeses!

Cheeses with a whiff of sanctity

Did you enjoy the cheeses served at Christmas? Then take the opportunity, during this religious festival, to pay homage to generations of monks, many of them Benedictines, without whom Europe would not have the richest cheese heritage in the world.

Whether or not they are believers, all those who love cheese should give thanks to the generations of monks responsible for creating the vast diversity of the European cheese heritage. Without them, there would probably have been no Maroilles, no German Munster, Roquefort, Pont-l'Évêque, Livarot and countless others. Originator of this vocation was Saint Benoît de Nursie, 'father of the monks', founder of the Benedictine Order and author of a *règle* (rule book) which he wrote in AD 540. This sets out, in 73 chapters, how the everyday life of a monastery should be organized. Benoît lived at the top of Monte Cassino, south of Rome, where cheese was the staple food of the local population. Cheese-making is never directly mentioned in the *règle* but it does state that work and voluntary poverty are the defining marks of a monk; more specifically, in chapter 48, that 'they will truly be monks if they work with their hands'.

In the cellars at Orval Abbey in the Belgian Ardennes, Brother Paul prepares cheese ready to eat. The abbey is also famous for its triple-fermented beer.

Making farmhouse Munster at Graine Johe near Col du Bonhomme. The equipment used for moulding has not changed in half a century.

FOOD OF THE POOR, of all those not able to afford meat, cheese could not be other than appreciated by monks who had vowed to live a life of complete detachment. Many monasteries were created after the end of the first millennium, and they all undertook to use the milk productively from herds kept on the land they had cleared. The cheese recipes, if necessary adapted to suit local conditions (land, climate, type of animals), passed from monastery to monastery, all, in fact, linked by a system of sponsorship and community interests under which the less fortunate monks were helped by those who were better off.

NUMEROUS CREATIONS originally invented by monks were subsequently made by others outside the monasteries and became well-known names with no further links to a monastic tradition. This happened in the case of Roquefort, for example; its recipe probably came from the Saint-Foy Abbey at Conques, in the Aveyron region.

ONLY A DOZEN OR SO CHEESES are still made in monasteries. I have a weakness for these products, which don't always reach the top as far as flavour is concerned, but often have a very sensual texture. In 1986 they were all put together under the commercial brand name of Monastic. The monks, tired of having their products pirated by commercial cheese dairies, are no

longer innocents in business matters. So many labels incorporate the name, or picture, of a well-rounded monk with the smile of a bon vivant. The Monastic label brings together more than a dozen abbeys and allows the customer to recognize those cheeses that are made by genuine monks. Among them, Orval Abbey in the Belgian Ardennes, is celebrated both for its cheese and its triple-fermented beer. Like quite a number of others, it almost disappeared when the axe of the Revolution fell. Destroyed in 1793, it was only reinstated by the monks in 1926, and 30 or so of them now live in this peaceful setting. The cheese dairy is situated behind the massive walls of an ancient barn, close to the Abbey. The ultra-modern workrooms are as good as those in the best cheese dairies. Its impeccable cleanliness and

Port Salut is not sure to which saint it owes allegiance!

Port Salut's history is, to say the least, eventful. Its name comes from the Port-du-Salut Abbey at Entrammes, south of Laval. It was there that the cheese was created, around 1815, when the Trappist monks regained possession of the abbey after being expelled during the Revolution. The cheese quickly became so famous – it made its appearance on the market stalls of Paris in 1873 – that a great many imitations were made under the name Port Salut, Port-du-Salut having been registered as a trademark in 1876. Feeling this competition to be unjust, the monks initiated a legal action against the makers, using a name so close to that of their product, which they won in January of 1938. In 1946 the losers decided to adopt the name Saint-Paulin. The monks of Entrammes ended up selling their brand name to a major cheese-producing company but continued making cheese at the abbey until 1988 and marketing it under the name 'Entrammes'.

Let's break bread in the simplest way

• *If you serve only one kind of bread* with the cheese, don't go in for eccentricities; it must please everybody, have a good flavour and go well with the cheeses offered. A good, leavened baguette of the right quality would be perfect. Choose one with a crisp crust and a creamy crumb with plenty of holes.

• *If you find baguette too commonplace,* you could choose a good country loaf, made with yeast; that would go well with any kind of cheese.

• *Bread from a sandwich-type loaf* is unsuitable as it is too soft and relatively sweet, which detracts from the flavour of the cheese; at best it can be used spread with Crème de Roquefort to accompany an aperitif.

• *Nut breads can be interesting.* In some regions walnuts are automatically served with cheese, for their aroma is a perfect foil for the roasted or damp woodland notes found in some cheeses. Try some mature Comté with Vin Jaune du Jura and nut-bread rolls. You will find all these products playing in perfect harmony in exactly the same key.

gleaming stainless steel are almost incongruous in this environment dedicated to tradition. It was the monks from the Sept-Fons Abbey, in the Allier region, who took cheese technology there. To be honest, the recipe is not among the most sophisticated.

AT ORVAL as in the other abbeys, the production is quite small. Lacking a real vocation, the number of Monastic cheeses is diminishing. In recent years, both the abbey at Campénéac and that of Soligny-la-Trappe have stopped making cheese. Total production is steady at around 1,000 tonnes a year. Some cheeses bear the name of an abbey that still exists but whose monks or nuns no longer make any cheese themselves, having sold the brand name. This happened at Maredsous in Belgium, and also at the Trappist one at Bricquebec, in the Cotentin area. The situation at the Belgian Chimay Abbey is rather different; there the production of its cheese is subcontracted to an industrial cheese dairy but the abbey retains ownership of the brand name. For its part, Pierre-qui-Vire Abbey keeps its own animals, but the cheese production and ripening are done by a subcontractor in the grounds of the abbey. It's all very well consecrating oneself to the Lord, but one still has to move with the times…

Making farmhouse Munster.
The word 'Munster' is a
corruption of 'Monastère'.
Munster was originally made
by monks who came here
from Rome.

The preferences of today

The current fashion is for sensual textures and delicate flavours. Certain cheeses are admirably suited to these preferences, but we must also leave room for those cheeses with a stronger character that cheese lovers delight in, and not condemn them to being toned down and rendered soulless.

When I look at photographs taken in my shop 30 years ago I am astonished at the way the appearance of the cheeses has changed. Today I would no longer dare offer my customers such brownish Camemberts, such blue goat's milk cheeses, Roquefort with such yellowed paste. Our tastes have undoubtedly evolved and our cheeses also. Generally speaking, flavours now are less

pronounced, strong odours are rejected and excessive moulds are discouraged. What a long way we have come since Zola's description of Les Halles, the central market in Paris, more than a century ago, as 'high in colour (and in smells)'… Look at all the new, pasteurized items that appear every year; they are flawless, often quite pleasant, all-purpose products; at times, it is impossible to tell whether they were made from cow's, ewe's or goat's milk.

At Verrières, near Millau, the flock of ewes whose milk serves to make Jean-François' Pérail des Cabasse.

Preparing the moulds for Manchego
in the Spanish cheese dairy of Sainte
Cuquerella. The curd is wrapped in
a cloth that leaves its mark on the rind.
Below: where it is made.

CERTAIN AREAS OF FRANCE, which once had a long tradition of producing strong cheeses, have tempered the character of their output. Think of the Rhône-Alpes region, where all the most exuberant cheeses are losing ground – Pâtefine (cow's milk cheese with added white wine and various spices), the strong cheese from Mont Vertoux (goat's or ewe's milk cheese with cognac or eau-de-vie and spices), the aromas of Lyons (Rigottes or Pélardons put to ferment with undistilled marc) or Cachat (goat's milk cheese macerated in marc). In northern France, Vieux Lille, the strong cheese from Béthune and the Boulette d'Avesnes are all struggling to keep their following.

ALL THESE CHEESES were solidly structured, no doubt less by design than from ignorance of preservation techniques and the inability to control temperature. Rancidity, bitterness and piquancy were for a long time common to all of them. At an ambient temperature, biological – and notably enzymatic – activity develops all too rapidly and secondary fermentation is unleashed. Fatty acids tend to deteriorate, producing metallic, soapy and rancid odours.

WITH THESE POWERFUL FLAVOURS becoming less and less acceptable, strong cheeses have been obliged to learn a little discretion. Gone are the aggressive and fiery flavours, the abiding smells. In response to a clientèle that prefers products that are sensual rather than virile, more urbane than rustic, cheesemakers have learned to restrain the ardour of their products. In the case of Boulette d'Avesnes, for example, they add fresh white cheese to only slightly ripened Maroilles; in the eyes of the purists this completely changes the nature of the original recipe. As for the 'vehement Maroilles, whose thunderous flavour resounds like the sound of a saxophone in a cheese symphony' as Curnonsky put it, it belongs to another era.

BUT LET'S NOT HANKER FOR THE CAMEMBERTS our grandparents knew, because if we could taste them now we would probably pull a face. Few among us today would be capable of enjoying, as did Maurice Astruc, of the Roquefort Society, a 'thirty-month old Roquefort from which the blue has completely disappeared and which makes one sweat'. What do worry me, however, are the irreparable changes made to some cheeses, rendering

The art of imbuing a cheese with flavour

Apart from the ripening process, the cheesemaker has a number of tools at his disposal with which to impart flavour to his product.

• *By spicing them.* Many cheeses are made with whey or pieces of cheeses damaged in the making, one being Gaperon, which is flavoured with pepper and garlic, and Boulette d'Avesnes, peppered and mixed with chives and tarragon.

• *Flavouring them with alcohol.* Boulette d'Avesnes is traditionally washed with beer, Epoisses with Marc de Bourgogne, and Banon is sprinkled with eau-de-vie. This can often be a way of hiding what is underneath – of giving flavour to a product which may have been totally bland, or on the other hand, of masking unpleasant odours or ones that have got out of hand.

• *By macerating them.* Fermentation in a sealed container, with spices and alcohol, is a speciality of the south-east quarter of France. This process gives the cheese a very powerful flavour, like that of Cachat, for example.

• *By washing the rind.* Maroilles, Munsters and other Livarots can be distinguished by their strong flavour, caused by the presence on the rind of the 'red mould' (*Bacteria linens*), which gives them their characteristic orange colour. This bacteria accelerates the breaking down of the proteins in the dough, leaving it creamy and giving it flavour. Since the 'red mould' needs moisture in order to develop, the cheeses are regularly washed with salt water during ripening.

How cheeses should be dispatched

What should you do if an expatriate friend asks you to send him a good Camembert made with raw milk? How can you send your son, who is on an exchange visit to New Caledonia, his favourite cheeses, Comté and Saint-Nectaire? Sealed in a package the cheeses risk suffering damage during the journey. The changes of temperature will inevitably accelerate the breakdown of the cheese. Give preference, therefore, to hard-pressed cheeses, which develop more slowly than the soft-curd ones. If you must send soft-curd cheeses, send a whole cheese, so that it is protected by the rind, choose one that is not too mature and keep it in its original wrapping. And leave it room to breathe. Put it in a polystyrene or cardboard box, allowing room for the air to circulate. A little powdered charcoal will help to stop some of the odour. And be careful, some countries regulate the importation of farm produce and your parcel could find itself held in customs.

them insipid. Cheeses – without mentioning names – which were once excellent and which have become bland and lost their soul.

WAS THIS BROUGHT ABOUT BY CONSUMER DEMAND or was it, on the contrary, the new production methods, backed up by advertising, that gave rise to altered behavioural patterns and other expectations? A difficult question to answer. I can simply state that these changes have gone

Page opposite: the dispatch area for Manchego. The cheeses are sorted and packed according to their final destination.

hand in hand with a production-driven revolution in methods of collecting the milk and transforming it, with the often excessive back up of hygiene regulations and a deep concern for rapid turnover which leaves the cheeses no time to ripen.

MANY SOFT-CURD CHEESES have thus undergone a change in their aspect; formerly made by lactic coagulation, they were very chalky in the first weeks; now they have a smoother, more supple texture due to the use of rennet. Among the most significant examples of this change in coagulation methods are Feuille de Dreux, Munster and Maroilles. The ultimate result is a risk that products may become completely banal and lose their characteristic features. Curd made with rennet needs more time to ripen, but unfortunately, these days, this cannot be allocated. No doubt we have already gone too far along this road.

WE MUST BE CAREFUL THAT EXCELLENCE, richness and diversity are not cut off at their roots. The optimists among us hope that the balance will be redressed; that the interchangeable cheeses that have invaded the supermarket shelves will at last come to be recognized for their individuality and not just as a plastic-wrapped source of protein and calcium. It is rare these days for cheese dairies to put bad products on the market, but we are still waiting for them to astonish, stimulate and delight our taste buds rather than sending them to sleep.

ON THE FOLLOWING PAGES I SHALL INTRODUCE YOU to some cheeses of which the profile, or the history, are indicative of these changes. Boulette de Cambrai is a milder version of Boulette d'Avesnes. The ewe's milk Tomme d'Arles tends to be more successful than its fresh counterpart. Brie de Melun is less and less reddish and strong-flavoured and increasingly resembles a Brie de Meaux. Perail and Mascaré both have the melting texture that corresponds to present-day taste. As for Manchego, none of its many versions, from the most everyday to the most exigent, is likely to fall out with anyone.

Bottom right: an *affineur* who is proud of his product. The maker's label is engraved on the rind.

Boulette de Cambrai

Northern France
Buttermilk (from cow's milk)

This is a product made from leftover ingredients that only farmers could have invented. Boulette de Cambrai is made from buttermilk left after the butter has been churned, reinforced with pieces of cheeses too damaged in the making to be saleable – Maroilles, for the most part. It is all meticulously kneaded and then moulded by hand, usually into a rough pear shape, 6 to 7 centimetres (2¼–2¾ inches) high and weighing barely 200 grams (7 ounces); it is also made in the form of a ball. Pepper, tarragon, parsley or chives are sometimes mixed in the paste. In the old days, these were added for extra keeping quality, but now they are just used as flavouring. The cheese also exists in versions made with raw milk and pasteurized milk. Unlike its close relative the Boulette d'Avesnes, which can be eaten fairly well ripened, Boulette de Cambrai is usually eaten fresh, spread on bread. That is how they like it in the Cambrai region, outside of which it is unfortunately rarely seen.

Brie de Melun

France (Ile de France)
Cow's milk

With red streaks peeking through the white bloom on its rind, Brie de Melun is the most rustic of the French Bries. One of the oldest, too, since it originated at least a thousand years ago. It is stronger flavoured, saltier and more characteristic than the rather more refined Brie de Meaux. While the latter enjoys long-standing success and is known all over the world, Brie de Melun has never had a conquering instinct, nor any inclination to travel. For a long time it was a farmhouse cheese, made for domestic consumption, as its size – smaller than Brie de Meaux – indicates. A longer coagulation time and a ripening technique that brings out the 'red mould' explains its temperament. It has always been very tricky to handle, its saltiness being quick to gain the upper hand. Traditionally it was sold fairly young, barely ripened. I like to ripen it for eight to ten weeks. One can also find some that have been *affiné* for even longer, but they become dry, with a darker centre and a very strong flavour, reminiscent of the 'harvest Bries' – inferior cheeses that were left to dry and given to the workers in the fields. The *Confrèrie du Brie de Melun* (brotherhood of Brie de Melun) never fails to celebrate this tradition at the end of spring.

Manchego

Spain (La Mancha)
Ewe's milk

Originally from La Mancha, where it got its name, Manchego is one of the most famous of Spanish cheeses, no doubt because its thick rind and the firmness of its interior made it easy to transport. Naturally, it makes an appearance in Cervantes' *Don Quixote*, but the Romans ate it long before then. Made from ewe's milk, it traditionally takes the form of a small wheel, with an orange rind decorated with inter-linked motifs on the sides, a reminder of plaited alfalfa-grass moulds which were used to hold the curd. When it is ripened in olive oil (for up to two years!) the rind becomes bronze and then black. This is called Manchego en Aceite. Very popular in Spain, it is sometimes grated and used in cooking. In my opinion, this does not do it justice. Cheeses of two to three months old are called *semi-curado* or *mediocurado* (demi-sec), after which they become *curado* or *viejo*. After a year they are *anejo*, and it is at this stage that they begin to reveal their full aromatic potential. Like all self-respecting ewe's milk cheeses, it is slightly piquant and acidic when young, but gradually acquires splendid depth as the months go by.

Mascaré

France (Provence-Côte d'Azur)
Goat's and Ewe's milk

This square-shaped cheese is very popular in the Forcalquier region, where it is eaten creamy. It is original in that it is made with a mixture of raw milk from both goats and ewes in the true tradition of all cheeses from Provence where, because of the animals' different lactation cycles, the peasants used whichever milk was available. The modern mania for regulation and calibration had not yet taken hold. Mascaré is well-balanced on the palate, the ewe's milk softening its 'goaty' character. It is wrapped in a chestnut leaf and its top adorned by a Provençal herb. My colleague, Claudine Mayer, originally from Auvergne, is very taken with this cheese, which she ripens to great effect. She has just opened a shop equipped with magnificent, twelfth-century vaulted cellars at Saint-Rémy-de-Provence. The Mascaré cheeses are splendidly at ease there, like all the other Provençal specialities she is so fond of – fresh Tomme des Alpilles, in olive oil, Camarguais (a pressed-curd ewe's milk Tomme) and Trident (fresh Tomme made with ewe's milk from the Arles region). She may invite you to taste her Mascaré with a white wine from the Baux valley. Pure pleasure!

Pérail

France (Midi-Pyrénées)
Ewe's milk

This succulent little disc-shaped cheese made from ewe's milk has taken centuries to emerge from the shadow of the imposing local star, Roquefort. In the past, Pérail was only made during that period when Roquefort was out of production – that is to say during the second half of the year, when the ewe's are still giving milk but in lesser quantities. This was particularly rich and was used to make Pérail. This cheese now has a life of its own and is made all year round. One of the prime movers of its emancipation is Jean-François Dombre, cheesemaker-*affineur* and producer of Perail des Cabasses who fortunately, 30 years ago, declined an opportunity to leave the area and become a government official in Paris. The milk is collected in a wide area that runs from the Grands Causses to the Mediterranean scrub, via the foothills of the Cevennes mountains, traditional sheep-farming lands. The ewe's milk is generally used to make either Tommes or Roquefort. In Pérail it shows a more restrained, more subtle side to its character; made into this attractive little cheese, it is a real delicacy.

Tomme de Brebis d'Arles

France (Bouches-du-Rhône)
Ewe's milk

Tommes d'Arles must be one of Provence's most ancient cheeses. In days gone by it was the staple diet of farmworkers and their families in all the farmhouses of the Camargue. Sheep and goats have always grazed freely on the impoverished soil of the area. This was an unpretentious cheese and only a small part of its production was sent to local markets. According to the way it was stored, Tomme d'Arles was either round (its normal format) or square, after being squashed into boxes. Nowadays it is more often made with raw ewe's milk, although it can happen that it is mixed with goat's milk. Among the local people, it is beginning to oust the Picodons and Pélardons that had been quick to take advantage of its earlier drop in production. Relaunched a decade or so ago, this little disc is slowly but surely making a place for itself beneath the Provençal sun. It also comes in a fresh version – enthusiasts need only add a drizzle of olive oil.

Classifications are not recognized in Nature. Grouping, sorting, cataloguing – these are bound to involve simplification and a certain deviation from the facts. The list of 1,200 cheeses that appears on the following pages is no exception. It is constructed around 50 or so categories, each identified with one basic, representative cheese. Purists will no doubt feel that some of these groups are a trifle audacious and some more coherent than others. We have simply tried to look at this through the eyes of the vast number of consumers who ask us for 'a cheese of the such-and-such family'. Some of these 'families' are based on milk from one animal species, some on the shapes of the cheeses, others on a specific method of production. This attempt at simplification is aimed at making these appendices as readable and accessible as possible to all those lovers of good cheeses who are put off by technical terms. The other difficulty we encountered – one common to any written material – is that of trying to work from a fixed point in a constantly changing landscape. Every day some cheeses disappear and are replaced by others. Some, while retaining the same name, are produced by different methods. The scale on which some cheeses are produced can change, for example, from farmhouse cheeses made from raw milk to a factory-style product using pasteurized milk. We hope the reader will forgive these errors or potential inaccuracies.

As far as possible we have given the precise geographical origin of each cheese, in the full knowledge that it may now be produced in a much wider area than that with which it is historically associated. For some cheeses more than one animal species is mentioned; these are made with a mixture of milks, either on a regular or seasonal – or even alternating – basis. A number of cheeses are made in raw, pasteurized or partially pasteurized milk versions. Some are covered by a controlled appellation of origin (AOC) or its European equivalent, the protected appellation of origin (AOP). This system of recognition, which began in France with Roquefort, is based on a product being very strongly rooted in a well-defined area. Little by little it has been taken up by other European countries. (Switzerland only adopted it in the year 2000.) Elsewhere, another European label, the IGP (protected geographic location), defines and protects those cheeses that can claim a certain attachment to a specific locality. These appellations have not yet found favour in more distant places, like North America or the Antipodes, where the idea of *terroir* does not have the same importance.

As to the optimum maturation periods indicated, these are based on personal opinion which should, of course, be adjusted according to the cheese, the skill of the *affineur*, the season and so on. This list is not selected on the basis of quality or personal preference; many of the cheeses mentioned have never graced the shelves of Roland Barthélemy's establishment – nor ever will. Rather, its purpose is that of an inventory, to give an idea of the extraordinary diversity of our cheese heritage.

The Chaource family
and related cheeses

The cow's milk cheeses belonging to this family, made in the north-eastern quarter of France, characteristically have a fairly acidic, very fine-grained paste. They never become creamy when ripened.

Cheese	Other names	Country	Area of origin	Cow	Goat	Ewe	Buffalo	Unpasteurized	Heated	Pasteurized	Farm	Cottage industry	Factory	AOC-AOP	IGP	Monastic	Optimum maturation
Bray Picard		France	Picardy	•						•		•					1 month
Butte de Doué		France		•						•		•					1 month
Carré de Bray		France	Normandy	•				•		•	•	•	•				1 month
Chaource		France	Aube and Yonne	•				•		•		•		•			1 month
Maromme		France		•				•			•						1 month
Neufchâtel	Cœur de Bray	France	Pays de Bray	•				•		•	•	•	•	•			3 weeks
Vignotte		France		•									•				1 month
Villebarou		France	Orléans	•				•				•					2 months
Villedieu		France		•				•					•				1 month

The Epoisses family
and related cheeses

This is the orange-coloured, washed rind version of the Chaource family, and has a much more pronounced flavour. Alcohol or undistilled marc is used in the ripening of some of these cheeses.

Cheese	Other names	Country	Area of origin	Cow	Goat	Ewe	Buffalo	Unpasteurized	Heated	Pasteurized	Farm	Cottage industry	Factory	AOC-AOP	IGP	Monastic	Optimum maturation
Abbaye de la Pierre-qui-Vire		France	Burgundy	•				•			•						1 month
Affidélis		France	Burgundy	•				•			•						2 months
Aisy Cendré	Cendré d'Aisy	France	Burgundy	•				•		•	•						2 months
L'Ami du Chambertin		France	Burgundy – Gevrey-Chambertin	•				•		•	•						2 months
Chablis		France	Burgundy	•						•	•						2 months
Chaumont		France	Champagne	•				•			•						3 months
Epoisses		France	Burgundy	•				•	•	•	•			•			2 months
Langres		France	Plateau de Langres	•				•		•	•			•			2 months
Plaisir au Chablis		France	Brochon Côte-d'Or	•						•	•						1 month
Prestige de Burgundy		France	Burgundy	•						•			•				1 month
Soumaintrain		France	Burgundy	•				•		•	•	•					2 months
Trou du Cru	Cœur d'Epoisses	France	Burgundy	•				•			•						1 month

The Brie de Meaux family
and related cheeses

This family originated in the area east of Paris. These cheeses, made from cow's milk, are an elegant disc shape, covered with a fine white bloom (bloomy-rind cheeses) with a texture that readily becomes creamy as it ripens.

Cheese	Other names	Country	Area of origin	Cow	Goat	Ewe	Buffalo	Unpasteurized	Heated	Pasteurized	Farm	Cottage industry	Factory	AOC-AOP	IGP	Monastic	Optimum maturation
Bath cheese	Bath soft cheese	England	Avon	•				•		•	•						1 month
Melbury		England		•						•			•				2 months
Sharpam		England	Devon	•				•		•	•						2 months
Somerset brie		England	Somerset	•						•			•				1 month
Grape Vine Ash Brie		Australia	New South Wales	•						•		•					1 month
Jindi Brie		Australia	Victoria	•					•	•							1 month
Timboon Farmhouse Blue		Australia	Victoria	•						•			•				2 months
Vermont Farmhouse Brie		USA	Vermont	•						•			•				1 month
Brie		France		•						•			•				1 month
Brie de Coulommiers	Brie Petit Moule	France	Seine-et-Marne	•				•				•	•				2 months
Brie de Macquelines		France	Ile de France	•				•			•						2 months
Brie de Malhesherbes		France	Seine-et-Marne	•				•			•						6 weeks
Brie de Meaux	Brie de Valois	France	Seine-et-Marne	•				•			•		•	•			3 months
Brie de Melun		France	Seine-et-Marne – Brie	•				•				•	•	•			3 months
Brie de Montereau		France	Ile de France	•				•			•						2 months
Brie de Nangis		France	Ile de France	•				•			•						2 months
Brie de Provins		France	Ile de France	•				•			•						2 months
Brie Fermier		France	Ile de France	•				•				•					2 months
Brie Noir		France	Ile de France	•				•			•						6 month
Chevru		France	Ile de France	•				•		•	•						3 months
Fougeru		France	Ile de France	•				•			•		•				1 month
Abbey Blue Brie		Ireland		•				•				•					2 months
Dunbarra		Ireland		•						•			•				1 month
Pencarreg		Wales	Cardiganshire	•						•		•					1 month

A descendant of Brie, it is smaller and thicker. Its convenient format was an important factor in the rapid development of its popularity. A great many versions of it are made all over the world.

| Cheese | Other names | Country | Area of origin | Animal species | | | | Milk | | | Product | | | Label | | | Optimum maturation |
				Cow	Goat	Ewe	Buffalo	Unpasteurized	Heated	Pasteurized	Farm	Cottage industry	Factory	AOC-AOP	IGP	Monastic	
Weisse lady		Germany	Bavaria	●						●			●				1 month
Somerset Camembert		England	Somerset	●						●		●					1 month
Waterloo		England	Berkshire	●				●				●					1 month
Bouquet des Moines		Belgium		●						●		●					1 month
Bonchester		Scotland	Roxburghshire	●				●	●			●			●		2 months
Teviotdale		Scotland		●				●	●			●			●		3 months
Airiños		Spain	Asturias	●						●		●					1 month
Barberey	Fromage de Troyes	France	Champagne	●				●				●					1 month
Belle-des-Champs		France		●						●			●				3 weeks
Bouysette		France	Rouergue	●				●				●					3 weeks
Brillador		France		●						●			●				1 month
Brique de Jussac		France		●						●		●					1 month
Briquette de Coubon		France	Auvergne	●				●			●						3 weeks
Camembert		France	Southern Normandy	●						●			●				3 weeks
Camembert au calvados		France	Normandy	●				●					●				1 month
Camembert de Normandie		France	Normandy	●				●			●	●	●	●			1 month
Caprice des Dieux		France	Champagne	●						●			●				2 weeks
Carré		France		●						●		●					1 month
Carré de l'Est		France	Lorraine – Champagne	●						●			●				1 month
Carré de Lorraine		France	Lorraine	●						●			●				1 month
Cendré d'Argonne		France	Champagne-Ardenne	●						●		●					2 months
Cendré de Champagne	Fromage Cendré	France	Champagne-Ardenne	●				●		●		●					1 month
Chécy		France	Orléans	●						●		●					1 month
Chiberta		France	Basque Country	●						●			●				1 month
Colombier		France	Burgundy – Auxois	●				●			●						1 month
Coulommiers		France	Ile de France	●				●				●	●				1 month
Crème des Prés		France		●						●			●				1 month
Crémet du Cap Blanc-Nez	Cap Blanc-Nez	France	Nord – Pas-de-Calais	●						●		●					3 weeks
Évry-le-Châtel		France	Champagne	●				●		●		●					1 month
Feuille de Dreux	Dreux à la feuille – Marsauceux	France	Dreux	●				●		●		●					1 month
Feuille de Sauge		France	Orléans	●						●		●					1 month
Frinault		France	Orléans	●						●		●					1 month
Galette des Monts du Lyonnais		France	Lyons	●				●				●					3 weeks
Géramont		France		●						●			●				1 month
Henri IV		France		●						●			●				1 month
Olivet Bleu		France	Loiret	●				●	●	●		●					1 month
Olivet Cendré		France	Loiret	●				●	●	●		●					1 month
Olivet Foin		France	Loiret	●				●	●	●		●					1 month
Oreiller de Ciboulette		France		●						●		●					1 month
Pannes cendré		France	Loiret	●				●				●					3 months
Pas de l'Escalette		France	Southern Aveyron	●	●			●			●						1 month
Patay		France	Loiret	●						●		●					2 months
Pavé d'Affinois		France		●						●			●				1 month
Petit-Bessay		France	Bourbonnais	●				●			●						1 month
Pithiviers au foin	Bondaroy au foin	France	Loiret	●				●				●					1 month
Riceys	Cendré des Riceys	France	Champagne	●				●				●					2 months
Rigotte de Sainte-Colombe		France	Savoie	●						●		●					3 weeks
Saint-Benoît		France	Orléans	●				●				●					1 month
Saint-Félicien		France	Vivarais	●				●		●		●	●				1 month
Saint-Marcellin		France	Dauphiné	●	●			●	●			●	●				1 month
Saint-Morgon		France	Mayenne	●						●			●				2 weeks
Tomme de Romans	Romans	France	Drôme and Ardèche	●						●		●	●				2 weeks
Val des Moines		France		●						●			●				1 month
Vendôme cendré	Vendôme-Bleu	France	Orléans	●				●			●						2 months
Voves		France		●						●		●					2 months
Cooleeney		Ireland	Tipperary	●				●			●						6 weeks
Saint Killian		Ireland	Wexford	●						●		●					1 month
Formaggella		Italy	Italian pre-Alps	●						●		●					1 month
Tomme de Rougement		Switzerland	Vaud canton	●				●				●					3 weeks
Tomme Vaudoise		Switzerland		●				●				●					3 weeks

The Munster family

and related cheeses

All these cheeses have a very strong character caused by washing the rind during ripening, which encourages the development of the 'red ferment mould'. They readily become soft and runny.

Cheese	Other names	Country	Area of origin	Cow	Goat	Ewe	Buffalo	Unpasteurized	Heated	Pasteurized	Farm	Cottage industry	Factory	AOC-AOP	IGP	Monastic	Optimum maturation
Andescher		Germany	Bavaria	•						•		•					3 months
Knappenkäse		Germany		•						•			•				2 months
Münster		Germany	Black Forest	•					•	•		•	•				2 months
Romadur	Romadurkäse	Germany		•						•			•				2 months
Weinkäse		Germany		•						•			•				2 months
Weisslaacker Bierkäse	Weisslacker	Germany		•						•			•				2 months
Stinking Bishop		England	Gloucestershire	•						•		•					2 months
Polkolbin smear ripened		Australia		•						•		•					6 weeks
Bierkäse		Austria		•						•		•					3 months
Mondseer		Austria	Salzburg	•						•		•					2 months
Schlosskäse		Austria		•						•			•				2 months
Beaux Prés		Belgium		•						•			•				2 months
Fromage de Bruxelles	Brusselse Kaas	Belgium	Brabant	•						•			•				1 month
Herve	Herve Kaas	Belgium	Herve	•					•	•		•	•	•			3 months
Remedou	Piquant	Belgium	Liège	•					•	•	•	•					4 months
Ange Cornu		Canada (Quebec)	Quebec	•				•				•					2 months
Laracam		Canada (Quebec)	Lanaudière	•				•				•					3 months
Lechevalier-Mailloux		Canada (Quebec)	Quebec	•				•				•					2 months
Pied-de-Vent		Canada (Quebec)	Iles-de-la-Madeleine	•				•				•					2 months
Pont Couvert		Canada (Quebec)	Mauricie-Bois-Francs	•				•				•					2 months
Bishop Kennedy		Scotland	Perthshire	•				•				•	•				2 months
Tetilla		Spain	Galice	•						•		•	•	•			2 months
Tronchón		Spain	La Mancha	•	•					•		•	•				2 months
Ulloa		Spain	Galice	•						•		•					1 month
Liederkranz		USA		•						•			•				2 months
Baguette Laonnaise	Baguette de Thiérache	France	Picardy	•						•			•				3 months
Bergues		France	Maritime Flanders (Dunkirk)	•				•			•	•					2 months
Chaumes		France	Dordogne–Pyrenees	•						•			•				1 month
Cœur d'Arras		France	Artois	•						•		•					1 month
Cœur d'Avesnes		France	Nord	•						•		•					1 month
Cœur de Thiérache		France	Picardy	•						•		•					1 month
Craquegnon affiné à la Bière 'La Gauloise'		France	Nord	•				•				•					3 months
Crayeux de Roncq		France	Flanders	•				•			•						2 months
Creux de Beaufou		France	Vendée	•				•			•						2 months
Croquin de Mayenne		France	Mayenne	•						•		•					3 weeks
Curé Nantais	Cheese from Nantes – Petit Breton – Fromage du Curé	France	Pays Nantais	•						•		•	•				1 month
Dauphin		France	Flanders	•				•		•		•	•				3 months
Fleur de Bière		France	Meurthe-et-Moselle	•						•			•				1 month
Fromage de Foin		France	Picardy	•				•				•					3 months
Fromage Fort de Béthune		France	Flanders	•				•				•					3 months
Gauville		France	Normandy	•				•	•	•	•						2 months
Gérardmer		France	Vosges	•						•			•				2 months
Gris-de-Lille	Puant Macéré – Vieux Lille – Maroilles Gris – Vieux-Gris-de-Lille	France	Flanders	•				•		•		•	•				4 months
Guerbigny		France	Picardy	•				•				•					1 month
Le Quart (Maroilles)		France	Nord	•				•	•	•	•	•			•		3 months
Lisieux	Petit Lisieux	France	Pays d'Auge	•				•	•	•	•	•		•			2 months
Livarot	Colonel	France	Pays d'Auge	•				•	•	•	•	•		•			2 months
Lozange-de-Saint-Pol		France	Nord	•				•		•		•					3 months
Mamirolle		France	Doubs	•						•			•				2 weeks
Maroilles		France	Nord et Aisne	•				•		•	•	•		•			4 months
Mignon (Maroilles)		France	Flanders	•				•		•		•		•			3 months
Mignot	Mignot Blanc	France	Pays d'Auge	•						•		•					2 months
Munster	Géromé	France	Vosges	•				•	•	•	•	•	•	•			3 months
Pas de l'Ayau		France	Nord	•						•		•					2 months
Pavé d'Auge	Pavé de Moyaux	France	Southern Normandy	•				•		•	•	•					3 months

→

Cheese	Other names	Country	Area of origin	Cow	Goat	Ewe	Buffalo	Unpasteurized	Heated	Pasteurized	Farm	Cottage industry	Factory	AOC	IGP	Monastic	Optimum optimal
Pavé de Moyeux		France	Normandy – Pays d'Auge	●				●		●	●	●					2 months
Pavé du Plessis		France	Northern Normandy	●				●					●				3 months
Pont l'Evêque		France	Normandy	●				●	●	●	●	●	●	●			2 months
Récollet		France	Lorraine	●						●			●				1 month
Rigotte d'Échalas		France	Lyons	●						●			●				3 weeks
Rigotte de Condrieu		France	Lyons	●	●			●			●						1 month
Rigotte des Alpes		France	Dauphiné, Lyons	●				●		●			●				2 weeks
Rigottes		France	Dauphiné, Lyons, Loire	●				●		●			●				1 month
Rocroi	Cendré des Ardennes	France	Ardennes	●				●			●						2 months
Rollot	Cœur de Rollot	France	Picardy	●				●			●	●	●				2 months
Roucoulons		France	Franche-Comté	●						●			●				1 month
Rougette		France		●						●			●				1 month
Rouy		France	Burgundy	●						●			●				1 month
Saint-Albray		France	South-west	●						●			●				3 weeks
Saint-Aubin		France	Anjou	●						●			●				1 month
Saint-Rémy		France	Franche-Comté – Vosges	●						●			●				2 months
Saulxurois		France	Champagne-Ardenne	●					●				●				2 months
Sorbais (Maroilles)		France	Flanders	●				●				●		●			3 months
Tomme de Séranon		France	Provence	●				●				●					3 weeks
Trouville		France	Normandy	●						●		●					2 months
Vacherol		France		●						●			●				3 months
Vieux-Boulogne		France	Boulogne	●				●									2 months
Vieux Pané		France	Mayenne	●						●			●				3 weeks
Vieux-Boulogne		France	Boulogne	●				●				●					3 months
Void		France	Lorraine	●						●		●					3 months
Ardrahan		Ireland	Cork	●						●		●					2 months
Brescianella		Italy	Lombardy	●						●		●					3 months
Quartirolo Lombardo		Italy	Lombardy	●				●		●		●		●			1 month
Robiola della Valsasina		Italy	Lombardy	●				●				●					3 weeks
Salva		Italy	Lombardy	●				●				●					3 months
Taleggio		Italy	Piedmont, Lombardy, Veneto	●				●		●		●	●	●			2 months

The Pérail family
and related cheeses

These ewe's milk cheeses are quite mildly flavoured for the most part. Covered with a white bloom, they become creamy as they ripen.

Cheese	Other names	Country	Area of origin	Cow	Goat	Ewe	Buffalo	Unpasteurized	Heated	Pasteurized	Farm	Cottage industry	Factory	AOC-AOP	IGP	Monastic	Optimum maturation
Emlett		England	Avon			●		●				●					6 weeks
Flower Mary		England	Sussex			●		●				●					6 weeks
Little Rydings		England	Avon			●		●				●					2 months
Weisser Prinz		Austria				●				●			●				1 month
Berger Plat		France	Bresse			●		●			●						1 month
Brebiou		France	Jurançon			●				●			●				2 weeks
Ewe de Meyrueis		France	Languedoc–Roussillon – Corsica			●		●			●						3 weeks
Caldegousse		France	Aveyron			●		●				●					2 weeks
Castagniccia		France	Corsica			●		●				●					1 month
Fedo		France	Provence		●	●		●				●					2 weeks
Fromageon Fermier		France	Rouergue			●		●			●						2 weeks
La Gayrie		France	Rouergue			●		●			●						6 weeks
Lacandou		France	Rouergue			●		●				●					3 weeks
Nabouly d'en Haut		France	Pyrenees			●		●				●					3 weeks
Notle		France	Touraine			●		●				●					3 weeks
Pérail		France	Rouergue			●		●			●	●					3 weeks
Tomme de Brebis d'Arles		France	Camargue			●		●			●						3 weeks
Vieux Corsica		France	Northern Corsica			●											3 months
Paglietta		Italy	Piedmont	●		●			●			●			●		1 month
Azeitão		Portugal	Estremadura			●		●				●					1 month

The Rotolo family
and related cheeses

These ewe's milk cheeses have a rather stronger flavour than those belonging to the Perail family; this is caused by frequent washing in the ripening cellars. These cheeses, too, readily take on a creamy texture.

Cheese	Other names	Country	Area of origin	Animal species				Milk			Product			Label			Optimum maturation
				Cow	Goat	Ewe	Buffalo	Unpasteurized	Heated	Pasteurized	Farm	Cottage industry	Factory	AOC-AOP	IGP	Monastic	
Herriot Farmhouse		England	Yorkshire			●				●	●						3 months
Brebichon de Haute-Provence		France	Northern Provence			●		●			●						5 weeks
Brebis du Lochois		France	Touraine			●		●			●						1 month
Caussedou		France	Quercy			●		●			●						1 month
Fium' Orbo		France	Corsica		●	●		●			●	●					2 months
Moularen		France	Provence			●		●			●						1 month
Niolo		France	Corsica – Niolo plateau		●	●		●			●	●					3 months
Rotolo		France	Corsica			●		●			●						6 months
U Rustino		France	Northern Corsica			●		●			●	●					4 months

The Saint-Nectaire family
and related cheeses

The curd for these cow's milk cheeses is lightly pressed in the course of production. During *affinage*, which takes place in a damp environment, their quite close texture softens and becomes creamy.

Cheese	Other names	Country	Area of origin	Animal species				Milk			Product			Label			Optimum maturation
				Cow	Goat	Ewe	Buffalo	Unpasteurized	Heated	Pasteurized	Farm	Cottage industry	Factory	AOC-AOP	IGP	Monastic	
Northumberland		England	Northumberland	●						●	●						3 months
Spenwood		England	Berkshire	●	●			●				●					6 months
Torville		England	Somerset	●				●				●					2 months
Beauvoorde		Belgium		●						●	●						2 months
Victor et Berthold		Canada (Quebec)	Lanaudière	●				●			●						3 months
Bethmale	Oustet	France	Ariège – Comté de Foix	●				●			●		●				6 months
Chambérat		France	Bourbonnais	●				●	●		●						3 months
Colombière		France	Alpes	●				●			●						3 months
Doux de Montagne		France	Northern Garonne, Arriège	●				●				●					4 months
E Bamalou		France	Ariège – Comté de Foix	●				●			●						2 months
Fourme de Rochefort		France	Auvergne	●				●			●						3 months
Fromage de Lège		France	Central Pyrenees	●				●			●						6 months
Fromage du Pic de la Calabasse		France	Comté de Foix	●				●			●						3 months
Le Montagnard		France	Franche-Comté	●				●				●					2 months
Moulis		France	Pyrenees – Comté de Foix	●				●				●					3 months
Murol		France	Auvergne	●						●			●				2 months
Murolait	Trou de Murol	France	Auvergne	●						●			●				2 weeks
Pavin		France	Auvergne	●						●			●				2 months
Le Petit Pardou		France	Béarn	●				●			●						2 months
Phébus		France	Comté de Foix	●				●			●						3 months
Reblochon		France	Aravis	●				●			●	●	●	●			6 weeks
Rogallais		France	Comté de Foix	●				●			●						2 months
Saint-Nectaire		France	Auvergne	●				●	●	●	●		●	●			3 months
Savaron		France	Auvergne	●						●	●						2 months
Tomme de Montagne des Vosges		France	Vosges	●				●			●						3 months
Toupin		France	Haute-Savoie	●				●			●						4 months
Durrus		Ireland	Cork	●				●			●						3 months
Gubbeen		Ireland	Cork	●						●		●					3 months
Milleens		Ireland	Cork	●				●			●						4 months
Branzi		Italy	Lombardy	●				●		●	●						6 months
Caerphilly		Wales		●				●	●	●	●						2 months
Tournagus		Wales		●				●			●						3 months
Wedmore		Wales		●				●				●					1 month

These cheeses are made in a very similar way to Saint-Nectaire. The main difference is in the ripening, the rind of the Tomme being simply brushed. It is generally greyish and the interior is drier.

Cheese	Other names	Country	Area of origin	Cow	Goat	Ewe	Buffalo	Unpasteurized	Heated	Pasteurized	Farm	Cottage industry	Factory	AOC-AOP	IGP	Monastic	Optimum maturation
Coquetdale		England	Northumberland	●						●	●						3 months
Cotherstone		England	Durham	●				●				●					3 months
Menallack Farmhouse		England	Cornwall	●				●				●					6 month
Saint-Basile		Canada (Quebec)	Quebec	●				●			●						3 months
Cantabria		Spain	Santander	●						●	●		●	●			6 month
Formatge de la Selva		Spain	Catalonia	●				●		●	●						4 months
Queso Ahumado		Spain	Navarre	●	●	●		●			●						6 month
Bargkass		France	Vosges	●				●	●		●						2 months
Bourricot		France	Auvergne	●						●			●				2 months
Esbareich		France	Central Pyrenees	●				●			●						3 months
Fouchtra		France	Cantal	●				●			●	●					6 month
Fromage de Poubeau		France	Central Pyrenees	●				●			●						3 months
Fromage de Vache Brulé		France	Basque Country	●				●			●						3 months
Lou Magré		France	Gascony	●				●			●						3 months
Montségur		France	Pyrenees	●						●			●				3 months
Persillé du Semnoz		France	Savoie	●	●			●			●						2 months
Petite Tomme Beulet		France	Haute Savoie	●						●	●						6 weeks
Pyrénées de Vache		France	Pyrenees	●						●	●						3 months
Tome des Bauges		France	Bauges	●				●			●		●				2 months
Tomette de Yenne		France	Rhône-Alpes	●				●				●					2 months
Tomme au Marc de Raisin		France	Savoie	●				●				●					2 months
Tomme d'Alpage de la Vanoise		France	Savoie	●				●			●						3 months
Tomme d'Auvergne		France	Auvergne	●				●		●		●					2 months
Tomme de Bonneval		France	Haute-Maurienne	●				●				●	●				2 months
Tomme de Chèvre from the Novel Valley		France	Savoie		●			●			●						6 month
Tomme de l'Aveyron		France	Larzac	●				●			●						3 months
Tomme de la Frasse		France	Savoie	●				●			●						6 month
Tomme de Lomagne		France	Gascony	●				●				●					2 months
Tomme de Lullin		France	Savoie	●				●				●					6 month
Tomme de Ménage	Boudane	France	Haute-Tarentaise	●				●			●						3 months
Tomme de Morzine		France	Savoie		●			●			●						6 month
Tomme de Pont-Astier		France	Doubs	●				●		●		●					2 months
Tomme de Savoie		France	Pays de Savoie	●				●	●	●	●	●	●		●		4 months
Tomme de Thônes		France	Savoie – the Aravis Chain	●				●			●						2 months
Tomme de Val d'Isère		France	Savoie – Haute-Tarentaise	●				●			●						2 months
Tomme des Allobroges		France	Savoie	●				●			●						3 months
Tomme des Allues		France	Savoie	●				●		●	●						3 months
Tomme des Aravis		France	Savoie	●				●			●	●					3 months
Tomme du Beaujolais		France	Beaujolais	●						●	●	●					2 months
Tomme du Bougnat		France	Auvergne	●				●			●						2 months
Tomme du Faucigny		France	Savoie	●				●			●						5 months
Tomme du Mont-Cenis		France	Savoie	●				●			●						3 months
Tomme du Pelvoux		France	Savoie	●				●			●						3 months
Tomme du Revard		France	Savoie	●				●		●	●						3 months
Tomme Fermière des Lindarets		France	Savoie	●				●			●						6 months
Tomme Grise de Seyssel		France	Savoie	●				●				●					6 months
Tomme le Gascon		France	Gascony	●				●				●					2 months
Tommette de l'Aveyron		France	Rouergue			●		●			●						2 months
Vachard		France	Auvergne	●				●				●					2 months
Bra		Italy	Piedmont	●	●	●		●			●	●	●	●			6 months
Raschera		Italy	Piedmont	●	●	●		●			●	●		●			3 months
Sora		Italy	Piedmont	●		●		●				●					1 year
Toma Brusca		Italy	Piedmont	●				●			●	●					4 months
Toma del Maccagno		Italy	Piedmont	●				●			●	●					2 months
Toma di Capra		Italy	Piedmont	●				●				●					4 months
Toma di Lanzo		Italy	Piedmont	●				●				●					3 months
Toma Piemontese		Italy	Piedmont	●				●				●		●			4 months
Toma Valle Elvo		Italy	Piedmont	●				●			●	●					3 months
Toma Valsesia		Italy	Piedmont	●				●			●	●					3 months
Valle d'Aosta Fromadzo		Italy	Lombardy, Val d'Aoste	●				●				●					9 months
Alvorca		Portugal		●	●	●		●				●					6 months

The Vacherin family
and related cheeses

A speciality of Franco-Swiss origin, this category offers rich, generous cheeses that need to be wrapped and kept in boxes so that their creamy interior does not collapse.

Cheese	Other names	Country	Area of origin	Cow	Goat	Ewe	Buffalo	Unpasteurized	Heated	Pasteurized	Farm	Cottage industry	Factory	AOC-AOP	IGP	Monastic	Optimum maturation
				Animal species				**Milk**			**Product**			**Label**			
Vacherin Chaput		Canada (Quebec)	Montérégie	•				•			•						1 month
Cabri Arriègeois		France	Comté de Foix		•			•				•					6 weeks
Mont-d'or	Vacherin du Haut-Doubs	France	Doubs	•				•				•	•	•			1 month
Vacherin d'Abondance		France	Savoie – Abondance valley	•				•			•						1 month
Vacherin des Aillons		France	Bauges	•				•			•						3 months
Vacherin des Bauges		France	Bauges	•				•			•						2 months
Vacherin Mont d'Or	Mont d'Or de Joux	Switzerland	Swiss Jura	•					•	•	•						1 month

The Venaco family
and related cheeses

The soft ewe's milk Tommes of this family are recognizable by their fine, full flavour, the strength of which depends on whether or not the rinds were washed during ripening.

Cheese	Other names	Country	Area of origin	Cow	Goat	Ewe	Buffalo	Unpasteurized	Heated	Pasteurized	Farm	Cottage industry	Factory	AOC-AOP	IGP	Monastic	Optimum maturation
				Animal species				**Milk**			**Product**			**Label**			
Aragón	Tronchón	Spain	Aragon		•	•		•			•	•					2 weeks
Penamellera		Spain	Asturias		•	•		•			•						2 months
A filetta	Fougère	France	Northern Corsica		•	•		•				•					1 month
Amou		France	South-west			•		•			•						4 months
Barousse		France	Pyrenees	•				•			•						2 months
Ewe de Bersend		France	Savoie			•		•			•						2 months
Brebis du Pays de Grasse		France	Provence			•		•			•						2 months
Corsica		France	Corsica			•				•		•					1 month
Fromage des Pyrenees		France	Pyrenees			•				•			•				2 months
Galette du Val de Dagne		France	Corbières			•		•			•						3 months
Napoléon		France	Corsica			•		•				•					6 weeks
Ourliou		France	Lot			•				•		•					2 months
Tomme de Brebis		France	Savoie			•		•			•						1 month
Tomme de Brebis de Haute-Provence		France	Northern Provence			•		•			•						2 months
Tommette des Corbières		France	Corbières			•		•			•						2 months
Venaco		France	Northern Corsica		•	•		•			•						2 months
Orla		Ireland	Cork			•		•				•					6 months
Caciotta Toscana		Italy	Tuscany	•		•				•		•					3 weeks
Casciotta di Urbino		Italy	Marche	•		•		•		•	•			•			1 month
Marzolino		Italy	Tuscany	•		•				•	•						2 months
Queijo da Ovelha		Portugal				•		•				•					2 months
Serpa		Portugal	Alentejo			•		•				•		•			2 months
Serra da Estrela		Portugal	Serra da Estrela			•		•			•	•		•			2 months

The Chevrotin family
and related cheeses

Characteristic of these goat's milk cheeses, of which there are a great many in the Alps, is the process of pressing the curd during production. They have a quite dense texture and a pronounced goat's milk flavour.

Cheese	Other names	Country	Area of origin	Cow	Goat	Ewe	Buffalo	Unpasteurized	Heated	Pasteurized	Farm	Cottage industry	Factory	AOC-AOP	IGP	Monastic	Optimum maturation
Basing		England	Kent		●			●			●						2 months
Loddiswel Avondale		England	Devon		●			●			●						2 months
Ribblesdale		England	Yorkshire		●			●			●						2 months
Ticklemore		England	Devon		●			●			●	●					3 months
Vulscombe		England	Devon		●			●			●						1 month
Wigmore		England	Berkshire		●			●			●						2 months
Le Capra		Canada (Quebec)	Lanoudière		●			●			●						1 month
Breña		Spain			●			●				●					3 months
Garrotxa		Spain	Catalonia		●				●		●	●					3 months
Ibores		Spain	Estremadura		●			●			●	●					3 months
Queso del Montsec	Cendrat	Spain	Catalonia		●			●				●					3 months
Queso Majorero		Spain	Canary Islands		●			●			●	●		●			2 months
Annot		France	Inland Nice region		●			●				●					2 months
Asco		France	Northern Corsica		●	●		●				●					3 months
Aubisque		France	Pyrenees – Ossau valley		●	●		●				●					3 months
Cabrioulet	Tomme Loubières	France	Foix		●			●				●					3 months
Caprinu		France	Corsica		●			●				●					6 months
Chevre Fermier des Pyrenees		France	Béarn-Gascony Midi-Pyrenees		●			●				●					1 month
Chevrotin de Macôt		France	Savoie – Tarentaise		●			●			●						2 months
Chevrotin de Montvalezan		France	Savoie – Tarentaise		●			●			●						2 months
Chevrotin de Morzine		France	Savoie		●			●			●						3 months
Chevrotin de Peizey-Nancroix		France	Savoie		●			●			●						3 months
Chevrotin des Aravis		France	Haute-Savoie – Aravis		●			●			●						2 months
Chevrotin des Bauges		France	Bauges		●			●			●						2 months
Chevrotin du Mont-Cenis		France	Savoie		●			●			●						2 months
Figue		France	Périgord		●			●				●					3 weeks
Fort de la Platte		France	Briançon		●			●				●					6 months
Grataron d'Arèches		France	Savoie		●			●			●						2 months
Grataron de Haute-Luce		France	Savoie		●			●			●						2 months
Lou Pennol		France	Southern Quercy		●			●			●						3 months
Palouse des Aravis		France	Alps – Aravis		●			●			●						6 months
Péchegros		France	Tarn		●			●			●	●					1 month
Sarteno		France	Corsica		●	●		●			●						3 months
Tomme de Chèvre de Gascogne		France	Gascony		●			●			●						2 months
Tome Pressée		France	Provence		●	●		●			●						1 year
Tomme au Muscadet		France	Loire valley		●			●				●					6 months
Tomme de Chèvre Corse		France	Corsica		●			●			●						3 months
Tomme de Chèvre de Belleville		France	Savoie – Tarentaise		●			●			●						2 months
Tomme de Chèvre de la Vallée de Morzine		France	Savoie		●			●			●						2 months
Tomme de Chèvre de Provence		France	Provence		●			●				●					1 month
Tomme de Chèvre Pays Nantais		France	Nantes		●			●			●						6 weeks
Tomme de Courchevel		France	Savoie		●			●			●						2 months
Tomme de Crest		France			●			●			●						2 months
Tomme de Huit Litres		France	Provence		●			●			●						6 months
Tomme de Vendée		France	Vendée		●			●				●					2 months
Tomme du Pays Basque		France	Basque Country		●	●		●			●						3 months
Tomme du Vercors		France	Vercors		●			●			●						2 months
Tomme Fermière des Hautes-Vosges		France	Hautes-Vosges		●				●		●	●					3 months
Tomme mi-Chèvre de Lécheron		France	Savoie	●	●			●			●						3 months
Tomme mi-Chèvre des Bauges		France	Savoie	●	●			●			●						2 months
Tomme Sainte-Cécile		France	Burgundy		●			●			●						6 months
Tommette mi-Chèvre des Bauges		France	Bauges	●	●			●			●						2 months
Valde Blore		France	Inland Nice region		●			●			●	●					2 months
Kefalotyri		Greece			●	●		●			●	●					3 months
Croghan		Ireland	Wexford		●			●			●						3 months
Gjetost		Norway		●	●					●			●				1 month

and related cheeses

Those great travellers, the Dutch, invented pressed-curd cheeses, often coated with a protective paraffin-wax crust, which could be stacked perfectly into the holds of ships without getting damaged.

Cheese	Other names	Country	Area of origin	Animal species				Milk			Product			Label			Optimum maturation
				Cow	Goat	Ewe	Buffalo	Unpasteurized	Heated	Pasteurized	Farm	Cottage industry	Factory	AOC-AOP	IGP	Monastic	
Bianco		Germany		•						•			•				2 months
German Trappistenkäse		Germany		•						•			•				2 months
Geheimratskäse		Germany		•						•			•				1 month
Geltinger		Germany	Schleswig-Holstein	•						•			•				3 months
German Gouda	Deutscher gouda	Germany		•						•			•				6 months
Schwäbischer landkäse		Germany		•						•			•				2 months
Steppe		Germany		•						•			•				6 months
Tilsit		Germany	Lithuania	•						•			•				3 months
Tollenser		Germany	Eastern Germany	•						•			•				2 months
Vitadam		Germany		•						•			•				1 month
Wilster marschkäse	Wilstermarsch	Germany	Holstein	•						•			•				3 months
Coverdale		England	Yorkshire	•						•		•					2 months
Curworthy		England	Devon	•				•				•					4 months
Steirischer bauernkäse		Austria		•		•				•		•					2 months
Steirischer hirtenkäse		Austria		•		•				•		•					2 months
Esrom	Danish Bütterkäse	Denmark		•						•			•		•		3 months
Havarti	Danish Tilsit	Denmark		•						•			•				2 months
Maribo		Denmark	Isle of Lolland	•						•			•				4 months
Molbo		Denmark		•						•			•				3 months
Bola		Spain		•						•			•				3 months
Mahón		Spain	Balearics	•	•			•	•	•	•	•	•	•			1 year
San Simón		Spain	Galicia	•					•		•	•					2 months
Brick		USA	Wisconsin	•						•			•				2 months
Kesti		Finland		•						•			•				2 months
Kreivi		Finland		•						•			•				2 months
Lappi		Finland		•						•			•				3 months
Babybel		France		•						•			•				1 month
Bonbel		France		•						•			•				1 month
French Gouda		France		•						•			•				6 months
Mimolette	Boule de Lille-Vieux Lille	France	Nord	•					•	•	•		•				2 years
Pavé de Roubaix		France	Nord	•						•	•						1 year
Baby Gouda	Lunchies Kaas	Netherlands		•						•			•				3 months
Boerenkaas		Netherlands	Southern Holland	•				•			•	•		•			1 year
Edam	Tête de Maure-Manbollen-Katzenkopf-Tête de chat	Netherlands	Northern Holland	•						•			•	•			6 months
Friese nagelkaas		Netherlands		•						•		•	•				3 months
Friese Nelkenkaas		Netherlands	Friesland	•						•		•	•				3 months
Friesekaas	Frise	Netherlands	Friesland	•						•		•	•				3 months
Gouda	Goudse kaas	Netherlands	Southern Holland	•						•	•	•	•	•			6 months
Kernhem		Netherlands		•						•			•				2 months
Kruidenkaas		Netherlands		•						•			•				3 months
Kummel		Netherlands		•						•			•				3 months
Leidener	Leidsekaas-Leiden Commissiekaas	Netherlands	Leiden	•						•		•	•				1 year
Mimolette		Netherlands		•						•			•				6 months
Minell		Netherlands		•						•			•				1 month
Nagelkaas		Netherlands		•						•			•				3 months
Pardano		Netherlands		•						•			•				1 month
Roomkaas		Netherlands		•						•			•				3 months
Coolea		Ireland	Cork	•				•				•					1 year
Doolin		Ireland	Waterford	•						•		•					3 months
Bel Paese		Italy	North	•						•			•				2 months
Italico		Italy		•						•			•				2 months
Edda		Norway		•						•			•				2 months
Nökkelost		Norway		•						•			•				3 months
Norvegia		Norway		•						•			•				3 months
Penbryn		Wales	Carmarthenshire	•						•			•				2 months
Teifi		Wales	Carmarthenshire	•				•					•				3 months
Flamengo		Portugal		•						•		•					6 months
São Jorge		Portugal	Azores	•				•				•	•	•			6 months
Ambrosia		Sweden		•						•			•				3 months
Drabant		Sweden		•						•			•				3 months

Cheese	Other names	Country	Area of origin	Cow	Goat	Ewe	Buffalo	Unpasteurized	Heated	Pasteurized	Farm	Cottage industry	Factory	AOC	IGP	Monastic	Optimum maturation
Gårda		Sweden		•						•			•				3 months
Gräddost		Sweden		•						•			•				2 months
Kryddal		Sweden		•						•			•				2 months
Prästost		Sweden		•						•		•	•				2 months
Sveciaost	Svecia	Sweden		•						•			•		•		3 months

The Cheddar family
and related cheeses

Undoubtedly brought by the Romans to Britain following their passage through Cantal in France, the recipe for Cheddar, which involves breaking up the curd (hence the uneven texture of the cheese), has become universal.

Cheese	Other names	Country	Area of origin	Cow	Goat	Ewe	Buffalo	Unpasteurized	Heated	Pasteurized	Farm	Cottage industry	Factory	AOC-AOP	IGP	Monastic	Optimum maturation
Buffalo		England	Hereford-Worcester				•					•					3 months
Cheddar		England	Somerset	•				•	•	•	•		•	•			1 year
Cheshire	Chester	England	Cheshire	•				•		•	•	•	•				3 months
Cornish Yarg		England	Cornwall	•						•		•					2 months
Cotswold		England		•						•			•				4 months
Denhay Dorset drum		England	Dorset	•						•	•						2 months
Derby		England	Derbyshire	•						•		•					4 months
Devon Garland		England	Devon	•				•				•					2 months
Double Gloucester		England	Gloucestershire	•				•		•	•	•					6 months
Double Worcester		England	Worcestershire	•				•			•						9 months
Gospel Green		England	Surrey	•				•									3 months
Hereford Hop		England	Gloucestershire	•				•		•	•						4 months
Lancashire		England	Lancashire	•						•	•	•	•				6 months
Leicester	Red Leicester	England	Midlands	•						•		•					6 months
Lincolnshire Poacher		England	Lincolnshire	•				•			•						6 months
Sage Derby		England	Derby	•						•		•					1 year
Sage Lancashire		England		•						•	•	•					4 months
Single Gloucester		England	Gloucestershire	•				•		•	•		•			9 months
Staffordshire Organic		England	Staffordshire	•				•			•						4 months
Swaledale		England	Yorkshire	•		•				•	•		•			3 months
Wellington		England	Berkshire	•				•			•						2 months
Wensleydale	White Wensleydale-White cheese	England	Yorkshire	•						•	•	•				6 months
Cheedam		Australia		•						•		•				1 year
Pyengana Cheddar		Australia	Tasmania	•						•	•					18 months
Cheddar l'Ancêtre		Canada (Quebec)	Bois-Francs	•				•			•					3 months
Aran		Scotland		•				•			•					1 year
Dunlop		Scotland	Ayrshire	•				•			•	•				1 year
Gowrie		Scotland	Perthshire	•						•	•					4 months
Isle of Mull		Scotland	Isle of Mull	•				•			•					6 months
Lairobell		Scotland	Orkney	•				•			•					6 months
Loch Arthur Farmhouse		Scotland	Dumfries–Galloway	•				•			•					1 year
Orkney		Scotland	Orkney	•						•	•					1 year
Scottish Farmhouse Cheddar		Scotland		•				•			•					1 year
Shelburne Cheddar		USA		•				•			•					1 year
Colby Crowley		USA	Wisconsin-Vermont	•						•	•		•			6 months
Grafton Cheddar		USA	Vermont	•				•			•					1 year
Longhorn		USA		•						•		•				6 months
Monterey	Monterey Jack–Jack Bear flag	USA	California	•						•		•				10 months
Cantal	Fourme du Cantal	France	Cantal	•				•	•	•	•	•	•	•		1 year
Laguiole		France	Aubrac (Aveyron, Cantal, Lozère)	•				•			•	•		•		18 months
Salers	Fourme de Salers-Cantal Salers	France	Cantal	•				•			•		•		18 months
Lavistown		Ireland	Kilkenny	•				•			•					3 months
Llanboidy		Wales	Pembrokeshire	•				•		•						6 months
Llangloffan Farmhouse		Wales	Pembrokeshire	•				•			•					6 months
Tyn Crug		Wales	Cardiganshire	•				•			•					6 months

The Pélardon family
and related cheeses

A great many goat's milk cheeses are made in the form of a disc of varying diameter and thickness. They are found in every region, without exception. The format is used for cheeses made from both lactic curd and those coagulated with rennet.

Cheese	Other names	Country	Area of origin	Cow	Goat	Ewe	Buffalo	Unpasteurized	Heated	Pasteurized	Farm	Cottage industry	Factory	AOC-AOP	IGP	Monastic	Optimum maturation
Bosworth		England	Staffordshire		•			•			•						1 month
Cerney Village		England	Gloucestershire		•					•	•						1 month
Capriole Banon	Indiana	USA	Indiana		•					•	•						1 month
Alpicrème		France	Alpilles		•			•			•						2 weeks
Anneau de Vic-Bilh		France	Pyrenees		•			•			•						2 weeks
Arôme à la Gêne de Marc	Arôme de Lyon	France	Lyons	•	•			•				•					3 months
Arôme au Vin Blanc		France	Lyons	•	•			•				•					3 months
Banon	Banon à la Feuille	France	Provence	•	•	•		•			•	•					1 month
Banon Poivré		France	Provence	•	•	•		•			•	•					1 month
Banon Sarriette		France	Provence	•	•	•		•			•	•					1 month
Beaujolais pur Chèvre		France	Beaujolais		•			•			•						1 month
Bigoton		France	Orléans		•			•			•						2 weeks
Bruyère de Joursac		France	Auvergne		•			•			•						1 month
Cabécou d'Entraygues		France			•			•			•						3 weeks
Cabécou de Cahors		France	Lot		•			•			•						3 weeks
Cabécou du Béarn		France			•			•			•						3 weeks
Cabécou du Fel		France	Quercy		•			•			•						3 weeks
Cabécou du Périgord		France	Aquitaine		•			•			•	•					3 weeks
Cabri de Parthenay		France	Deux-Sèvres		•			•			•						2 weeks
Cabri des Gors		France	Deux-Sèvres		•			•			•						3 weeks
Cabécou Lezéen		France	Poitou		•			•			•						2 weeks
Capricorne de Jarjat		France	Ardèche-Vivarais		•			•			•						1 month
Cendré de la Drôme		France	Drôme Provençal		•			•			•						2 weeks
Château Vert		France	Mont Ventoux		•			•			•						2 weeks
Chèvre à la Sarri		France	Provence		•			•			•						3 weeks
Chèvre Affiné au Marc de Bourgogne		France	Burgundy		•			•			•						1 month
Goat de l'Ariège		France	Pyrenees		•			•			•						2 weeks
Goat de Provence		France	Provence		•			•			•						1 month
Goat des Alpilles		France	Provence		•			•			•						3 weeks
Goat du Larzac		France	Larzac		•			•			•						2 weeks
Goat du Morvan		France	Morvan		•			•				•					3 weeks
Goat du Ventoux		France	Provence		•			•			•						2 weeks
Chevriou		France	Saône-et-Loire		•			•			•	•					1 month
Cujassous de Cubjac		France	Périgord		•			•			•						3 weeks
Fromage Corse (Manenti)		France	Southern Corsica		•	•		•			•						2 months
Fromage du Jas		France	Provence		•			•			•						3 weeks
Galet de Bigorre		France	Pyrenees		•			•			•						2 weeks
Galet Solognot		France	Orléans		•			•			•						2 weeks
Galette de La Chaise-Dieu		France	Auvergne	•	•			•			•						1 month
Gavotine		France	Provence		•	•		•			•						1 month
Gramat		France	Quercy		•			•			•						1 month
Groû du Bâne		France	Provence		•			•			•						3 weeks
Livernon du Quercy		France	Quercy		•			•			•	•					3 weeks
Lunaire		France	Quercy		•			•			•						2 weeks
Lusignan		France	Poitou		•			•				•					3 weeks
Mont d'or du Lyonnais	Mont d'or de Lyon	France	Lyons	•	•			•			•	•					1 month
Mothais sur Feuille		France	Poitou		•			•			•						3 weeks
Pélardon		France	Cévennes		•			•			•	•	•	•			3 weeks
Pélardon des Corbières		France	Corbières		•			•			•	•					1 month
Petit Pastre Camarguais		France	Provence			•		•			•						3 weeks
Petit Quercy		France	Quercy		•			•			•						3 weeks
Petite Meule		France	Quercy		•			•			•						1 month
Picadou		France			•			•				•					3 weeks
Picodon		France	Rhône Valley		•			•	•	•	•			•			3 weeks
Poivre d'âne	Pèbre d'Aï	France	Provence	•	•	•		•			•	•					2 weeks
Pougne Cendré		France	Gâtine		•			•				•					1 month
Provençal		France	Provence		•			•			•						1 month
Rocamadour	Cabécou de Rocamadour	France	Quercy		•			•			•			•			2 weeks

Cheese	Other names	Country	Area of origin	Cow	Goat	Ewe	Buffalo	Unpasteurized	Heated	Pasteurized	Farm	Cottage industry	Factory	AOC-AOP	IGP	Monastic	Optimum maturation
Rogeret de Lamastre		France	Vivarais	●	●			●			●	●					1 month
Rond'oc		France	Tarn		●			●			●						3 weeks
Rouelle du Tarn	Rouelle blanche	France	Tarn		●			●			●						1 month
Ruffec		France	Poitou		●			●			●						3 weeks
Saint-Félicien		France	Vercors	●	●			●		●	●	●	●				3 weeks
Saint-Félicien de Lamastre		France	Vivarais		●			●			●						3 weeks
Saint-Gelais		France	Poitou		●			●			●						3 weeks
Saint-Héblon		France	Périgord	●						●	●						3 weeks
Saint-Mayeul		France	Northern Provence – Valensole plateau		●			●			●						1 month
Saint-Nicolas de l'Hérault		France			●			●			●						3 weeks
Saint-Pancrace		France	Rhône-Alpes		●			●			●						3 weeks
Saint-Rémois		France	Saint-Rémy-de-Provence		●			●			●						2 weeks
Séchon		France	Dauphiné		●			●			●						4 weeks
Selles-sur-Cher		France	Berry		●			●			●	●		●			2 weeks
Tomme Capra		France	Rhône valley		●			●			●						3 weeks
Tomme de Banon		France	Provence	●	●	●		●			●	●					3 weeks
Tomme de Chèvre d'Arles		France	Provence		●			●			●						3 weeks
Tomme de Provence à l'Ancienne		France	Camargue		●			●			●						3 weeks
Tomme de Saint-Marcellin		France	Dauphiné	●	●			●	●	●	●	●	●				2 weeks
Tomme des Quatre Reines de Forcalquier		France	Northern Provence		●			●			●						1 month
Tommette à l'Huile d'Olive		France	Provence		●			●			●						2 weeks
Vieillevie		France	Lot		●			●			●						2 weeks
Robiola della Langhe		Italy	Piedmont – Cuneo Province	●	●	●		●	●		●						3 weeks
Scimudin		Italy	Lombardy	●	●			●			●						1 month

The Trappiste family
and related cheeses

The recipe for these pressed-curd cheeses, which are better known as Port-Salut, was handed down over the centuries by monasteries and abbeys. They are often washed-rind cheeses but, on the whole, their flavour remains fairly mild.

Cheese	Other names	Country	Area of origin	Cow	Goat	Ewe	Buffalo	Unpasteurized	Heated	Pasteurized	Farm	Cottage industry	Factory	AOC-AOP	IGP	Monastic	Optimum maturation
Bruder Basil		Germany	Bavaria	●						●			●				1 month
Butterkäse		Germany		●						●			●				2 months
Limbourger	Limburger	Germany		●						●			●				3 months
Steinbuscher		Germany		●						●			●				2 months
King River Gold		Australia	Victoria	●						●		●					2 months
Trappistenkäse		Austria		●						●			●				2 months
Abbaye de Leffe		Belgium		●						●		●	●				3 months
Brigand		Belgium		●						●			●				2 months
Chimay		Belgium	Wallonia	●						●		●					3 months
Loo Véritable		Belgium		●						●			●				2 months
Maredsous		Belgium		●						●							3 months
Orval	Abbaye d'Orval	Belgium	Ardennes	●						●	●					●	1 month
Passendale		Belgium	Flanders	●						●		●	●				2 months
Plateau de Herve		Belgium	Herve	●						●		●	●				3 months
Postel		Belgium		●						●		●					3 months
Rubens		Belgium	Flanders	●				●			●	●					2 months
Saint Andrews		Scotland	Perthshire	●						●	●						2 months
Abbaye de Citeaux	Trappe de Cîteaux, Trappiste de Cîteaux	France	Burgundy	●				●			●	●				●	2 months
Abbaye de la Coudre		France	Brittany	●						●	●	●					3 months
Abbaye de la Joie Notre-Dame		France	Brittany	●				●			●	●					2 months
Abbaye de Timadeuc		France	Morbihan	●						●	●	●				●	2 months
Beaumont		France	Savoie	●				●			●		●				2 months
Belval	Trappe de Belval	France	Flanders – Artois – Picardy	●				●			●	●				●	2 months
Bricquebec	Abbaye de Bricquebec, Trappe de Bricquebec	France	Cotentin	●						●	●	●					3 months
Campénéac		France	Brittany	●						●		●					2 months

Cheese	Other names	Country	Area of origin	Animal species				Milk			Product			Label			Optimum maturation
				Cow	Goat	Ewe	Buffalo	Unpasteurized	Heated	Pasteurized	Farm	Cottage industry	Factory	AOC	IGP	Monastic	
Chambarand	Trappiste de Chambarand	France	Dauphiné	●						●		●				●	2 months
Entrammes	Port-Salut – Trappiste d'Entrammes	France	Mayenne	●				●					●				2 months
Fleuron d'Artois		France	Nord	●				●		●	●						4 months
Fromage d'Hesdin		France	Artois	●				●				●					2 months
Galette de Frencq		France	Nord	●				●			●						3 months
Igny	Trappiste d'Igny	France	Champagne	●				●				●					3 months
Laval	Trappiste de Laval	France	Maine	●				●				●					3 months
Meilleraye		France	Brittany	●						●		●					3 months
Monts-des-Cats	Trappe de Bailleul	France	Nord – Mont-des-Cats	●						●		●				●	3 months
Oelenberg		France	Alsace	●						●		●					2 months
Port-Salut		France	Mayenne – Maine	●						●			●				3 months
Saint-Paulin		France	Brittany and Maine	●						●			●				2 months
Saint-Winoc		France	Flanders	●				●			●						2 months
Tamié	Abbaye de Tamié	France	Massif des Bauges	●				●				●				●	2 months
Trappe (Abbaye de la Coudre)		France	Maine	●						●		●				●	1 month
Trappe d'Échourgnac		France	Périgord	●						●		●				●	3 months
Troisvaux		France	Ternois	●				●				●					2 months
Crimlin		Ireland		●						●			●				2 months
Cushlee		Ireland		●						●		●					2 months
Ridder		Norway		●						●			●				2 months
Celtic Promise		Wales	Carmarthenshire	●				●				●					2 months
Saint David's		Wales	Monmouthshire	●						●		●					2 months
Ridder		Sweden		●						●			●				2 months

The Gruyère family
and related cheeses

Originally from the Fribourg area, these cheeses, which sometimes contain small holes, were intended to be ripened for long periods; the curd is pressed to extract the maximum moisture. Their aromas develop very slowly but very intensely.

Cheese	Other names	Country	Area of origin	Animal species				Milk			Product			Label			Optimum maturation
				Cow	Goat	Ewe	Buffalo	Unpasteurized	Heated	Pasteurized	Farm	Cottage industry	Factory	AOC-AOP	IGP	Monastic	
Allgäuer Bergkäse	Alpkäse	Germany	Bavaria	●				●		●	●	●		●			1 year
Heidi Gruyère		Australia	Tasmania	●						●		●	●				18 months
Bergkäse		Austria		●				●				●					1 year
Beaufort		France	Beaufortin – Tarentaise – Maurienne	●				●			●	●		●			12 months
Le Brouère		France	North-east	●						●			●				2 months
Comté	Gruyère de Comté	France	Jura mountains	●				●				●		●			18 months
Graviera		Greece	Epirus – Crete	●						●			●				6 months
Favorel		Netherlands		●						●							6 months
Gabriel		Ireland	Cork	●				●				●					9 months
Asiago		Italy	North-east	●				●				●		●			18 months
Asiago d'Allevo	Asiago d'Allievo	Italy	North-east	●				●				●					18 months
Asiago Grasso di Monte		Italy	North-east	●				●				●					18 months
Asiago Pressato	Pressato	Italy	North-east	●						●		●					1 month
Bergkäse		Italy	Alps	●				●		●		●					6 months
Latteria		Italy	Frioul, Trentino, Vénitie, Lombardy	●				●		●		●					1 year
Montasio		Italy	Veneto-Friuli	●				●				●	●	●			1 year
Monte Veronese		Italy	Veneto	●				●				●		●			2 years
Puzzone di Moena		Italy	Trentino	●				●				●					1 year
Silter		Italy	Lombardy	●				●				●					1 year
Ubriaco		Italy	Veneto	●						●		●					6 months
Vezzena		Italy	Trentino	●				●		●		●					2 years
L'Étivaz		Switzerland	Vaud Canton	●				●			●			●			18 months
Fribourg		Switzerland	Swiss Romande	●				●				●					18 months
Gruyère		Switzerland	Swiss Romande	●				●				●		●			18 months
Rebibes		Switzerland		●				●				●					3 years
Spalen	Spalenkäse	Switzerland	Central Switzerland	●				●				●					6 months
Tête-de-Moine	Bellelay	Switzerland	Bernese Jura	●				●				●		●			6 months

The Manchego family
and related cheeses

Hard ewe's milk Tommes are the great speciality in the Iberian Peninsular. They will easily keep for up to two years but only the best of them ever become piquant.

Cheese	Other names	Country	Area of origin	Cow	Goat	Ewe	Buffalo	Unpasteurized	Heated	Pasteurized	Farm	Cottage industry	Factory	AOC-AOP	IGP	Monastic	Optimum maturation
Berkswell		England	Midlands			•		•			•						3 months
Duddleswell		England	Sussex			•		•				•					4 months
Friesla		England	Devon			•				•	•						3 months
Leafield		England	Oxfordshire			•				•		•					2 months
Malvern		England	Worcestershire			•		•				•					4 months
Tala		England	Cornwall			•		•			•						6 months
Tyning		England	Somerset			•		•			•						1 year
Cairnsmore		Scotland	Dumfries–Galloway			•		•				•					1 year
Aralar		Spain	Basque Country			•		•				•	•				6 months
Castellano		Spain	Castile and Leon			•		•			•	•	•				6 months
Gorbea		Spain	Basque Country			•		•				•	•				6 months
Grazamela		Spain	Cadiz			•		•		•		•					6 months
Idiazábal		Spain	Basque Country			•		•			•	•		•			6 months
Manchego		Spain	La Mancha			•		•		•	•	•	•	•			1 year
Manchego an Aceite		Spain	La Mancha			•		•		•	•	•					6 months
Orduña		Spain	Basque Country			•		•				•	•				6 months
Oropesa de Tolède		Spain	Toledo			•		•			•	•					6 months
Pedroches de Cordoue		Spain	Cordoba			•		•			•	•					6 months
Queso Iberico		Spain	Centre	•	•	•		•				•	•				4 months
Roncal		Spain	Navarre			•		•			•	•	•	•			1 year
Serena		Spain	Andalusia–Cordoba			•		•		•	•	•	•	•			6 months
Sierra di Zuheros		Spain	Estremadura			•		•		•	•	•					6 months
Urbasa		Spain	Basque Country			•		•				•	•				6 months
Urbia		Spain	Basque Country			•		•				•	•				6 months
Zamorano		Spain	Castile and Leon			•		•						•			6 months
Abbaye de Belloc		France	Basque Country			•				•		•	•				6 months
Ardi-Gasna	Iraty	France	Basque Country			•		•			•	•					18 months
Arnéguy		France	Pyrenees			•		•			•	•					6 months
Aulus		France	Ariège	•		•					•						6 months
Cayolar		France	Basque Country			•		•				•					6 months
Cierp de Luchon		France	Ariège	•		•					•						6 months
Etorki		France	South-west			•		•		•		•					2 months
Laruns		France	Pyrenees			•		•				•					6 months
Lavort	Médiéval	France	Auvergne			•		•			•						3 months
Matocq		France	Pyrenees	•		•		•				•					6 months
Ossau-Iraty		France	Béarn–Basque Country			•		•	•	•	•	•	•	•			6 months
Oustet		France	Ariège	•		•					•						6 months
Saint-Lizier		France	Ariège	•		•					•	•					6 months
Tardets		France	Pyrenees			•		•				•					6 months
Tomme de Brebis Corse		France	Corsica			•		•			•	•					3 months
Tomme de Brebis de Camargue		France	Camargue			•		•				•					1 year
Tomme des Grands Causses		France	Rouergue			•		•				•					8 months
Tommette du Pays Basque		France	Basque Country			•		•	•			•	•				1 month
Tourmalet		France	Béarn			•		•				•					2 months
Canestrato Pugliese		Italy	Apuglia			•		•	•		•			•			1 year
Formaggio de Fossa		Italy	Emilie – Romagne – Marche	•		•		•		•	•						3 months
Formaggio di Grotta Sulfurea		Italy	Emilie – Romagne			•		•				•					6 months
Pecorine Lucarno		Italy	Basilicata		•	•		•				•					3 months
Pecorino Filiano		Italy	Basilicata		•	•		•				•					3 months
Pecorino di Moliterno	Canestrato di Moliterno	Italy	Basilicata		•	•		•				•					3 months
Pecorino di Pienza		Italy	Tuscany			•		•				•					6 months
Pecorino 'Foja de Noce'	Pecorino di Montefeltro, Caciotta di Montefeltro	Italy	Marche			•		•				•					2 months
Pecorino Romano		Italy	Lazio – Sardinia – Tuscany			•		•	•			•		•			9 months
Pecorino Sardo	Fiore Sardo-Pecorino Fiore Sardo	Italy	Sardinia			•		•				•		•			6 months
Pecorino Siciliano	Canestrato Siciliano	Italy	Sicily			•		•		•	•	•		•			6 months
Pecorino Toscano	Pecorino Toscanello	Italy	Tuscany			•		•		•	•	•		•	•		6 months
Piacintinu		Italy	Sicily			•		•				•					2 months
Acorn		Wales	Cardiganshire			•		•			•						6 months
Cwmtawe Pecorine		Wales	Swansea			•		•			•						6 months
Evora		Portugal			•	•		•			•	•		•			4 months

The Emmenthal family
and related cheeses

Easily recognizable by its large holes, this cheese originated in Switzerland before being imitated all over the world. Often produced by large, industrialized cheese dairies, it is generally used in grated form.

Cheese	Other names	Country	Area of origin	Animal species				Milk			Product			Label			Optimum maturation
				Cow	Goat	Ewe	Buffalo	Unpasteurized	Heated	Pasteurized	Farm	Cottage industry	Factory	AOC-AOP	IGP	Monastic	
Alpsberg		Germany		•						•			•				6 months
Bavarian Emmenthal	Allgäuer Emmentaler	Germany	Bavaria	•						•			•	•			4 months
Austrian Emmenthal		Austria		•						•			•				4 months
Murbodner		Austria		•						•			•				4 months
Tiroler Alpkäse		Austria		•				•		•			•	•			6 months
Colombier des Aillons		France	Bauges	•	•			•		•	•	•					2 months
Emmental de Savoie		France	Haute-Savoie – Savoie	•				•					•		•		6 months
Emmenthal Français		France	Savoie – Haute-Savoie	•				•	•	•			•				6 months
Emmental Grand Cru		France	Franche-Comté – Savoie	•				•					•				6 months
Leerdamer		Netherlands	South	•						•			•				1 month
Maasdamer	Maasdam	Netherlands		•						•			•				1 month
Jarlsberg		Norway		•						•			•				6 months
Grevéost	Grevé	Sweden		•						•			•				1 year
Emmental		Switzerland	Emme valley	•				•					•				1 year

The Gorgonzola family
and related cheeses

These blue cheeses have a much more creamy texture than those of the Stilton type. Their flavour is generally less pronounced, possibly also because they are now produced on an industrial scale.

Cheese	Other names	Country	Area of origin	Animal species				Milk			Product			Label			Optimum maturation
				Cow	Goat	Ewe	Buffalo	Unpasteurized	Heated	Pasteurized	Farm	Cottage industry	Factory	AOC-AOP	IGP	Monastic	
Bayerhofer Blue		Germany	Bavaria	•						•			•				2 months
Bavarian Blue		Germany	Bavaria	•						•			•				1 month
Cambozola		Germany		•						•			•				1 month
Montagnolo		Germany		•						•			•				2 months
Exmoor Blue		England	Somerset	•	•	•	•			•	•				•		2 months
Lymeswold		England		•						•			•				2 months
Gippsland Blue		Australia	Victoria	•						•		•					3 months
Milawa Blue		Australia	Victoria	•						•		•					3 months
Mycella		Denmark		•						•			•				2 months
Dunsyre Blue		Scotland	Lanarkshire	•				•			•						3 months
Bleu de Bresse	Bresse Bleu	France		•						•			•				2 months
Bleu du Vercors-Sassenage		France	Vercors	•				•		•	•			•			3 months
Montbriac		France	Auvergne	•						•		•					2 weeks
Saingorlon		France		•						•			•				2 months
Saint-Agur		France	Forez	•						•			•				1 month
Bavarian Blue		Italy		•						•			•				1 month
Dolcelatte		Italy	Lombardy	•						•			•				3 months
Dolcelatte Torta		Italy	Lombardy	•						•			•				1 month
Gorgonzola		Italy	Piedmont–Lombardy	•						•		•	•	•			4 months

The Parmesan family
and related cheeses

A great Italian speciality, these cheeses, with their extra-hard, dry and granular texture and their strong flavour, are primarily used as a seasoning for any number of dishes. Some of them are matured for as long as four years.

Cheese	Other names	Country	Area of origin	Animal species				Milk			Product			Label			Optimum maturation
				Cow	Goat	Ewe	Buffalo	Unpasteurized	Heated	Pasteurized	Farm	Cottage industry	Factory	AOC-AOP	IGP	Monastic	
Parmesello		Germany		•						•			•				6 months
Creusois		France	Limousin Marche	•					•	•	•						6 months
Mizen		Ireland	Cork	•					•			•					1 year
Bagos		Italy	Lombardy	•					•			•					1 year
Bitto		Italy	Lombardy	•					•			•		•			1 year
Grana		Italy	North	•					•		•	•	•				18 months
Grana Padano		Italy	Northern Italy – Po valley	•					•			•	•	•			2 years
Grana Trentino		Italy	Trentino	•					•			•					2 years
Parmigiano Reggiano		Italy	Lombardy – Emilia-Romagna	•					•			•	•	•			3 years
Västerbottenost	Västerbotten	Sweden	Bothnia	•					•			•	•				1 year
Saanen	Hobelkäse	Switzerland	Fribourg	•					•			•					2 years
Sbrinz		Switzerland	Central Switzerland	•					•			•					18 months
Schabzieger	Sapsago (Swiss Romande) – Kraüterkäse (German-speaking Switzerland)	Switzerland	Eastern Switzerland	•					•	•		•					2 months

The Raclette family
and related cheeses

Produced in the past in less isolated areas than those producing Gruyère, these wheel-shaped cheeses have a supple texture and a milder flavour. The curd is heated to a lesser degree and these cheeses can be eaten much younger, principally as raclette.

Cheese	Other names	Country	Area of origin	Animal species				Milk			Product			Label			Optimum maturation
				Cow	Goat	Ewe	Buffalo	Unpasteurized	Heated	Pasteurized	Farm	Cottage industry	Factory	AOC-AOP	IGP	Monastic	
Cave cheese		Denmark		•						•			•				4 months
Danbo		Denmark		•						•			•				6 months
Elbo		Denmark		•						•			•				6 months
Fynbo		Denmark		•						•			•				6 months
Samsø		Denmark		•						•			•				6 months
Tybo		Denmark		•						•			•				6 months
Abondance	Tomme d'Abondance	France	Haute-Savoie – Chablais	•				•			•	•	•	•			6 months
Morbier	Faux Septmoncel	France	Franche-Comté	•				•			•	•	•	•			4 months
Raclette		France	Alps	•				•			•	•	•				2 months
Almkäse		Italy	Bolzano Province	•				•				•					1 year
Fontal		Italy	Val d'Aosta	•						•			•				3 months
Fontella		Italy	Val d'Aosta	•						•			•				3 months
Fontina		Italy	Val d'Aosta	•				•				•	•	•			6 months
Fontinella		Italy	Val d'Aosta	•						•			•				3 months
Formai de Mut dell'Alta Val Bambrena		Italy	Lombardy	•				•				•		•			6 months

The Cabrales family
and related cheeses

The family of blue goat's milk cheeses is a very small one, largely centred on Spain. The blue mould appears in the form of fairly irregular marbling; the flavour is incomparable.

Cheese	Other names	Country	Area of origin	Animal species				Milk			Product			Label			Optimum maturation
				Cow	Goat	Ewe	Buffalo	Unpasteurized	Heated	Pasteurized	Farm	Cottage industry	Factory	AOC-AOP	IGP	Monastic	
Beenleigh Blue		England	Devon		●	●		●				●					8 months
Harbourne Blue		England	Devon		●			●				●					2 months
Goat-Noit		Canada (Quebec)	Eastern Cantons		●					●			●				3 months
Cabrales	Cabraliego	Spain	Asturias	●	●	●		●	●		●			●			6 months
Gamonedo		Spain	Gamoneu		●			●			●						6 months
Picón		Spain	Cantabrian mountains	●	●	●		●			●						3 months
Picos de Europa		Spain	Cantabrian mountains	●	●	●		●			●						3 months
Champignon de Luxe		France		●						●			●				1 month
Blue Rathgore		Ireland	North		●					●			●				6 months

The Roquefort family
and related cheeses

Ewe's milk gives these most glorious of the blue cheeses something extra in the way of strength and spirit that makes them easily distinguishable from cheeses made from cow's milk. What a pity that they are sometimes used to make sauces!

Cheese	Other names	Country	Area of origin	Animal species				Milk			Product			Label			Optimum maturation
				Cow	Goat	Ewe	Buffalo	Unpasteurized	Heated	Pasteurized	Farm	Cottage industry	Factory	AOC-AOP	IGP	Monastic	
Yorkshire Blue		England	Yorkshire			●				●	●						2 months
Meredith Blue		Australia	Victoria			●				●		●					2 months
Bleu de la Moutonnière		Canada (Quebec)	Bois-Francs			●				●		●					4 months
Lanark Blue		Scotland	Lanarkshire			●		●				●					3 months
Bleu de Brach	Tomme de Brach	France	Limousin			●		●				●					3 months
Bleu de Corse		France	Corsica			●		●			●	●					2 months
Bleu de Séverac		France	Aveyron			●		●				●					3 months
Roquefort		France	Rouergue			●		●				●	●	●	●		6 months

The Termignon family
and related cheeses

This small family is made to a very unusual recipe that involves heating the curd. The flavour is quite acidic, the blue mould appears spontaneously, in an irregular manner, in the form of veining and marbling.

Cheese	Other names	Country	Area of origin	Animal species				Milk			Product			Label			Optimum maturation
				Cow	Goat	Ewe	Buffalo	Unpasteurized	Heated	Pasteurized	Farm	Cottage industry	Factory	AOC-AOP	IGP	Monastic	
Bleu de Termignon		France	Haute-Maurienne	●				●			●						6 months
Castelmagno		Italy	Piedmont	●	●	●		●			●	●		●			6 months
Murianengo		Italy	Piedmont	●	●	●		●			●						6 months

The Chabichou family
and related cheeses

The more or less compact tower or plug shape is quite common in goat's milk cheeses. Made with lactic curd, they generally become dry when ripened.

Cheese	Other names	Country	Area of origin	Cow	Goat	Ewe	Buffalo	Unpasteurized	Heated	Pasteurized	Farm	Cottage industry	Factory	AOC-AOP	IGP	Monastic	Optimum maturation
Capricorn Goat		England	Somerset		●					●	●		●				1 month
Chabis Sussex Goat Cheese		England	Sussex		●			●			●						1 month
Autun		France	Burgundy	●	●			●			●						2 weeks
Bonde de Gâtine		France	Deux-Sèvres		●			●			●	●					1 month
Bouca		France	Centre		●			●			●						2 weeks
Bressan		France	Bresse	●	●			●			●						2 weeks
Cabardès		France	Aude		●			●			●						1 month
Chabichou du Poitou		France	Haut-Poitou		●			●	●	●	●	●	●	●			1 month
Charolais	Charolles	France	Burgundy Charolais	●	●			●			●	●					1 month
Civray		France	Poitou-Charentes		●			●			●						2 weeks
Clacbitou		France	Burgundy		●			●			●						1 month
Cornilly		France	Berry		●			●			●						3 weeks
Dornecy		France	Nivernais		●			●			●						1 month
Fourme de Chèvre de l'Ardèche		France	Rhône-Alpes		●			●			●						2 months
Gien		France	Orléans	●	●			●			●	●					1 month
Mâconnais	Chevreton de Mâcon, Cabrion de Mâcon	France	Burgundy – Mâcon	●	●			●			●						2 weeks
Montoire		France	Orléans		●			●			●						3 weeks
Montrachet		France	Burgundy		●			●				●					3 weeks
Troo		France	Orléans		●			●			●						3 weeks
Villageois		France	Charentes		●			●			●		●				3 weeks
Villiers-sur-Loire		France	Orléans		●			●			●						3 weeks
Mine-Gabhar		Ireland	Wexford		●			●			●						1 month

The Sainte-Maure family
and related cheeses

This family undoubtedly owes its popularity to its very practical and easily cut shape. Almost all are cheeses made from lactic curd, which gradually become dry.

Cheese	Other names	Country	Area of origin	Cow	Goat	Ewe	Buffalo	Unpasteurized	Heated	Pasteurized	Farm	Cottage industry	Factory	AOC-AOP	IGP	Monastic	Optimum maturation
Golden Cross		England	Sussex		●			●				●	●				1 month
Rosary Plain		England	Wiltshire		●			●			●						2 weeks
Bouchon Lyonnais		France	Lyons		●			●			●						1 month
Bûchette d'Anjou		France	Anjou		●			●				●					2 weeks
Bûchette de Banon		France	Provence		●			●			●						1 week
Chouzé		France	Berry		●					●			●				3 weeks
Graçay		France	Berry		●			●			●						1 month
Ile d'Yeu		France	Ile d'Yeu		●			●			●						1 month
Joug		France	Berry		●			●			●	●					1 month
Ligueil		France	Berry		●					●			●				3 weeks
Loches		France	Berry		●			●			●						3 weeks
Saint-Loup		France	Berry		●			●			●						3 weeks
Sainte-Maure		France			●			●			●	●	●				2 weeks
Sainte-Maure-de-Touraine		France	Touraine		●			●			●	●		●			1 month
Tournon-Saint-Pierre		France	Touraine		●			●			●						1 month
Vazerac		France	Quercy		●			●			●						3 weeks

The Brique du Forez family
and related cheeses

Generally made from curd coagulated with rennet, unlike the previous category, these cheeses become creamy as they ripen – the more so because of their relatively slender format. Their flavour is quite mild.

Cheese	Other names	Country	Area of origin	Cow	Goat	Ewe	Buffalo	Unpasteurized	Heated	Pasteurized	Farm	Cottage industry	Factory	AOC-AOP	IGP	Monastic	Optimum maturation
Brique Ardéchoise		France	Ardèche		●			●			●						1 month
Brique du Bas Quercy		France	Rouergue			●		●			●						1 month
Brique du Forez		France	Monts du Forez	●	●			●		●	●	●					1 month
Brique du Livradois	Cabrion	France	Livradois	●	●			●	●		●	●					1 month
Briquette d'Allanche		France	Cantal		●			●			●						3 weeks
Briquette de la Dombes		France	Dombes		●			●					●				2 weeks
Chêne		France	Quercy		●			●			●						2 weeks
Lingot Ardéchoise		France	Ardèche		●			●			●						1 month
Lingot du Berry		France	Berry		●			●		●			●				1 month
Rieumoise		France	Pyrenees		●			●			●						1 month
Saint-Nicolas-de-la-Dalmerie		France	Haut-Languedoc		●			●			●						1 month

The Bougon family
and related cheeses

This is a Camembert-type goat's milk cheese, with a white bloomy rind. In the professional jargon of the cheesemaker, the modern, pasteurized-milk version of this is called *chèvre boîte* – (goat's milk boxed cheese).

Cheese	Other names	Country	Area of origin	Cow	Goat	Ewe	Buffalo	Unpasteurized	Heated	Pasteurized	Farm	Cottage industry	Factory	AOC-AOP	IGP	Monastic	Optimum maturation
Bougon		France	Poitou-Charentes		●			●					●				2 weeks
Cathare		France	Laurageais		●			●			●						1 month
Chabris		France	Touraine – Berry		●			●			●						1 month
Mothe-Saint-Héray		France			●					●			●				1 month
Saint-Cyr		France	Poitou-Charentes		●					●			●				3 weeks

The Boulette family
and related cheeses

Generally eaten very fresh, Boulettes are a great speciality in northern France. They are fairly low-fat cheeses, kneaded with herbs and spices.

Cheese	Other names	Country	Area of origin	Cow	Goat	Ewe	Buffalo	Unpasteurized	Heated	Pasteurized	Farm	Cottage industry	Factory	AOC-AOP	IGP	Monastic	Optimum maturation
Boulette de Charleroi		Belgium		●						●	●						Fresh
Boulette de Namur		Belgium		●						●	●						Fresh
Boulette de Romedenne		Belgium		●						●		●					Fresh
Boulette d'Avesnes		France	Avesnois (Flanders)	●					●	●	●	●	●				3 months
Boulette de Cambrai		France	Cambrésis	●					●	●	●	●					Fresh
Boulette des Moines		France	Burgundy	●						●							Fresh

The Carré du Tarne family
and related cheeses

Square cheeses seem to be losing popularity with consumers, for some mysterious and incomprehensible reason. Here are a few survivors that are not afraid of angles.

Cheese	Other names	Country	Area of origin	Cow	Goat	Ewe	Buffalo	Unpasteurized	Heated	Pasteurized	Farm	Cottage industry	Factory	AOC-AOP	IGP	Monastic	Optimum maturation
Cabra		France	Corsica		●			●				●					6 weeks
Calenzana		France	Northern Corsica		●	●		●			●						3 months
Carré de Chavignol		France	Centre		●			●				●					1 month
Chèvrefeuille	Goat à la feuille	France	Deux-Sèvres		●			●			●						1 month
Couhé-Vérac		France	Poitou		●			●			●	●					1 month
Curac	Pavé du Quercy	France	Quercy		●			●			●	●					2 weeks
Couhé-Vérac	Brindamour – Brin d'Amour	France	Corsica		●	●		●			●	●					3 months
Fleury du col des Marousses		France	Pyrenees		●			●			●						6 weeks
Lauzeral		France	Quercy		●			●			●						1 month
Mascaré		France	Provence		●	●		●				●					1 month
Mouflon		France	Southern Corsica – Calgese		●			●			●						3 months
Pavé Ardéchois		France	Ardèche		●			●			●						1 month
Pavé Blésois		France	Blois		●			●			●						1 month
Pavé de Gâtine		France	Poitou-Charentes		●			●			●						1 month
Pavé de la Ginestarie	Carré du Tarne – Pavé du Tarne	France	Albi		●			●			●						1 month
Pavé des Dombes		France	Dombes		●	●		●			●	●					2 weeks
Saint-Maixent		France	Poitou		●			●			●						1 month
Sublime de Verdon		France	Verdon		●			●			●						1 month
Tarnisa		France	Quercy		●			●					●				2 weeks

The Chavignol family
and related cheeses

Crottins came into being in poor wine-growing areas where milk that agricultural workers obtained from their goats was insufficient to make larger cheeses. Stocky and rustic, these cheeses are often very close textured.

Cheese	Other names	Country	Area of origin	Cow	Goat	Ewe	Buffalo	Unpasteurized	Heated	Pasteurized	Farm	Cottage industry	Factory	AOC-AOP	IGP	Monastic	Optimum maturation
Bilou du Jura		France	Jura		●			●			●						10 days
Bouchon de Sancerre		France	Sancerrois		●			●			●						1 month
Cabécou de Thiers		France	Auvergne		●			●			●						1 month
Caboin		France	Berry		●			●			●						3 weeks
Cathelain		France	Savoie		●			●			●						2 weeks
Châtaignier		France	Quercy		●			●			●						3 weeks
Chèvroton du Bourbonnais		France	Bourbonnais	●	●			●			●						3 weeks
Crézancy	Sancerre	France	Sancerrois		●			●			●						1 month
Crottin d'Ambert	Ambert	France	Auvergne		●			●			●						2 weeks
Crottin de Chavignol	Chavignol	France	Cher – Loiret – Nièvre		●			●			●			●	●	●	1 month
Lyonnais		France	Lyons		●			●			●						3 weeks
Marchal		France	Lorraine		●			●			●						2 weeks
Quatre-Vents		France	Dauphiné		●			●			●						3 weeks
Roncier		France	Vaucluse		●			●			●						2 weeks
Saint-Amand-Montrond		France	Sancerrois		●			●			●						1 month
Santranges		France	Sancerrois		●			●			●						1 month
Toucy		France	Burgundy		●			●			●	●					2 weeks
Vendôme		France	Vendômois		●			●			●						2 weeks

The Bouton de Culotte (trouser button) family
and related cheeses

These cheeses are, of course, intended as an accompaniment to an aperitif. They can be eaten either fresh or slightly ripened. Some of them are flavoured with various herbs or spices.

Cheese	Other names	Country	Area of origin	Cow	Goat	Ewe	Buffalo	Unpasteurized	Heated	Pasteurized	Farm	Cottage industry	Factory	AOC-AOP	IGP	Monastic	Optimum maturation
Grabetto		Australia	Victoria		●					●		●					1 month
Apérobic		France	Burgundy	●	●			●			●						10 days
Baratte de Chèvre		France	Burgundy		●			●			●						10 days
Bouton d'Oc		France	Midi–Pyrenees		●			●			●						10 days
Bouton de Culotte		France	Burgundy	●	●			●			●	●					2 weeks
Caillou du Rhône		France	Mâcon		●			●			●						2 weeks
Chevry		France	Saône-et-Loire		●			●			●	●					2 weeks
Gasconnades		France	Gers		●			●			●						1 week
Rigotton		France	Val-d'Oise		●			●			●						15 weeks

The cottage cheese family
and related cheeses

Cow's milk is made into a whole range of more or less fat-free cheeses for eating fresh. They are sometimes augmented with crème fraîche or mixed with herbs and spices of all kinds.

Cheese	Other names	Country	Area of origin	Cow	Goat	Ewe	Buffalo	Unpasteurized	Heated	Pasteurized	Farm	Cottage industry	Factory	AOC-AOP	IGP	Monastic	Optimum maturation
Dopplerahmfrischkäse		Germany		●						●			●				Fresh
Körniger Frischkäse		Germany		●						●			●				Fresh
Quark	Speisequark	Germany	Bavaria	●						●		●	●				Fresh
Rahmfrischkäse		Germany		●						●			●				Fresh
Schitkäse		Germany		●						●			●				Fresh
Cambridge		England		●					●	●			●				Fresh
Colwick Cheese		England		●						●			●				Fresh
Cornish Pepper		England	Cornwall	●						●		●					Fresh
Lactic Cheese		England		●						●			●				Fresh
Paneer		England		●						●			●				Fresh
Single Cream Cheese		England		●						●			●				Fresh
York		England		●					●	●			●				Fresh
Kugelkäse		Austria	Danube	●				●				●					Fresh
Sauerkäse		Austria		●						●		●	●				Fresh
Topfen		Austria		●						●			●				Fresh
Caboc		Scotland	Ross & Cromarty	●						●		●					Fresh
Crowdie		Scotland	Ross & Cromarty	●						●	●						Fresh
Afuega'l Pitu		Spain	Asturias	●				●			●						Fresh
Cream Cheese		USA		●						●			●				Fresh
Aligot	Tomme Fraîche de l'Aubrac	France	Midi–Pyrenees – Rouergue – Auvergne	●				●			●	●	●	●			Fresh
Bibbelkäse		France	Alsace	●						●		●					Fresh
Boulamour		France		●				●					●				Fresh
Boursin		France	Normandy	●						●			●				Fresh
Cailles Rennaises		France	Brittany	●				●				●					Fresh
Carré Frais		France		●						●			●				Fresh
Cervelle de Canut	Claqueret Lyonnais	France	Lyons	●						●		●	●				Fresh
Goat frais du Berry		France	Berry	●				●			●	●					Fresh

Cheese	Other names	Country	Area of origin	Animal species				Milk			Product			Label			Optimum maturation
				Cow	Goat	Ewe	Buffalo	Unpasteurized	Heated	Pasteurized	Farm	Cottage industry	Factory	AOC-AOP	IGP	Monastic	
Coulandon		France	Bourbonnais	•				•				•					Fresh
Crémet Nantais		France	Nantes	•				•		•	•	•					Fresh
Demi-Sel		France	Pays de Bray	•				•		•		•	•				Fresh
Fontainebleau		France	Ile de France	•				•		•		•					Fresh
Fromage à la Pie		France	West	•				•		•		•					Fresh
Gournay Frais	Malakoff	France	Normandy	•				•		•		•					Fresh
Jonchée Niortaise		France	Poitou	•	•			•				•					Fresh
Petit Suisse		France		•				•				•		•			Fresh
Poustagnac		France	Guyenne	•		•		•				•					Fresh
Saint-Florentin		France	Auxerrois	•						•		•	•				Fresh
Saint-Moret		France		•						•			•				Fresh
Samos 99		France		•						•			•				Fresh
Ségalou		France	Quercy	•				•			•						Fresh
Tartare		France		•						•			•				Fresh
Quark		Netherlands		•						•		•	•				Fresh
Bresso		Italy		•				•				•					Fresh
Crescenza		Italy	Lombardy	•						•		•	•				Fresh
Giuncata		Italy	Southern Italy	•		•		•				•	•				Fresh
Graukäse		Italy	Tirol	•				•			•						Fresh
Mascarpone		Italy	Lombardy	•						•		•	•				Fresh
Murazzano		Italy	Piedmont	•				•				•	•	•			Fresh
Pannarello		Italy	Veneto-Friuli	•						•		•					Fresh
Prescinsêua		Italy	Genoa	•						•		•					Fresh
Raviggiolo		Italy	Emilia-Romagna	•				•				•	•				Fresh
Squacquerone		Italy	Emilia-Romagna	•						•		•	•				Fresh
Stracchino		Italy	Lombardy	•						•		•	•				Fresh
Cottage cheese		Universal		•				•	•			•	•				Fresh
Fromage blanc		Universal		•				•	•		•	•	•				Fresh
Fromage frais		Universal		•				•	•	•		•	•				Fresh

The Rove des Garrigues family
and related cheeses

There is a plethora of fresh cheeses made with goat's milk. Unlike ewe's milk, the flavour develops more quickly. They can be eaten just as they are without any enhancement.

Cheese	Other names	Country	Area of origin	Animal species				Milk			Product			Label			Optimum maturation
				Cow	Goat	Ewe	Buffalo	Unpasteurized	Heated	Pasteurized	Farm	Cottage industry	Factory	AOC-AOP	IGP	Monastic	
Button	Innes button	England	Staffordshire		•			•				•					Fresh
Cerney		England	Gloucestershire		•			•				•					Fresh
Perroche		England	Kent		•			•			•						Fresh
Kervella		Australia	West		•					•	•						Fresh
Galloway Goat's Milk Gems		Scotland	Dumfries–Galloway		•			•			•						Fresh
Cabra del Tietar		Spain	Avila		•			•			•						Fresh
Flor de Oro		Spain	Valencia Province	•	•	•		•			•	•					Fresh
Queso de Murcia		Spain	Murcia		•			•			•	•					Fresh
Besace de Pur Chèvre		France	Savoie		•			•			•						Fresh
Bouchée de Chèvre		France	Centre		•			•				•					Fresh
Brousse du Rove		France	Provence	•	•	•		•	•		•						Fresh
Cabrette du Périgord		France	Aquitaine		•			•				•					Fresh
Camisard		France	Cévennes		•			•				•					Fresh
Champdenier		France	Poitou		•			•			•						Fresh
Pastille de Chèvre		France	Périgord		•			•				•					Fresh
Petit Frais de la Ferme		France	Berry		•			•			•						Fresh
Rove des Garrigues		France	Languedoc–Roussillon		•			•			•						Fresh
Cacioricotta		Italy	South		•			•			•						Fresh
Caprini Freschi		Italy			•			•			•	•					Fresh
Pant ys Gawn		Wales	Monmouthshire		•					•		•					Fresh

The Persillé de la Tarentaise family
and related cheeses

The goat's milk cheeses belonging to this family, produced in quite small quantities, are made by an ancient technique that allows the cheeses to keep longer by heating the curd and then crushing it. Blue mould appears (or doesn't) in a haphazard way.

Cheese	Other names	Country	Area of origin	Animal species				Milk			Product			Label			Optimum maturation
				Cow	Goat	Ewe	Buffalo	Unpasteurized	Heated	Pasteurized	Farm	Cottage industry	Factory	AOC-AOP	IGP	Monastic	
Bleu de Sainte-Foy		France	Rhône-Alpes	•	•			•			•						3 months
Persillé de La Clusaz		France	Haute-Savoie	•	•			•			•						2 months
Persillé de la Haute Tarentaise		France	Haute-Tarentaise		•			•			•						3 months
Persillé de la Tarentaise		France	Savoie – Tarentaise		•			•			•						2 months
Persillé de Thônes		France	Haute-Savoie	•	•			•			•						2 months
Persillé de Tignes	Bleu de Tignes – Tignard	France	Savoie		•			•			•						3 months
Persillé des Aravis		France	Haute-Savoie – Aravis		•			•			•						2 months
Persillé du Grand-Bornand		France	Haute-Savoie	•	•			•			•						2 months
Persillé du Mont-Cenis		France	Savoie	•	•			•			•						2 months
Tarentais		France	Tarentaise		•			•			•						1 month

The Pouligny-Saint-Pierre family
and related cheeses

Another way to get noticed! The pyramid is not the most convenient-shaped cheese to cut, but is certainly one of the most attractive.

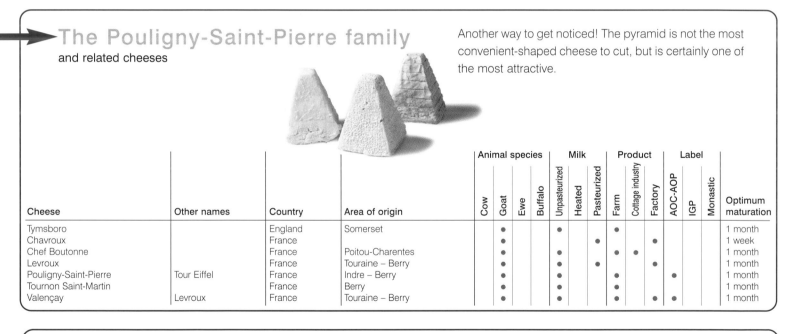

Cheese	Other names	Country	Area of origin	Animal species				Milk			Product			Label			Optimum maturation
				Cow	Goat	Ewe	Buffalo	Unpasteurized	Heated	Pasteurized	Farm	Cottage industry	Factory	AOC-AOP	IGP	Monastic	
Tymsboro		England	Somerset		•			•			•						1 month
Chavroux		France			•					•			•				1 week
Chef Boutonne		France	Poitou-Charentes		•			•			•		•				1 month
Levroux		France	Touraine – Berry		•			•			•		•				1 month
Pouligny-Saint-Pierre	Tour Eiffel	France	Indre – Berry		•			•			•			•			1 month
Tournon Saint-Martin		France	Berry		•			•			•						1 month
Valençay	Levroux	France	Touraine – Berry		•			•			•			•	•		1 month

The Dôme de Poitou family
and related cheeses

This quite recent family of cheeses is made in an original shape and seems set for a great future. In the case of goat's milk cheeses, often very similar in appearance, the shape can sometimes make all the difference.

Cheese	Other names	Country	Area of origin	Animal species				Milk			Product			Label			Optimum maturation
				Cow	Goat	Ewe	Buffalo	Unpasteurized	Heated	Pasteurized	Farm	Cottage industry	Factory	AOC-AOP	IGP	Monastic	
Dôme		France	Berry		•			•			•	•					3 weeks
Dôme du Poitou		France	Poitou		•			•				•					1 month
Petit Fermier		France	Provence		•			•			•						3 weeks
Taupinière des Charentes		France	Poitou-Charentes		•			•			•						3 weeks
Truffe de Valensole		France	Northern Provence		•			•			•						3 weeks

The Novelty Goat's Milk cheese family

and related cheeses

Triangular, heart-shaped, tetrahedron, bell-shaped, or formed like a falling drop of water – these cheeses are always a great hit on the cheeseboard. But it is well worth seeking out those that have other attractions beside their shape.

Cheese	Other names	Country	Area of origin	Animal species				Milk			Product			Label			Optimum maturation
				Cow	Goat	Ewe	Buffalo	Unpasteurized	Heated	Pasteurized	Farm	Cottage industry	Factory	AOC-AOP	IGP	Monastic	
Cabrigan		France	Northern Provence		●			●			●						3 weeks
Chevrion		France	Agen		●			●			●						1 month
Clochette		France	Charente		●			●			●						2 weeks
Cœur d'Alvignac		France	Périgord		●			●				●					2 weeks
Cœur de Chèvre Cendré		France	Centre		●			●				●					2 weeks
Cœur de Saint-Félix		France	Lauragais		●			●			●						3 weeks
Cœur du Berry		France	Berry		●			●				●					2 weeks
Cœur Téotski		France	Tarn		●			●			●						3 weeks
Goutte		France	Agen		●			●			●						2 weeks
Iétoun		France	Northern Provence – Valensole Plateau		●			●			●						2 weeks
Tricorne de Marans		France	Poitou	●	●	●		●			●						2 weeks
Trois Cornes de la Vendée	Sableau – Tribèche – Trébèche	France	Vendée	●	●	●		●			●						1 month

The Corsican Maquis family

and related cheeses

Ewe's milk is excellent for making cheeses to be consumed fresh. They are often flavoured with herbs and spices.

Cheese	Other names	Country	Area of origin	Animal species				Milk			Product			Label			Optimum maturation
				Cow	Goat	Ewe	Buffalo	Unpasteurized	Heated	Pasteurized	Farm	Cottage industry	Factory	AOC-AOP	IGP	Monastic	
Old York		England	Yorkshire			●				●		●					Fresh
Sussex Slipcote		England	Sussex			●		●			●	●					Fresh
Burgos		Spain				●		●				●					Fresh
Queso Fresco Valenciano		Spain		●	●	●		●			●						Fresh
Villalón	Pata de Mulo	Spain				●		●			●	●					Fresh
Brebis de Haute-Provence		France	Northern Provence			●		●			●						Fresh
Brousse de la Vésubie		France	Provence			●		●			●	●					Fresh
Caillebotte d'Aunis		France	Poitou – Charentes			●		●				●					Fresh
Gastanberra		France	Basque Country			●		●	●		●						Fresh
Jonchée d'Oléron	Oléron	France	Aunis			●		●			●						Fresh
Maquis Brunelli		France	Corsica			●		●			●						Fresh
Pigouille		France	Ile d'Oléron			●		●			●						Fresh

The Gardian family
and related cheeses

In areas where dairy farming is extensively practised, milks from different animal species are traditionally used together or alternately, according to the various lactation cycles. The cheeses vary greatly as a result.

Cheese	Other names	Country	Area of origin	Animal species				Milk			Product			Label			Optimum maturation
				Cow	Goat	Ewe	Buffalo	Unpasteurized	Heated	Pasteurized	Farm	Cottage industry	Factory	AOC-AOP	IGP	Monastic	
Cádiz		Spain	Andalusia		•	•		•		•	•						Fresh
Cervera		Spain	South		•	•		•		•	•						Fresh
Cuajada		Spain			•	•		•		•	•	•					Fresh
Malaga		Spain	Andalusia		•	•		•		•	•						Fresh
Mato		Spain	Catalonia	•				•				•					Fresh
Puzol		Spain	South		•	•		•		•							Fresh
Juustoleipä		Finland		•						•	•	•	•				Fresh
Munajuusto	Ilves	Finland		•						•	•	•	•				Fresh
Caillebotte	Jonchée	France	Poitou-Charentes	•	•			•			•	•	•				Fresh
Gardian		France	Provence		•	•		•			•	•	•				Fresh
Feta		Greece		•	•	•		•	•	•	•		•				Fresh
Caciotta		Italy	Centre	•	•	•	•	•				•					Fresh
Robiola		Italy	Piedmont–Lombardy	•	•	•		•		•	•	•					Fresh
Robiola di Roccaverano		Italy	Piedmont	•	•	•		•			•	•		•			Fresh

The Provolone family
and related cheeses

The 'drawn-curd' technique – a great Italian speciality – produces cheeses that, if left to ripen for long enough (up to two or three years!), develop a very dry interior that can be smoked. They are used primarily in cooking.

Cheese	Other names	Country	Area of origin	Animal species				Milk			Product			Label			Optimum maturation
				Cow	Goat	Ewe	Buffalo	Unpasteurized	Heated	Pasteurized	Farm	Cottage industry	Factory	AOC-AOP	IGP	Monastic	
Pastorello		Australia	État de Victoria	•						•			•				6 months
American Provolone		USA		•						•			•				6 months
Kasseri	Kaseri	Greece			•	•		•			•	•	•	•			3 months
Cacciocavallo		Italy	Southern Italy	•						•	•	•	•	•			1 year
Cacciocavallo Silano		Italy	Southern Italy	•						•	•	•	•	•			1 year
Provolone		Italy	Lombardy	•			•			•			•				6 months
Provolone del Monaco		Italy	Campania	•				•					•				1 year
Provolone Valdapana		Italy	Northern Italy	•						•		•	•	•			1 year
Ragusano		Italy	Sicily	•						•				•			6 months

The mozzarella family
and related cheeses

The 'drawn-curd' cheeses made with cow's or buffalo's milk are very acidic and fill the mouth with an intense freshness. These very malleable cheeses can be made in any shape the imagination can come up with.

Cheese	Other names	Country	Area of origin	Cow	Goat	Ewe	Buffalo	Unpasteurized	Heated	Pasteurized	Farm	Cottage industry	Factory	AOC-AOP	IGP	Monastic	Optimum maturation
Haloumi		Cyprus		•	•	•		•	•	•		•					Fresh
Bocconcini		Italy	All Italy	•						•			•				Fresh
Burrata		Italy	Apuglia	•						•	•	•					Fresh
Burrata di Andria		Italy		•						•	•	•					Fresh
Burrino	Butirro, Burri	Italy	Southern Italy	•						•		•	•				1 month
Fior di Latte	Mozzarella di vacca	Italy	Campania–Latium	•			•	•		•		•	•	•			Fresh
Mozzarella di Bufala Campana		Italy	Campania–Latium				•	•		•	•	•	•	•			Fresh
Scamorza		Italy	Southern Italy	•						•	•	•					1 week
Vastedda del Belice		Italy	Sicily			•				•	•	•					Fresh

The Brocciu family
and related cheeses

Using the whey left from the production of cheese to make another, different form of cheese is a universal practice. It gives very varied resulting cheeses, which are sometimes enriched with cream, or flavoured with herbs or spices to give them more character.

Cheese	Other names	Country	Area of origin	Cow	Goat	Ewe	Buffalo	Unpasteurized	Heated	Pasteurized	Farm	Cottage industry	Factory	AOC-AOP	IGP	Monastic	Optimum maturation
Requeson		Spain				•		•					•				Fresh
Brebis Frais du Caussedou		France	Quercy			•		•			•						Fresh
Breuil	Cenberona	France	Basque Country			•		•			•						Fresh
Brocciu	Broccio – Brucciu	France	Corsica		•	•		•	•	•				•			Fresh
Gaperon	Gapron	France	Auvergne	•				•		•	•	•					2 months
Greuilh	Zembera	France	Pyrenees			•		•									Fresh
Sérac	Recuite	France	Savoie	•	•	•		•									Fresh
Anthotyro		Greece			•	•		•			•	•					Fresh
Manouri		Greece	Crete – Macedonia		•	•		•			•	•		•			Fresh
Myzithra	Mitzithra	Greece			•	•		•			•	•					Fresh
Xynotyro		Greece			•	•		•									Fresh
Ricotta di Pecora		Italy				•		•			•	•	•				Fresh
Ricotta Piacentina		Italy		•				•			•	•	•	•			Fresh
Ricotta Romana		Italy		•				•			•	•	•				Fresh
Seirass		Italy	Piedmont	•		•		•			•	•					Fresh
Seirass del Fieno		Italy	Piedmont	•		•		•			•	•					Fresh
Requeijão		Portugal				•		•					•				Fresh
Mesost		Sweden		•						•			•				2 weeks
Zieger	Ziger	Switzerland	German-speaking Switzerland		•			•		•		•					Fresh

The Cancoillotte family
and related cheeses

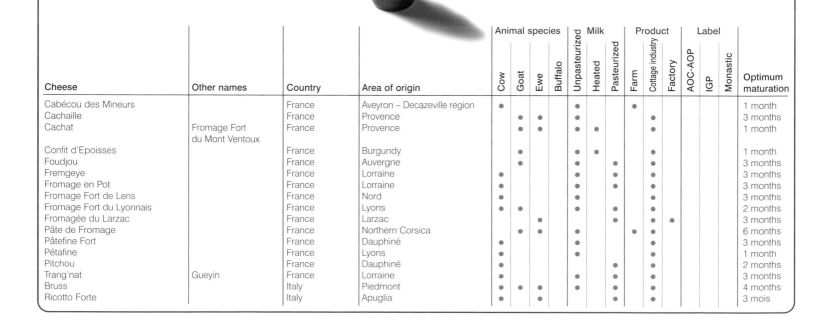

These melted cheeses are a by-product of cheese making. The majority of them are made from cheeses either left over or damaged in production, which are broken up and melted together.

Cheese	Other names	Country	Area of origin	Animal species				Milk			Product			Label			Optimum maturation
				Cow	Goat	Ewe	Buffalo	Unpasteurized	Heated	Pasteurized	Farm	Cottage industry	Factory	AOC-AOP	IGP	Monastic	
Abgesottener Käse		Germany		●						●			●				Fresh
Glundner Käse		Germany		●						●			●				Fresh
Kochkäse		Germany		●						●			●				Fresh
Kacheke's		Belgium		●						●			●				Fresh
Cook Cheese		USA		●						●			●				Fresh
Cancoillotte	Colle	France	Franche-Comté	●				●	●	●		●					Fresh
Rambol		France	Yvelines	●						●			●				Fresh
Vache qui Rit		France	Franche-Comté	●						●							Fresh
Smeltkaas		Holland		●						●		●	●				2 months
Fjäll Brynt		Sweden		●						●							Fresh
Crème de Gruyère		Switzerland		●						●			●				Fresh

The strong cheeses
and related cheeses

No longer in favour with many people, these strong cheeses were the everyday fare of generations of peasants who preserved them in sealed containers with alcohol and spices – both used for their antiseptic properties.

Cheese	Other names	Country	Area of origin	Animal species				Milk			Product			Label			Optimum maturation
				Cow	Goat	Ewe	Buffalo	Unpasteurized	Heated	Pasteurized	Farm	Cottage industry	Factory	AOC-AOP	IGP	Monastic	
Cabécou des Mineurs		France	Aveyron – Decazeville region	●				●			●						1 month
Cachaille		France	Provence		●	●		●				●					3 months
Cachat	Fromage Fort du Mont Ventoux	France	Provence		●	●		●	●			●					1 month
Confit d'Epoisses		France	Burgundy		●			●	●			●					1 month
Foudjou		France	Auvergne		●			●		●		●					3 months
Fremgeye		France	Lorraine	●				●		●		●					3 months
Fromage en Pot		France	Lorraine	●				●		●		●					3 months
Fromage Fort de Lens		France	Nord	●				●				●					3 months
Fromage Fort du Lyonnais		France	Lyons	●	●			●		●		●					2 months
Fromagée du Larzac		France	Larzac			●				●		●			●		3 months
Pâte de Fromage		France	Northern Corsica		●	●		●			●	●					6 months
Pâtefine Fort		France	Dauphiné	●				●				●					3 months
Pétafine		France	Lyons	●				●				●					1 month
Pitchou		France	Dauphiné	●				●		●		●					2 months
Trang'nat	Gueyin	France	Lorraine	●				●		●		●					3 months
Bruss		Italy	Piedmont	●	●	●		●		●		●					4 months
Ricotto Forte		Italy	Apuglia	●		●				●		●					3 mois

Further information

Useful sources

The magazine: *L'Amateur de Fromage*

This French magazine, which first appeared in 1994, is one of the rare publications anywhere in the world entirely dedicated to the subject of cheese. It contains popular favourites, advice on cheese and wine combinations, illustrations, articles, recipes and so on. It deals almost exclusively with traditional cheeses, particularly those made from raw milk. Aimed at both an amateur and a professional readership, this totally independent quarterly publication, which accepts no advertisements, is sold by subscription only. Further information from:

L'Amateur du Fromage
Éditions ADS
142, avenue de Paris
94300 Vincennes
Tel: +33 (0) 1 42 81 98 91
Fax: +33 (0) 1 42 82 71 59
Internet site:
www.amateur-fromage.com
Email: editionsads@freesurf.fr

Organizations

⊳ 'La Guilde des Fromagers – Confrèrie de Saint-Uguzon' (Cheesemakers' Guild – the Brotherhood of Saint Uguzon), created in 1969. Under the presidency of Roland Barthélemy, it is represented in 30 countries. Between amateurs and professionals, more than 4,000 people are, or have been, members. It organizes regular meetings and participates in professional events
Further information from:
25, rue du Maillard
94567 Orly Cedex 417
Tel: +33 (0) 1 46 87 55 72
Fax: +33 (0) 1 45 60 59 99

⊳ 'Confrèrie des Chevaliers du Taste Fromage de France' (Brotherhood of the Knights of Cheese-tasting of France). Created in 1954, the brotherhood has inducted more than 15,000 people. It is represented in about 20 countries.

Further information from:
André Ducoup
60, Boulevard de Clichy
75018 Paris
Tel/Fax: +33 (0) 1 42 64 54 18

⊳ The Specialist Cheesemakers' Association. 17, Clerkenwell Green, London EC1R 0DP,
Tel: +44 (0) 20 7253 2114.
www.specialistcheesemakers.co.uk

⊳ American Cheese Society. 304, West Liberty Street, Suite 201, Louisville, KY 40202
www.cheesesociety.org

⊳ British Cheese Board Dragon Court, 27 Macklin Street, London, WC2B 5LX.
Tel: +44 (0) 20 7921 1744

Some internet sites

⊳ www.camembert-aoc.org
The site of France's flagship cheesemaker. Learn about the history of Marie Harel. (French, English, Japanese)

⊳ www.fromagesdesuisse.com
All about the main Swiss cheeses. (French)

⊳ www.gruyere.com
The information site for Gruyère cheeses. (French, English, German, Italian)

⊳ www.fromages.com
The information site for the sale of cheeses on the internet. (French, English)

⊳ www.mozzco.com
To explore Paula Lambert's gastronomic site, see page 75.

⊳ www.stiltoncheese.com
All about Stilton.

⊳ www.cheese.com
To buy cheese on the internet.

⊳ www.cheesesof the world.com
To buy cheeses from around the world on the internet.

A few good cheese books

⊳ *The Cheese Lover's Cookbook Guide* by Paula Lambert, published by Simon and Schuster, 2000.

⊳ *The World Encyclopedia of Cheeses* by Juliet Harbutt and Roz Denny, published by Lorenz Books, 2002.

⊳ *Cheese Primer* by Steven Jenkins, published by Workman Publishing, 1996.

⊳ *Guide to the Finest Cheeses of Britain* by Juliet Harbutt (for Specialist Cheesemakers Association), 1999.

⊳ *French Cheeses* by Kazuko Masui and Tomoko Yamada, published by Dorling Kindersley, 2000.

⊳ *A Passion for Cheese* by Paul Gayler, published by St. Martin's Press, 2002.

⊳ *The Cheese Plate* by Max McCalman and David Gibbons, published by Crown Publications, 2002.

⊳ *Cheese: A Comprehensive Guide to Cheeses of the World* by Juliet Harbutt, 2002.

⊳ *Handbook of Cheese*, published by Hachette Illustrated, 2003.

⊳ *Cheeses of the World* by Bernard Nantet et al, published by Rizzoli, 2002.

⊳ *The Cheese Bible* by Christian Teubner, published by Penguin, 1998.

⊳ *The Real Cheese Companion*, Sarah Freeman, 1998.

⊳ *The All-American Cheese and Wine Book* by Laura Werlin and Andy Ryan, published by Stewart, Tabori & Chang, 2003.

⊳ *Simply British Cheese* by Matthew Greener et al, published by Storyman Publishing, 2002.

⊳ *Italian Cheese: Two Hundred Traditional Types: A Guide to their Discovery and Appreciation* by Piero Sardo et al, published by Slow Food Intl, 2001.

⊳ *The New American Cheese* by Laura Werlin, published by Stewart, Tabori & Chang, 2000.

⊳ *The Cheese Room* by Patricia Michelson, published by Michael Joseph.

Places to visit

⊳ **Cheddar Gorge Cheese Company**, The Cliffs, Cheddar, Somerset.
Tel: +44 (0) 1934 742810.
Cheddar cheese factory with cheese-making and craft demonstrations.

⊳ **Wensleydale Creamery Visitor Centre**, Hawes, Yorkshire.
Tel: +44 (0) 1969 667664.
Wensleydale's cheese museum, tracing development of the cheese from monastic times to the present. Visitors can watch cheese being prepared from the viewing gallery. Free tasting and shop.

⊳ **Alkmaar Cheese Market**, Alkmaar, Netherlands. Street market held at 10 a.m. every Friday from April to September.

⊳ **Dutch Cheese Museum (Hollands Kaasmuseum)**, Waagplein 2, Alkmaar, Netherlands.
Tel: +31 (0) 72 511 4284

⊳ **Fort des Rousses**, in the Rousses mountains (Jura). Comté cheeses by the thousand, as far as the eye can see. Visits by appointment.
Tel: +33 (0) 3 84 60 35 14

⊳ **Fromages Agour**, Route Louhossoa, Hélette (Basque Country), Spain. A delightful exhibition and retail outlet. Open Monday to Friday from 8 a.m. to midday and 2 p.m. to 6 p.m.
Tel: +34 (0) 5 59 37 63 86

Modern cheeses

As a result of pasteurization and marketing, modern factory cheeses do not pretend to be gastronomic cheeses. Produced on a vast scale and destined mainly for multiple outlets, their flavour is constant and reliable for consumption throughout the year. Their popularity is heavily dependent on major television advertising campaigns. In France, the two main specialist manufacturers are the Bongrain group and the Bel cheese company. These are some of the best known ones.

› **Babybel**
Modelled on Dutch Edam, Babybel was created in 1931. Its compact size and its red wax protective shell make it ideal for snacks and picnics.

› **Belle des Champs**
Made from cow's milk, this bloomy-rind, soft-curd cheese has a very mild flavour and an extremely supple texture.

› **Boursin**
Backed by a catchy advertising slogan that became a cult – *du vin, du pain, du Boursin* (wine, bread, Boursin – they all rhyme in French!) – this small fresh cheese, flavoured with garlic and fresh herbs, was created in 1963. Soft and creamy, it is made in Normandy from cow's milk. Enriched with cream, and with no rind, it is also made in pepper, chive or walnut versions.

› **Bresse Bleu**
Modelled on Gorgonzola, this blue cheese came into being in the Bresse region just after the Second World War. Made from cow's milk, it is made to be eaten while creamy.

› **Caprice des Dieux**
Eaten in 150 countries, this bloomy-rinded, lozenge-shaped cheese was created at Illoud-en-Bassigny, in Haute-Marne. Made from cow's milk, it is notable for its creamy texture.

› **Chaumes**
Launched in 1972, this cheese was modelled on Munster and is very similar to it in appearance. Its flavour, however, is much milder – more like the Trappiste cheeses. It is made in south-western France. It used to be cut and served by weight from supermarket cheese counters.

› **Chevroux**
Created in 1985, this truncated-pyramid-shaped fresh cheese is made from goat's milk. It leaves a great impression of freshness on the palate.

› **Etorki**
A copy of the traditional Pyrenean ewe's milk cheeses, this one is made in the Basque country. Not too strongly flavoured, it is firm with an almost creamy texture.

› **Kiri**
This 'cheese for gourmets in short trousers' was first made in 1968. It is a fresh cheese, melted and blended with cream and intended for sandwiches.

› **Leerdamer**
A Dutch version of Swiss Emmenthal, the flavour of Leerdamer is fruitier but less intense. Its dough is quite supple.

› **Port Salut**
Heir to the cheeses made by the monks of the Abbey at Entrammes in 1816, Port Salut is the most famous of the Trappiste cheeses. It is very mild, with a smooth texture.

› **Rouy**
Created at the beginning of the last century in Burgundy, it was modelled on Pont-l'Evêque. Beneath its streaked orange rind it has a delicate aroma of cow's milk.

› **Saint-Albray**
First made in the Béarn region in 1977, this cheese is easily recognized by its unusual shape – like a flower with six petals. It is soft and creamy beneath its orange rind with its fine white bloom.

› **Tartare**
Like Boursin – the cheese it was created to compete with – Tartare is made in several versions: garlic and fresh herbs, walnut, three peppers and so on. It is particularly good on toast.

› **Vache qui Rit**
Launched by Léon Bel in 1921, Vache qui Rit is recognized all over the world. Originally it was a melted cheese made with Gruyère pieces.

Glossary of cheese terms

Affinage (cheese ripening): process of bringing a cheese to the phase of maturity when it reaches its optimum flavour.

Appellation d'origine contrôlée (AOC) (Controlled appellation of origin): appellation (identifying name) that defines and protects cheeses that have a strict link to a specific area.

Appellation d'origine protegée (AOP) (Protected appellation of origin): European Union version of AOC.

Bloom: mould that develops on the surface of a cheese. It may be white, yellow, red, blue and so on, and distributed over the rind evenly or in patches.

Bloomy rind: rind covered with a white mould.

Brushed rind: often greyish rind that has been brushed during ripening to remove excessive moulds.

Buron: name given in Auvergne to a small workplace in the mountains where cheeses are made and ripened in the summer.

Buttermilk: whitish liquid left over after butter has been churned.

Casein: main protein contained in milk. The richer the milk the better it is for cheese making.

Cayolar (or etchola): Basque word for a mountain workplace where ewe's milk Tommes are made in the summer.

Coagulation: action of curdling milk by causing the proteins to agglomerate.

Cujala: mountain workplace in Béarn, where ewe's milk Tommes are made during the summer.

Curd: coagulated milk.

Curd cutter: implement used to cut curd into small pieces to help the whey drain from it.

Curdling: transforming milk into a solid form by coagulation.

Curd made with rennet (or sweet curd): milk coagulated mainly using rennet. This method is fairly fast and gives a quite firm curd.

Dairy: opposite of 'farmhouse'; it applies to cheeses made from milk collected from several dairy farms.

Double Cream: cheese enriched with fresh cream with at least a 60 per cent fat content (i.e. 60 per cent of the total solids without the water content).

Drawn curd: cheese in which the curd forms strings when stretched, after being boiled several times.

Dry extract: that which would be left if the water content of the cheese were removed. The fat-content figure quoted on the label is a percentage of this and not of the actual cheese.

Estive: summer period when the animals are taken to the high mountain pastures. The cheeses are made *in situ* during this time.

Etchola: see *Cavolar*.

Farmhouse: said of a cheese made by a single commercial concern from milk also produced by it.

Ferment: catch-all term that includes bacteria (including lactic bacteria), fungi, including the various species of mould, and yeasts.

Fermentation: process by which milk turns to cheese under the action of various micro-organisms.

Fissure: crack that can appear in hard cheeses. This is not a flaw but a natural phenomenon.

Fruitière: name given to cheese dairies in Alpine regions, to which farmers take their milk to be made into cheese.

Hâloir: drying room where the cheeses are placed immediately after they are made.

Indication géographique protégée (IGP) (Protected geographical area): European appellation defining and protecting cheeses that have the advantage of belonging to a specific area.

Jasserie: mountain workshop in the Forez area, where cheeses are made.

Lactic curd: milk coagulated mainly by the use of lactic ferments. It is quite acidic. This method of coagulation is fairly slow and the curds take some time to drain.

Lactic ferments: ferments that feed on the milk sugars (lactose), producing lactic acid in the process.

Lactose: milk sugar.

Morge: French word referring to the viscous substance that gradually forms on the surface of firm cheeses that are washed during ripening.

Mould: a microscopic fungus that can develop on the rind of cheeses or in the dough itself. The best known of these are the penicilliums.

Pasteurization: process of heating milk to a temperature between 75 and 90°C (170 and 200°F) for a few seconds, thus eliminating most of the micro-organisms it contained.

Penicillium: family of moulds.

Raw milk: milk direct from the udders (at approximately 37°C/100°F), which has not been heated above 40°C (105°F).

Rennet: digestive enzyme taken from the fourth stomach of young ruminants (this makes cheese a pre-digested product). Nowadays there are synthetic forms of rennet.

Rennet coagulation: 'setting' the milk by adding rennet to make it solidify.

Rennet stomach: abomasum, or lining of the fourth stomach of a young ruminant, used to produce traditional rennet.

Report: French word roughly meaning 'transfer' – used to describe a change in the way a foodstuff is consumed: e.g. milk, which is liquid, becomes cheese – a solid.

Rocou: orange colouring obtained from the seeds of the tropical annatto – a tree of the *bixaceae* family.

Saumure: water saturated with salt.

Sedge: strips of the leaves of these water reeds are used to bind Livarot cheeses. Paper strips are now largely used in their place.

Seeding: addition of ferments or moulds to the milk, the curd or the rind.

Thermization: a lesser form of pasteurization during which the milk is heated to between 63 and 68°C (145 and 155°F) for a few seconds up to a few minutes.

Triple cream: fresh cheese enriched with fresh cream of which the solid matter is made up of at least 75 per cent fat content.

Washed rind: damp rind, orange-ish in colour, with a strong smell resulting from repeated washing with salt water in the ripening process.

Whey (a 5 per cent solution of lactose in water): liquid left after the curd has been drained.

Index

This index lists the names of cheeses mentioned in the text (page numbers indicated in normal type). It also simplifies the process of finding a cheese in the '1,200 cheeses from around the world' tables in the appendix (page numbers indicated in bold). To research a specific cheese, first find the cheese family indicated and then the relevant country.

Acknowledgments

The authors would like to offer their warmest thanks to all those who have contributed their advice, help and availability to the production of this book: Philippe Abrahamse, Yves Adrian, Nicole Augoin, Jean-Charles Arnaud, Noël Autexier, Louis-Marie Barreau, Alain Barthélemy, Patrick Beaumont, Jean Berthaut, Frank Bertrand, M. Biet, Sylvie Boubrit, Daniel Boujon, Eric Bourges, Frédéric Brand, Madeleine and Jean-François Brunelli, José Luis Ordonnez Casal, Caseificio Rossi, Charles and Simone Chabot, Thierry Chévenet, Christiana Clerici, Bruno Collet, Consortium Parmigiano Reggiano, Daniel Delahaye, Domaine de Deves Nouvel, Jean-François and Rosine Dombre, Gilles Dubois, Michel Dubois, Jacques-Alain Dufaux, Jean and Peyo Etcheleku, Carlo Fiore, Christian Fleury, Philippe Garros, Bernard Gaud, Sébastian Gé, Claudine Gillet, André Girard, Gilles and Odile Goursat, Thierry Graindorge, Fromagerie Guiguet, La Graine Johé Didier Jean, Gérard Gratiot, Claire Guillemette, Dominique Guzman, Virginie and Jacque Haxaire, Alain Hess, Eric Jarnan, Philippe Jaubert, Joe Joffre, Gérard Leclère, Claude Leduc, Christian Le Gall, Magali Legras, Jean-Claude Le Jaouen, Claude Leroux, Luc Lesénécal, M. and Mme. Hervé Loussouarn, Jean Manuel Martinez Mora, Claudine Mayer, Philippe Meslon, Maryse Micheaud, Christian Moyersoen, Philippe Olivier, Joseph Paccard, Frère Paul, Marthe Pégourié, Roland Perrin, Denis Provent, Jean Puig, Batiste Raynal, Jeff Rémond, Claudia and Wolfgang Reuss, Patricia Ribier, Olivier Richard, Jean Salat, René Schertenleib, Simone and Rémi Seguin, Isabelle Seignemartin, Hélène Servant, M. Sigonneau, Dragan and Chantal Téotski, André Valadier, Rudi and Helen Vehren, M. Vermot, M. Veyrat, Claudine Vigier.

Roland Barthélemy would like to say a special thank you to Nicole and Claire, also the entire team at Rue de Grenelle, Michel Rougeault and all the members of the Cheesemakers' Guild, and all his friends. Without them this book could never have seen the light of day.

Arnaud Sperat-Czar wishes to offer his particular thanks to Anne-Sibylle Loiseau, to his close colleagues at *L'Amateur de Fromage*, Alexandre Espoir-Duroy, Jean Garsuault, Joseph Hossenlop, Loïc Kerjcan, Serge Michel, Hubert Richard and François Sperat-Czar; also Caroline and Joséphine for their support and infinite patience.

Daniel Czap thanks Marie-Line Salaün for her most competent assistance and 'Madame est Servie' for their invaluable transportation, and of course, Roland Barthélemy for being so generous with his time.

The editor thanks Marine Barbier for her invaluable assistance.

Despite all the care and attention that has gone into the preparation of this book the authors and the publisher feel that, in view of the changes that are constantly being made to the regulations, production methods and customs in the world of cheese-making, they are unable to accept responsibility for any errors, omissions or information contained herein. The explicitly declared objective of the book is that of providing a clear and practical guide for the consumer; it does not purport to be a reference book intended for the cheese specialist.

The photographs with which the book is illustrated are the work of Jacques Guillard. The photographs of the cheeses illustrating the 'favourites' columns were taken by Daniel Czap, apart from those that came from Roland Barthélemy's personal archives.

First published by Hachette Pratique, an imprint of Hachette-Livre
43 Quai de Grenelle, Paris 75905, Cedex 15, France
Under the title Fromages du Monde
© 2001, Hachette Livre
All rights reserved

English language translation produced by Translate-A-Book, Oxford

This edition published by Hachette Illustrated UK, Octopus Publishing Group Ltd,
2–4 Heron Quays, London, E14 4JP
English Translation © 2004, Octopus Publishing Group Ltd, London

Managing editor: Brigitte Éveno
Editor: Catherine Donzel
Artistic direction: Chine
Creation: Florence Cailly – Chine
Production: Felicity O'Connor

Printed by Tien Wah Press, Singapore
ISBN-13: 978-1-84430-115-7
ISBN-10: 1-84430-115-X